COLLECTOR'S ENCYCLOPEDIA OF

CALIFORNIA POTTERY

SECOND EDITION

by
Jack Chipman

COLLECTOR BOOKS
A Division of Schroeder Publishing Co., Inc.

DEDICATION

This second edition of the *Collector's Encyclopedia of California Pottery* is dedicated to these legends of the industry who were so kind and generous with their time during the preparation of the first edition of this book and, sadly, are no longer with us: Sascha Brastoff, Kay Finch, William Manker, Howard Pierce, and Hedi Schoop.

The current values in this book should be used only as a guide. They are not intended to set prices, which vary from one section of the country to another. Auction prices as well as dealer prices vary greatly and are affected by condition and demand. Neither the Author nor the Publisher assumes responsibility for any losses which might be incurred as a result of consulting this guide.

Searching For A Publisher?

We are always looking for knowledgeable people considered experts within their fields. If you feel that there is a real need for a book on your collectible subject and have a large comprehensive collection, contact Collector Books.

On The Cover

Clockwise from top left: Pacific vase; American Pottery 6¼" Pinocchio figurine (©Walt Disney); Bauer Ring pitcher; Vernon pierced plate and goblet designed by May and Vieve Hamilton; Catalina Island souvenir ashtray.
Cover Design: Beth Summers
Book Layout: Karen Geary

PRICING INFORMATION

Although it's been said many times, many ways, a price guide is simply a guide. It should not be a substitute for knowledge or experience!

Of all the factors influencing pricing, the most critical is the degree of desire on the part of a purchaser. It is the demand for a particular item which finally determines its value. Scarcity would follow as the second most important criteria. After these, condition is considered.

Prices given in this book are for ware in near-mint to mint condition, meaning no chips, cracks, or obvious signs of wear and tear. Prices also reflect first grade, meaning no factory flaws like underglaze chips, uneven glaze application, unfinished mold lines, or warpage. A moderate amount of crazing is acceptable on artware and to a lesser degree on dinnerware. In the case of rare pieces, a buyer may overlook these factors for the sake of adding a highly sought example to his or her collection. Again, it is demand which ultimately determines price. A plus (+) sign denotes a scarce-to-rare and/or a highly desirable example.

Geographic location is the final factor to consider. The prices given in this book largely reflect a specific market (California). Unless one is mail-order selling, the supply/demand factor of one's particular region must be carefully considered.

Collector Books
P.O. Box 3009
Paducah, KY 42002-3009

www.collectorbooks.com

Copyright © 1999 by Jack Chipman
Values Updated, 2002

CONTENTS

ACKNOWLEDGMENTS

I purchased my first piece of "made in California" pottery at a flea market near San Francisco in the mid- 1970s. But like most beginning pottery collectors at that time, I gravitated to the better known Ohio potteries at first. It took six years or so of fervent collecting and selling-off before I made the fateful decision to shift the collection's focus entirely to the ceramic heritage of my native state.

Due to a growing fascination with the objects of my desire and a desire to know more about them, I set for myself the daunting task of uncovering all I could about their origins. Even after many years of ardent research, I do not consider myself a true historian. A considerable amount has been learned, however, about the elusive industry that left behind the artifacts pictured in this book.

I have gotten the greatest pleasure (and most insight) from my many meetings and interviews with people directly connected with the Southern California ceramic industry. The following "industry people" helped with the compiling of the first edition of this book, and I want to thank them, above all, for their good will and encouragement: Michael Brayton, Johnnie Brutsche, Frances Climes, Carlotta Climes, Betty Davenport Ford, Douglas and Claudia Gabriel, Anna Haldeman, Bunny Hamilton, Ida Harris, Victor Houser, Tracy Irwin, Marie Johnson, Brad Keeler, Jr., Phil Keeler, John and Maxine Renaker, Susan Nikas, Richard Steckman, Roger (Bud) Upton, Bruce Winton, and Don Winton.

The following people contributed time and talent and thereby made a special contribution to the success of the first edition: Deborah Agata, Al Alberts, Melinda Avery, Danny Babcock, Gary Booth, Pam Bossick, Rena Bransten, Randall Bruce, Virginia Carpenter, Tony Cuñha, Harvey Duke, Delleen Enge, Al Fridley, Roger Goldstein, Norman Haas, Barbara Jean Hayes, Wilbur Held, Ann Kerr, Margaret Key, Bill Kochanski, Marianne Marchesini, Nancy Alison Martin, Maxine Nelson, Donna Obwald, Mary K. Poxon, Fred Pyrczak, Keith Robinson, Gayle Roller, Gloria Samario, Carl and Maire Schrenk, Jack Shafer, Howard Smith, Judy Stangler, Lou Volse, Marilyn Webb, and Buddy Wilson.

Many thanks to those who augmented this second edition with information, suggestions, or specific contributions: Diana Andrews; Rita Bee; Sharlene Beckwith; Debbie Clint; Victoria Damrel; Doris Dohn; Harvey Duke; Jimm Edgar; James Elliot and Patrick Berry of The Pottery Shop, Seattle, WA; Delleen Enge of Franciscan Matching, Ojai; Jan Fontes and George Alig, Jr. of The Antique Gallery, Fullerton, CA; Devin Frick; Carl Gibbs, Jr. of The California Connection, Houston, TX; Tamara Hodge; John M. Nichols; Susan Nikas of Hagen-Renaker, San Dimas, CA; Joyce Roerig; Walter Schirra; Joseph Smith of Joseph's Antiques, Coburg, OR; Stan Skee; Patti Smith; Doug Stanton; Bill Stern; Lou Volse; Marty Webster; Barbara Wills; Jack White; and Donna Yarrell. If I have forgotten anyone, I apologize. Everyone's help was appreciated!

Finally, I would like to express my gratitude to Lisa Stroup and the entire staff of Collector Books for their continuing support and for their attention to detail during the book's production.

INTRODUCTION

Boom and Bust: A Historical Perspective

"Wise indeed is a community which develops products that are indigenous to its surroundings." [1]

Fifty years ago, Helen E. Stiles began a critical chapter of her book, *Pottery In The United States* with these words. In concluding a brief but enthusiastic account of "Pottery Made in California," Ms. Stiles made the following observations:

"We in the East have opened our eyes to the ceramic products of the West, our shops display their wares, each new season brings new designs, but, as elsewhere, it is only when artists and craftsmen of integrity and ability are employed in this work, that we have a truly worthy product. Many such are today being produced in California, but there are those who fear that the wave of popularity may cheapen the products of some factories, and entice those of lesser abilities to set up their shops and cater to a not always discriminating public. Though this may, and probably has, occurred in some instances, California seems to be on the road to a period of prolific production and in many cases most outstanding ceramic wares. Southern California, especially, has every opportunity to produce indigenous design which will hold great interest, not only for the local consumer, but for many purchasers in all parts of the country." [2]

Predicting the future isn't easy, but Ms. Stiles was somehow able to see ahead to the unprecedented growth of Southern California's pottery industry.

Most people think of California Pottery as the vividly colored earthenware dishes manufactured in the thirties and forties by big industrial plants in and around Los Angeles. And they would be right. But California Pottery also embraces many other products of these companies as well as the decorative housewares and giftware turned out by a multitude of smaller potteries operating throughout Southern California between the early thirties and the early sixties.

The roots of the California Pottery industry are still observable today in the colorful tiles that embellish the numerous Spanish-style dwellings erected in Los Angeles in the twenties. Red-roofed minihaciendas dot the City of the Angels as well as many outlying suburbs, and are a fitting tribute to the Southland's Hispanic origins. Many of these homes conceal elaborately tiled bathrooms or kitchens made possible by skilled industrial artisans who duplicated ancient Spanish and Moorish designs.

But what appeared on the scene in 1930 was a strikingly original clay product which its creator, the J.A. Bauer Pottery Company of Los Angeles, called "California Colored Pottery." It was as ornamental as it was useful and was introduced to a mass market by utilizing the creative skills of both artists and industrial clay workers. Making it all the more remarkable, another local ceramic firm had been working on a strikingly similar line of goods. But due to its remote location on Catalina Island (about 25 miles off the coast of Southern California), rival Catalina Clay Products Company was unable to market its line nearly as quickly or successfully.

The ware devised by Bauer amounted to simple yet robust earthenware placesettings and accessories in a rainbow of solid colored glazes. The dishes could be purchased in mixed or matched sets at the whim of the consumer. Flower pots and vases glazed in the same bright colors as the dishes were also available to add a cheery note to indoor-outdoor settings.

This revolutionary concept instantly caught on with progressive minded "Angelinos" for two reasons. Prior to this the available dinnerware was either fussy European china or pseudo-European china manufactured in the East. Secondly, the new lines were specifically designed to accommodate Southern California's penchant for patio dining.

Bauer's California Colored Pottery, returning to Helen Stiles' remarks, was unique because it accommodated the Southland's peculiar lifestyle. Informal social interaction was fostered very early in this region by a benevolent climate and a population of diverse cultures. No single overriding ethic or ethnic attitude shaped the inhabitants into a cohesive union. Instead, a sense of opportunistic experimentation existed here. This extraordinary environment allowed a personal vision, no matter how unconventional, to make a difference.

That the origins of California Pottery coincided with the onset of the Great Depression is worth considering. The Southland, bolstered by the unique prosperity of Hollywood, offered at least a partial haven from this economic catastrophe. And the emerging pottery industry provided a significant measure of employment as surely as its output buoyed sagging spirits.

Ironically, California Colored Pottery reached its zenith with the introduction of the phenomenally successful "Fiesta" ware by the Homer Laughlin China Company of West Virginia in 1936. Every major ceramic plant located in or around L.A. had by this time marketed its own adaptation of the Bauer/Catalina wares. It was a simple matter of economic survival. Pottery yards which featured the various lines, like the famous Pottery Shack in Laguna Beach, multiplied rapidly throughout California in the thirties. Because it was cheerful and relatively inexpensive, colored pottery helped brighten the lives of Californians during the Depression years. By the late thirties it had been embraced by the rest of the country.

The Southern California potteries found themselves in a very favorable position as most of the ceramic raw materials they needed were obtainable within a short distance of Los Angeles. Adding to this was the fact that the city was at one time a leading producer of natural gas and fuel oil. Talc, a mineral mined in abundance in the California desert, proved to be a significant component in commercial clay bodies after it was found useful for tile production in the twenties. It was possible, as the chemists at Gladding, McBean & Company later discovered, to manufacture lightweight, durable and non-crazing dinnerware in a single firing cycle using talc as the primary ingredient. Most of the major producers of California Pottery – Bauer, Pacific, Gladding-McBean, Metlox, and Vernon (known as the "Big 5") – had turned to talc by the late thirties. Many of the smaller companies followed suit while the mineral was touted as one of the greatest advances in the history of pottery manufacturing. Still, it was the brightly colored glazes and the underglaze decorations offered by the various firms that sustained the industry in difficult times.

World War II ushered in the period of greatest growth for the ceramics trade in California. Although many government restrictions were placed on materials and a few companies converted to defense work, it was a boom period. The factor accounting for most of this productivity was the war-time curtailment of imports from Europe and Asia. With the traditional lines of china from the British, French and German factories and the ceramic goods from Italy and Japan no longer available, wholesale buyers for the nation's department stores found themselves in the awkward position of relying almost exclusively on domestic sources to stock their shelves.

A few Southern California firms, like Gladding-McBean, took full advantage of the situation and developed lines of porcelain dinnerware as fine as any imported china. The bulk of production, however, involved lines of earthenware dishes and decorative housewares. Much of the tableware, sporting trade names like "Franciscan" and Poppytrail," was decorated by hand. The housewares included figurines and related items for individual use or for gift-giving. The company that spearheaded this type of production was Brayton Laguna. Their acclaimed and highly successful hand-painted figurines gave rise to a multitude of competitors and before long the promise of something special became associated with the backstamp "made in California."

Small, usually family-owned, potteries sprang up all over the Southland during the war. By 1948, the peak year for the industry, over eight hundred ceramic concerns were in operation throughout California -- exceeding even that of Ohio. Hedi Schoop, Kay Finch, Florence Ward, Brad Keeler, and Will and George Climes were outstanding contributors to the local giftware explosion. But, as Helen Stiles had predicted, not all of the small businesses catered to a discriminating taste. Despite this warranted criticism, the Southern California spirit of ingenuity and abandon prevailed, resulting in a bumper crop of ware which certainly interested consumers nationwide.

The overseas goods which were unavailable during the war suddenly reappeared in the early fifties. Only a trickle at first, the imports grew to flood proportions as the Japanese, and later the Italians, dispatched an endless flow to rival the California designs. Unable to compete with the quality and low cost of the imports, many Southern California potteries began to close up shop.

Had it not been for the highly publicized ceramics career of Sascha Brastoff in the fifties and the many small businesses his success inspired, the local pottery industry would have succumbed much sooner than it did. Even so, the number of producers had been reduced to a fraction of the post-war high by the early sixties. Today only a handful remain. Their presence is an uneasy reminder of the boom and bust of California Pottery.

1 H.E. Stiles, *Pottery In The United States*, pg. 138.
2 Stiles, op. cit., pgs. 153-155.

AMERICAN CERAMIC PRODUCTS

The predecessor of American Ceramic Products was Cecil Jones' La Mirada Potteries. Jones was a talented and accomplished English ceramist with extensive experience working for potteries in England as well as the United States. He was affiliated with the Claycraft Potteries in Los Angeles prior to founding La Mirada in 1935.

The La Mirada Potteries began operations at 3221 San Fernando Road in Los Angeles, where only a year earlier the Robertson Pottery had been established. Jones' company produced a pioneering line of Chinese Modern-style housewares consisting of low bowls, vases, wall pockets, figurines, and figural planters. His Oriental designs were complemented by a series of brightly colored, transparent crackle glazes that were perfected with the help of George Robertson of the Robertson Pottery.

The La Mirada business was purchased by Thomas F. Hamilton in 1939 and renamed American Ceramic Products. With Jones remaining as plant superintendent, it continued unchanged until the early part of 1940, when a fire destroyed the factory. Operations were subsequently housed in a larger building constructed at 6205 Compton Avenue in Los Angeles. With completion of the new facility in 1941, American Ceramic Products was incorporated and full production, including a new line of square-shaped dinnerware called Mandarin, was resumed.

In 1945, the same year that Cecil Jones retired, owner Tom Hamilton was approached by the Winfield Pottery of Pasadena, desperately in need of assistance with a huge backlog of war-time dinnerware orders. After an unprecedented licensing arrangement was worked out and some new machinery installed, Winfield China was produced as a separate division of the business. Bamboo, Avocado and a few other patterns originated by the Pasadena company were turned out by both the Winfield Pottery and American Ceramic Products for a short time. (See Winfield chapter.)

With aggressive mass-marketing, Hamilton's Winfield line quickly expanded and in 1946 a separate manufacturing facility for it was constructed. The new Winfield Division of American Ceramic Products was a fully modern, 65,000 square foot factory and showroom located at 1825 Stanford Street in Santa Monica. Many hand-painted Winfield China patterns were designed and produced in the well-equipped plant. Bird of Paradise, designed by Ayako Okubo, was the most successful of the new lines which were marketed through major department stores across the country. After 1959, Winfield China was distributed by means of the direct sales approach used in the promotion of Tupperware products.

The La Mirada Division of American Ceramic Products maintained operations at the Compton Avenue location. By 1948, the original crackled

La Mirada Pottery, late thirties. Candle holder, 1½" x 4", $20.00. Vase, 4½", $35.00. Figurine, 9½", $50.00. Vase, 4½", $35.00.

glazes on artware had given way to a new collection of solid decorator colors, in combinations such as dawn pink and dusk gray. After 1948, the former low-fire La Mirada Mandarin dinnerware became a semi-porcelain line and was marketed under the Winfield China umbrella. Numerous new color combinations were employed on the Mandarin ware, including yellow-green, which was dubbed Daffodil. Hand-decorated patterns were also produced.

In 1963 Tom Hamilton sold the La Mirada plant. The Winfield China Division remained relatively prosperous as late as the mid sixties despite mounting competition from less-expensive Japanese china. The skill and dedication of the employees (about 250 at the time), and their willingness to work for less than union scale, helped sustain the business.

Thomas F. Hamilton died in 1964 and his son Tony took over management of American Ceramic Products until its sale in 1965. The new owners filed bankruptcy in 1967, with the company closing later that year.

The early La Mirada pottery was sometimes incised in-mold with the mark shown, (1) however, paper labels were used to identify much of the ware. "Winfield" (2) and "Winfield Ware" (3) were early Winfield China marks and were stamped on the unglazed bottoms of most items. The later mark shown (4) was an underglaze backstamp. "Winfield China Gourmet" (5) was a special line of the early sixties, with the mark being stamped underglaze. La Mirada dinnerware carried a circular backstamp reading "La Mirada Mandarin Los Angeles." After 1948 the ware bore the circular stamped mark "Winfield Handcraft China" but was actually a semi-vitreous product.

(1)

(2)

(3)

(4)

(5)

La Mirada Pottery from early forties. Water buffalo planter, 7" x 10", $60.00. Mandarin figure, 12", $45.00. Oriental child planter, 7½", $30.00.

La Mirada Pottery fish wall pocket, chartreuse crackle glaze, $75.00.

La Mirada Pottery "Lotus" vase (see mark below), 6", $35.00. Pony, turquoise crackle, 7" x 9½", $65.00.

In-mold mark on "Lotus" vase above.

La Mirada Pottery cock, 12½", light turquoise-maroon crackle glaze, in-mold mark, c. 1946, $75.00.

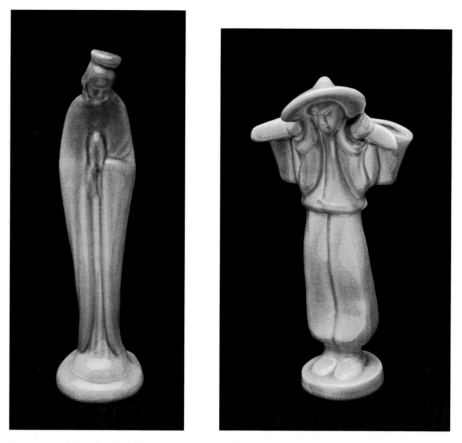

Left: La Mirada Madonna figurine, chartreuse and brown crackle, 11½", unmarked, $65.00. Right: La Mirada Oriental water bearer, chartreuse crackle, 12", no mark, $55.00.

Diminutive La Mirada deer figurines, turquoise crackle glaze, approximately 5", $25.00 each.

La Mirada shell-shaped wall pocket, 4", unmarked, $35.00.

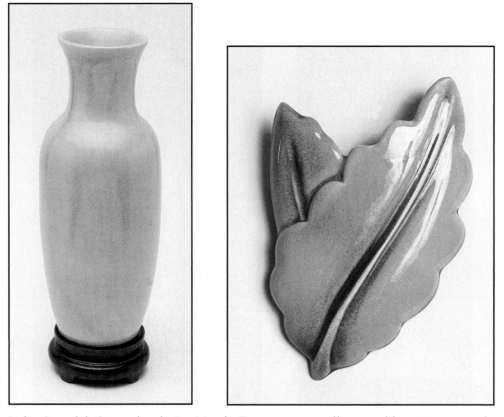

Left: Graceful Oriental-style La Mirada Pottery vase, yellow crackle, 12", no mark, $65.00. Vase seems at home on a Robertson Hollywood ceramic base, $65.00. Right: Attractive La Mirada leaf-shaped wall pocket, turquoise crackle, 9", in-mold mark on backside, $45.00.

Winfield China, Bird of Paradise pattern. Dinner plate, 10", $30.00; cup and saucer, $30.00; coffee pot, $65.00.

Winfield China, stamped marks. Mug, Bird of Paradise pattern, $30.00. Dinner plate, 10", Dragon Flower pattern, $25.00. Mug, Desert Dawn pattern, $25.00.

Winfield

TRUE PORCELAIN CHINA

Adds Beauty and Charm to Your Home

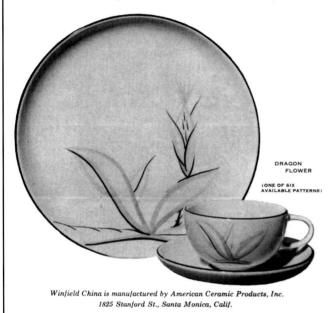

DRAGON
FLOWER

(ONE OF SIX
AVAILABLE PATTERNS)

Winfield China is manufactured by American Ceramic Products, Inc.
1825 Stanford St., Santa Monica, Calif.

DISTRIBUTED BY

WHAT *Winfield* CHINA WILL DO FOR YOU

Winfield CHINA will fill your every serving need with *one* set of dinnerware.

Winfield CHINA will last much longer than pottery and other china, because it is true one-fire porcelain, *double strength* and chip resistant.

Winfield CHINA will always look bright and new. The hand painted patterns are fired into the body *under the glaze*, protecting the designs from detergents. They can never be destroyed.

Winfield CHINA need not be dried. The *non-absorbent* glaze rejects moisture eliminating salt deposits that streak and spot.

Winfield CHINA's unusual serving pieces and versatile design make it possible for you to entertain graciously in any circumstance.

Winfield CHINA saves you time and effort because it eliminates the need for a variety of glass and metal bakers as *every piece* of *Winfield* CHINA is oven-proof.

Facts ABOUT POTTERY

POTTERY means the same as EARTHENWARE.

POTTERY is a comparably weak, porous clay body.

POTTERY is a low-fired product and both the glaze and the body will absorb water.

POTTERY leaves a salt deposit after washing that must be polished.

POTTERY *cannot* be used in restaurants because of laws governing health.

POTTERY is completely opaque and cannot show *any* translucency.

Winfield CHINA is a true Vitrified china and will outlast pottery 10 to 1.

Facts ABOUT *Winfield* CHINA

Winfield CHINA is a truly vitrified CHINA, unique in design and manufacturing process as it is a true high-fired porcelain.

Winfield CHINA is purposely made in a heavier weight for extreme durability.

Winfield CHINA is translucent when held over a strong light, particularly one of the thinner pieces.

Winfield CHINA is less translucent than fragile, impractical chinas, because of its durable weight and practical design.

Winfield CHINA can be tested as above to prove its quality conclusively as a true vitrified china must show some translucency.

PRINTED IN U.S.A.

Winfield China, Desert Dawn pattern, stamped marks. Coffee pot, $60.00; cup and saucer, $25.00; covered sugar, $30.00; creamer, $20.00.

Winfield China, Desert Dawn pattern. 14" chop plate, $95.00.

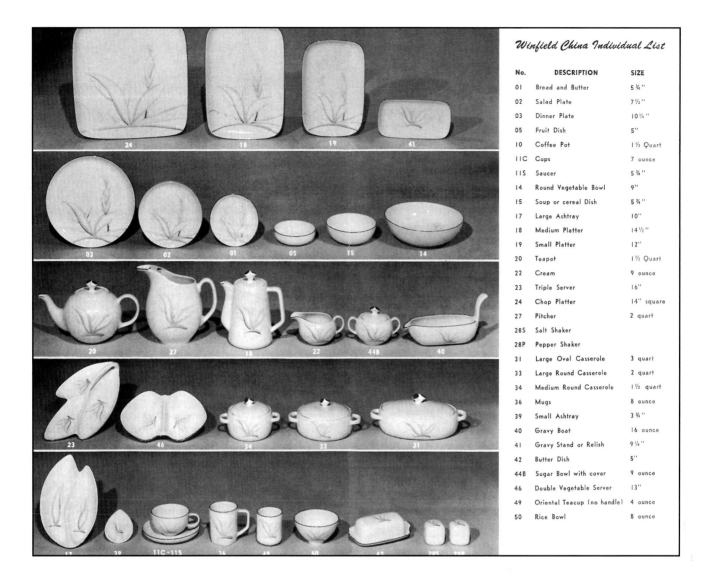

Winfield China Individual List

No.	DESCRIPTION	SIZE
01	Bread and Butter	5 ¾ "
02	Salad Plate	7 ½ "
03	Dinner Plate	10 ¼ "
05	Fruit Dish	5"
10	Coffee Pot	1 ½ Quart
11C	Cups	7 ounce
11S	Saucer	5 ¾ "
14	Round Vegetable Bowl	9"
15	Soup or cereal Dish	5 ¾ "
17	Large Ashtray	10"
18	Medium Platter	14 ½ "
19	Small Platter	12"
20	Teapot	1 ½ Quart
22	Cream	9 ounce
23	Triple Server	16"
24	Chop Platter	14" square
27	Pitcher	2 quart
28S	Salt Shaker	
28P	Pepper Shaker	
31	Large Oval Casserole	3 quart
33	Large Round Casserole	2 quart
34	Medium Round Casserole	1 ½ quart
36	Mugs	8 ounce
39	Small Ashtray	3 ¾ "
40	Gravy Boat	16 ounce
41	Gravy Stand or Relish	9 ¼ "
42	Butter Dish	5"
44B	Sugar Bowl with cover	9 ounce
46	Double Vegetable Server	13"
49	Oriental Teacup (no handle)	4 ounce
50	Rice Bowl	8 ounce

Winfield China, Pussy Willow pattern, hand painted, stamped mark (see above photo). Cup and saucer, $20.00. 7½" salad plate, $15.00.

Winfield China, hand-painted Spruce pattern. Fruit dish, 5", $15.00. 10¼" dinner plate, $20.00.

Winfield China dinner plate, 10¼", hand-painted Dainty Bess pattern, stamped mark, ca. 1949, $20.00.

Winfield China, Blue Pacific pattern, cheese dish and cover, stamped mark, $65.00.

La Mirada ware, hand-decorated in unknown patterns, stamped marks. 10" dinner plate, $15.00. Cup and saucer, $20.00.

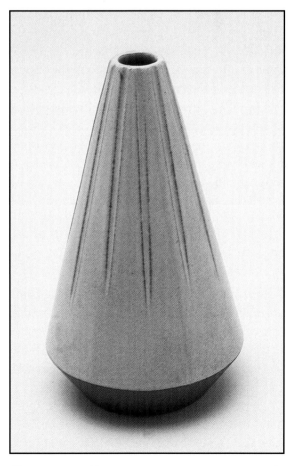

This curious 8½" stoneware vase appears positively threatening. Stamped "La Mirada/ Made in USA" with "303" in-mold, it evidently dates from the early sixties, $75.00.

BATCHELDER

One of the most influential figures of the American Arts and Crafts Movement was Ernest A. Batchelder. He was a dedicated and respected teacher, writer, and civic leader. The tiles he produced in Pasadena and Los Angeles served to advance his reputation as an authority in the design field of his day.

Batchelder was born in New Hampshire in 1875. He received his education at the Massachusetts Normal School in Boston, graduating in 1899. Summer classes with Denman Ross helped shape the design ethic which he espoused in the *Craftsman* magazine during the years 1906–09. In 1910, a compilation of this series of articles was published titled *Design In Theory and Practice*. It was his second book, the first being *Principles Of Design* which appeared six years earlier.

In 1904, Batchelder moved to California. Locating in Pasadena, he taught at Throop Polytechnic Institute (now California Institute of Technology) from 1904 to 1909. As an instructor there, Batchelder helped foster the manual arts movement, whose aim was the restoration of handiwork as an integral part of education. He left his post at Throop in order to establish a tile studio on land purchased in Pasadena in 1909. The following year a small workshop was erected on the property, which was located on the east side of the Arroyo, at 626 Arroyo Drive. By 1912, the Batchelder business had outgrown its modest beginnings and was relocated to a structure on what is now Arroyo Parkway in Pasadena. Frederick L. Brown was made a partner at this time, and sculptors Charles and Emma Ingels were employed as master mold makers.

Batchelder tiles of the period were formed by hand pressing slabbed clay into plaster molds. Relief tiles were sprayed with engobe in a variety of colors, the excess wiped off elevated areas before firing. Clays came from various regions of California, with both red and buff burning types used.

Business continued to expand at a rapid rate and by 1916 a new partner, Lucian H. Wilson, was associated with Batchelder. A larger and better-equipped factory was built on a six-acre site at 2633 Artesian Street in the Lincoln Heights district of Los Angeles. The new Batchelder-Wilson Company evolved into a full-service tile plant offering glazed faience tile in innumerable designs, along with architectural panels, moldings, corbels, fireplace facings, pavers and fountains. In addition, architectural terra cotta, garden pots, and bookends were produced.

Though showrooms were maintained in San Francisco, Chicago, and New York, the majority of the firm's trade was local, with Batchelder supplying an abundance of Spanish tile to contractors during the building boom of the twenties. Glaze colors ranged from the vivid hues of the outdoor Spanish tile to the more subdued "patina glazes" (ivory, tan, gray-blue, blue-green, orchid, lavender, and others) used in interior settings. The range of subjects depicted on figure tiles was as broad as the colors employed.

Batchelder unglazed (engobe) landscape with oak tree tile, 7¾". Impressed "Batchelder Los Angeles," $500.00.

William Manker, hired in 1926, became Batchelder's personal assistant after a brief apprenticeship and was responsible for many of the company's designs. By 1930, and the end of the construction boom, the effects of the Depression had set in. Bankruptcy was declared in 1932, with the Batchelder-Wilson plant and stock later sold to the Bauer Pottery.

In 1936, Batchelder began a second phase of his career with the establishment of Batchelder Ceramics at 158 Kinneloa Avenue in Pasadena. Batchelder Ceramics was a completely divergent line of fragile slip-cast bowls, vases, and related articles inspired by the success of former associate Manker. Batchelder, like Manker, designed and produced modern adaptations of classical Chinese forms in earthenware. The glazes he developed were extraordinary and added to the success of this later endeavor. Working closely with him was a handful of people who had been associated with the tile business.

Batchelder kept his second operation small so that he could supply a personal touch to the work, including hand-incising his name on most pieces. In this way he was able to continue the operating philosophy of his early tile business contained in the motto, "No two tiles the same." Batchelder Ceramics was distributed to department stores and gift shops throughout the country and in South America. In 1951, Ernest A. Batchelder retired; he died in 1957.

Unlike many tile businesses, Batchelder tiles were diligently marked. The mark shown was used by the Batchelder-Wilson Company in 1928. (The patent refers to the innovative spacing lugs that were added to the sides of the tile.) The most common mark was an impressed "BATCHELDER LOS ANGELES" in block letters. The early ware was similarly impressed "BATCHELDER PASADENA." Batchelder Ceramics pieces bore the hand-incised (most often by Batchelder himself) name of the owner. A few variations and abbreviations are shown. The words "Kinneloa Kiln" were occasionally included in the marking process.

Unglazed (engobe) hexagonal tile, 3½", advertising "Batchelder Tiles," $500.00+. Medieval hunting scene tile, 4", $300.00. Grapevine tile, 3", patina glazed, $125.00.

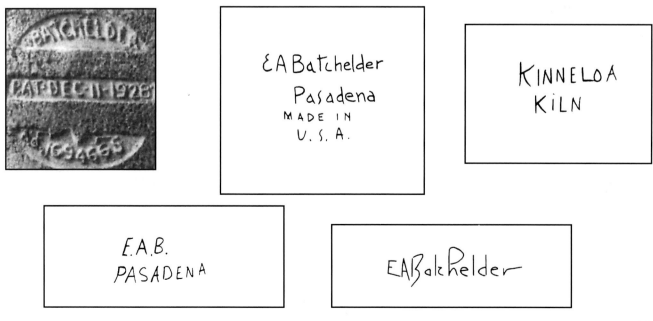

Top left: Partially glazed tile, 4", depicting medieval hunt, impressed "Batchelder Los Angeles," c. 1928, $300.00.

Top right: Unglazed (engobe) medieval landscape tile, 4", impressed "Batchelder Los Angeles," $250.00.

Bottom left: Unglazed (engobe) conventionalized bud with leaves tile, 3", impressed "Batchelder Los Angeles," $200.00.

Unglazed (engobe) peacock tile, 6", "Batchelder Los Angeles" impressed mark, $450.00.

Satin matte glazed Hispanic tile, 6", "Batchelder Los Angeles" impressed mark, c. 1928, $150.00.

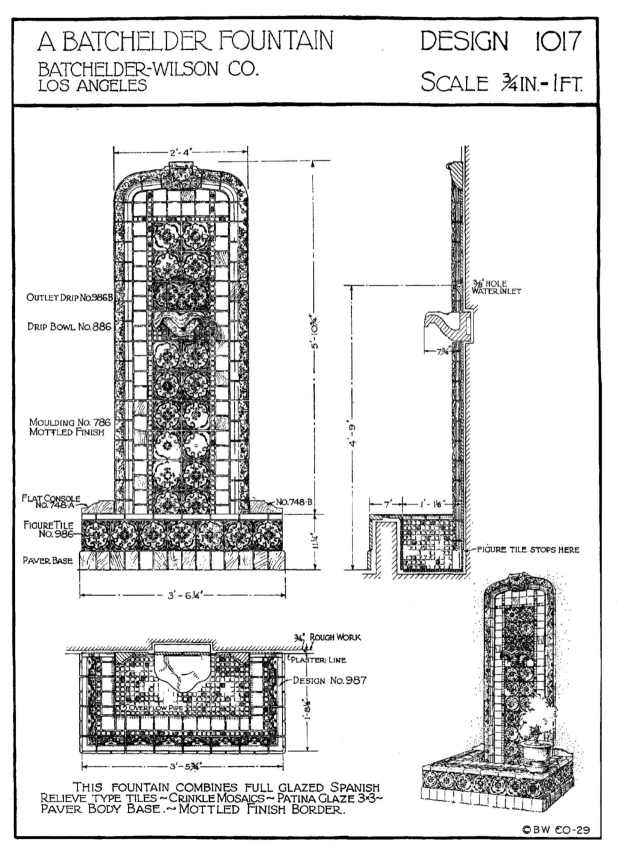

A BATCHELDER FOUNTAIN
BATCHELDER-WILSON CO.
LOS ANGELES

DESIGN 1017
SCALE ¾ IN. - 1 FT.

2'-4"

5'-10¾"

Outlet Drip No.986B

Drip Bowl No.886

Moulding No. 786
Mottled Finish

Flat Console
No.748-A
No.748-B

Figure Tile
No.986

Paver Base

11¼"

3'-6¼"

⅜" HOLE
WATER INLET

7¾"

4'-9"

7' 1'-1⅛"

FIGURE TILE STOPS HERE

¾" ROUGH WORK
PLASTER LINE
DESIGN No.987
OVERFLOW PIPE
1'-8½"

3'-5¾"

THIS FOUNTAIN COMBINES FULL GLAZED SPANISH
RELIEVE TYPE TILES ~ CRINKLE MOSAICS ~ PATINA GLAZE 3×3 ~
PAVER BODY BASE. ~ MOTTLED FINISH BORDER.

©BW CO-29

Architectural rendering for a Batchelder fountain design, dated 1929.

Extraordinary Batchelder tile, 14" x 15", depicting medieval dragon slayer in buff-colored bisque with glazed background and shield, deeply impressed on reverse "Batchelder/Los Angeles," $2,000.00+.

Unglazed (engobe) jardiniere, 12" x 13", base markings shown below, $1,000.00+.

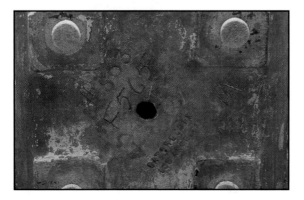

BATCHELDER ❖ TILES ❖

PATINA GLAZES

A FOUNTAIN IS DIFFERENT. It permits an infinite play of fancy in the choice of design and materials. There is no formula to apply, no precedent to violate. It is something to play with. There is always an appeal in the tinkle of dripping water or in the pool reflecting its bit of sky and trees . . . Tiles offer the logical medium for fountain construction. They are plastic in form, decorative in color, glaze and texture. The design for the fountain may be quite simple in character if ones purse limits expense, or quite ornate if ones taste is unfettered. In any case the result may be appropriate, imaginative and altogether lovely. No garden or sunroom is complete without a fountain.

This Batchelder Tiles advertisement appeared in the April, 1930 issue of *House Beautiful*.

BATCHELDER TILES   BATCHELDER-WILSON CO.

Colors have been carefully studied in order to offer harmonious combinations with our Patina Glaze Blends. These new colors allow desirable contrasts in almost any scheme which may be selected. They are not "just a few more colors". They have been chosen with definite chromatic values relative to our entire glazed product. They permit the use of two or more contrasting colors in the form of borders and liners with assurance of consistent results.

The Patina Glazes made available by Batchelder-Wilson were pictured in a brochure issued by the business, ca. 1929.

Batchelder Ceramics, incised marks. Back row: vase, 6", $175.00; vase, 9½", $300.00; vase, 7", $175.00. Front row: bowl, 3", $125.00; vase 4¾" x 5½", $150.00.

Batchelder Ceramics, incised marks. #49 vase, 6" x 8½", $150.00; #44 vase, 3½", $85.00; #49 vase, 6½" x 5", $150.00; #57 low bowl, 14", $200.00.

E. A. Batchelder's "Kinneloa Kiln" floral artware, incised marks. #218 vase, 8½", $125.00; #37 bowl, 3", $75.00; #44 vase, 3½", $85.00.

Batchelder Ceramics flower bowls, incised marks. 4" bowl (see mark in adjacent photo), $100.00; #72 bowl, 3" x 6", $125.00; #26 bowl, 3" x 7", $150.00.

Batchelder Ceramics vase, 6", incised mark, $175.00.
Flared bowl, 3¼" x 7½", incised mark, $150.00.

Batchelder Ceramics, incised marks. Oblong vase,
6¼" x 8", $175.00; low bowl, 1½" x 7", $125.00.

Monk bookends by Batchelder-Wilson of Los Angeles, 4½", unglazed
engobe patina, markings shown below, ca. 1923, $750.00+ pair.

BAUER

The J. A. Bauer Pottery was founded by Kentuckian John Andrew Bauer. In 1909–10, Bauer transferred a successful ceramics business from Paducah to Los Angeles seeking a more hospitable climate for an asthmatic condition. The new plant, which was sited near the intersection of Lacy Street and Avenue 33, in the Lincoln Heights district, boasted four large-capacity periodic kilns. By virtue of an aggressive sales force, the company quickly established a reputation as Southern California's foremost manufacturer of redware flower pots. Stoneware production followed, and by the twenties, the firm produced a wide range of items including mixing bowls, nappies, ramekins, bean pots, whiskey jugs, and covered crocks. During Prohibition the latter articles were utilized by enterprising individuals to concoct and bottle alcoholic beverages.

Around 1913, a skilled Danish designer by the name of Louis Ipsen was hired. A year or two later, Matt Carlton, an experienced potter from Arkansas, arrived, and the two men joined forces in the development of an artware line of glazed vases, flower bowls, and jardinieres. Molded forms were executed by Ipsen, while hand-throwing was Carlton's specialty. Matte green glazes were used almost exclusively on the standard redware body of the period. When the Bauer

Pottery exhibited their new art pottery at the Panama-California Exposition in 1915–16, it was awarded a Bronze Medal. Shortly afterward the firm's artware gave way to a line of molded stoneware vessels that was glazed only on the inside.

The Bronze Medal was a promising achievement, but founder John "Andy" Bauer was not destined to witness his company's greatest glory. Just prior to Bauer's death in 1922, the business was entrusted to a partnership that included his son-in-law, Watson E. Bockmon. It was Bockmon who oversaw production of the firm's inventive and very influential colored pottery.

Victor Houser, a ceramic engineer from the University of Illinois (hired in 1929), perfected the opaque colored glazes that enabled the Bauer business to popularize its concept of casual tableware in mix-n-match sets of bright colors. An initial line of dishes was modeled by Ipsen and introduced in 1930. In 1933, the popular and enduring "ring" ware followed and, combined with the earlier "plain" setting, comprised the organization's original California Pottery. The highly successful ring design was characterized by closely-spaced concentric ridges on hollow ware and a series of three ridges in relief on plates and platters. Included in the ring assortment of table and kitchen ware were more than one hundred different items for casual dining and food preparation.

So great was the demand for Bauer's colored pottery that a second plant was added in 1935 after neighboring Batchelder-Wilson ceased operations. Following Bockmon's purchase of the well-equipped facility, new tableware and artware designs were produced there on a regular basis. Bauer's successful tableware lines included Monterey (1936–1943), La Linda (1939–1961), Monterey Moderne (1949–1961), and Brusché Al Fresco (1950–1960). Gloss Pastel Kitchenware, fashioned by Ray Murray and introduced in 1941, included the distinctive "Aladdin" teapot design.

Technician Houser crafted a new series of glazes during World War II in response to the government's requisition of essential raw materials. Original colors —

Bauer's Watson E. Bockmon

jade green, Chinese yellow, orange-red, royal blue, delph blue, burgundy, ivory, black and white — were either reformulated or replaced by pastel hues. Artware, both cast and wheel thrown, continued to be produced; the latter work was performed by Carlton and his nephew Fred Johnson. Cast forms of the thirties and forties were designed by Jim Johnson and Ray Murray and were produced in the same monochrome glazes used for dinnerware.

Tracy Irwin, another talented Bauer designer, created an assortment of stylish floral containers during the company's final decade. He was also responsible for modeling the popular Monterey Moderne tableware, which was a sophisticated coupe design inspired in part by Russel Wright's American Modern.

By the fifties, with increased local competition and a flood of imports, Bauer no longer dominated the Los Angeles market as it had done in the thirties and forties. Because the company depended largely on its California accounts to sustain it, the slump in business experienced in the late fifties was inevitable. Management difficulties compounded the situation which culminated in a bitter strike in 1961. The Bauer pottery was closed by W. E. Bockmon's widow in 1962.

Various in-mold marks were used by Bauer. Shown is a selection of the more common ones in use from the thirties. Some Bauer ware was only marked "Made in U.S.A." The hand-thrown pottery of Matt Carlton and Fred Johnson was never marked. In addition, much of the regular jiggered and cast production was not marked. Paper labels were used briefly in the thirties.

Bauer "ring" covered water jug and six 6-ounce tumblers in metal caddy, $2,000.00+ complete. *Photo courtesy of Roger Gass.*

Bauer "ring" ware beer pitcher and mugs, ca. 1933. Beer pitcher, $1,000.00+; mugs, $400.00+ each. *Photo courtesy of Roger Gass.*

Ever popular nested set of "ring" mixing bowls, in-mold marks, $750.00 (in standard colors). *Photo courtesy of Richard N. Levine.*

Back row: Bauer "ring" ball jug, $350.00+; "ring" covered beater pitcher, $750.00+. Front row: Gloss Pastel Kitchenware, 4-cup teapot, $150.00; "plain" individual coffee pot, $150.00; "ring" 6-cup teapot with wood handle, $300.00.

"Ring" ware. Row 1: Covered baking dish, 4", $150.00+; individual casserole, $350.00+; cigarette jar, $750.00+; mustard jar, $750.00+; Hi-Fire style custard cup, $100.00+; ring custard cup, $75.00+. Row 2: Berry dish, $100.00+; lug soup with cover, 5½", $500.00+; soup plate, 7½", $150.00; cereal bowl, $85.00. Row 3: Refrigerator stack set in rack, 7½", $450.00; casserole in rack, $250.00; #3 spice jar, $500.00+; cookie jar, $750.00+. Note prices are color-specific. *Photo courtesy of C. L. McClanahan.*

Hi-Fire cylinder vase, 8", $150.00; (pieces following are "ring") salt and pepper shakers, $70.00; covered sugar, $75.00; creamer, $40.00; goblet, $150.00+; coffee cup and saucer, $85.00; dinner plate, 10½", $100.00+; salad plate, 7½", $50.00; cereal bowl, $55.00.

Bauer's winning "ring" dinnerware plates: 5" bread and butter in delph blue, $90.00+; 6" bread and butter in royal blue, $30.00; 7½" salad in orange-red, $45.00; 9" dinner in Chinese yellow, $35.00; 10½" dinner in jade green, $100.00+.

"Ring" 6-cup teapot with stack of 6" bread and butter plates, in-mold marks. Teapot, $350.00; plates, $20.00 – 30.00 each.

This classic teapot design, known to collectors as the Aladdin, was part of the Gloss Pastel Kitchenware line of the forties. Larger 8-cup size in yellow, in-mold mark, $250.00.

Used for leftovers, this stacking refrigerator jar set was part of Bauer's extensive "ring" line, in-mold marks, $400.00.

Decorative pots. Back row: 10" lion pot, $400.00+; 8" hanging basket, $350.00; 6" Indian bowl of the fifties, $150.00. Front row: 7" Indian bowl of the thirties, $600.00+; 8" Biltmore jar, $200.00. *Photo courtesy of C.L. McClanahan.*

"Ring" kitchenware, in-mold marks. Large batter bowl, $150.00; small batter bowl, $200.00.

A variety of Bauer mixing bowls. Top row: #24 Tracy Irwin design, $35.00; #24 Sears line, $35.00; #18 Gloss Pastel Kitchenware, $45.00. Center row: #24 "ring", $75.00; #26 Hi-Fire, $35.00; Bauer look-alike. Bottom row: #9 early "ring," $200.00+; "plain" design, $200.00+. *Photo courtesy of C. L. McClanahan.*

This "ring" 2-quart ice water pitcher is sometimes mistaken for Monterey, in-mold mark, $300.00.

Bauer-made similar custard cups in its ring design, no marks. The custard cups in the wire rack are from the Hi-Fire line of Plant #2, $25.00 – 75.00 each. The characteristic "ring" custard on the right was produced at Plant #1, $25.00.

Large hand-thrown art pottery vases by Bauer ca. 1915, no marks. Carnation vase, 24½", $1,800.00+; Rebekah vase, 24½", $2,500.00+.

Bauer's majestic oil jars in orange-red glaze. #122 oil jar, 20", $1,500.00+; #100 oil jar, 12", $1,200.00+; #100 oil jar, 22", $2,000.00+.

Imposing 24" handmade Rebekah vase in jade green by Matt Carlton, unmarked, $3,000.00+.

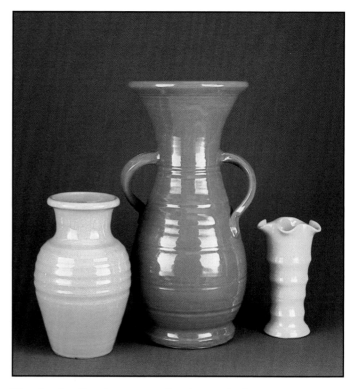

Handmade floral artware by Matt Carlton. Vase, 9½", $850.00+; handled vase, 17", $2,000.00+; ruffled vase, 7½", $350.00.

"Season's Greetings, 1930, Bauer Pottery Co." is the legend on this very hard-to-find ashtray in jade green, $500.00+.

Handmade garden vases by Fred Johnson in turquoise glaze, no marks. Vase with handles, 22", $1,000.00+; vase, 18", $800.00+.

Variations on a theme: Matt Carlton's handmade twist-handled vases, no marks. 18½" vase in orange-red, $1,800.00+; 14½" vase in delph blue, $2,500.00+; 12" vase in Chinese yellow, $1,200.00+.

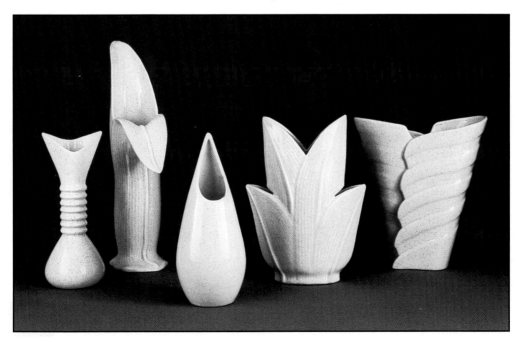

Bauer floral artware of the fifties designed by Tracy Irwin. Vase #506, 8", $50.00; vase #678, 13", $150.00; vase #505, 8", $50.00; vase #684, 8½", $65.00; vase #502, 8", $55.00.

Cal-Art Pottery designed by Ray Murray, in-mold marks. Top row: All in turquoise blue. Vase, 8", $85.00; vase, 6", $50.00; vase 7", $85.00. Bottom row: Bud vase, 7", in matte blue, $65.00; vase, 5", in matte blue, $35.00; vase pitcher, 5½" x 7" in matte green, $65.00.

Cal-Art ewer, 10", $125.00; Bauer dealer sign, $750.00+.

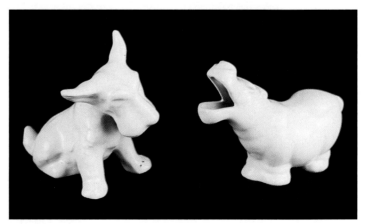

Cal-Art matte glazed Scottie, $500.00+; hippo, 3¼" x 4½", $350.00+.

Three swan planters from Bauer's Cal-Art line, produced at Plant #2. All have in-mold marks. Very rare black medium-size swan, 5½" x 10", $200.00+; small swan, 4" x 7", in matte white, $85.00; large swan, 6½" x 12", in matte white, $75.00.

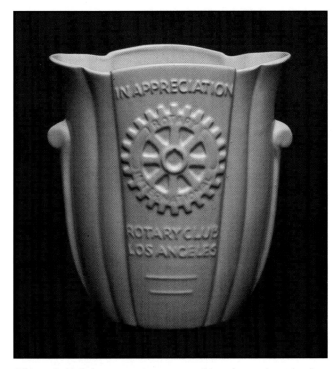

This rare oblong planter in white measures 6" x 13", in-mold marked "Bauer Los Angeles," $200.00+.

This 8" Cal-Art vase in matte white, honoring the Los Angeles Rotary Club, is not easy to find, $200.00+.

Bauer fish-shaped cookie jar, in speckled blue glaze, was originally a Cemar Potteries design, $150.00.

Gloss Pastel Kitchenware cookie jar, in-mold mark "Bauer Los Angeles," $175.00.

Bauer's Monterey Moderne line. Cup and saucer in burgundy, $35.00; 6" bread and butter plate in olive green, $8.00; 7½" salad plate in gray, $12.00; 9½" dinner plate in burgundy, $25.00; 10½" dinner plate in pink, $30.00; 13" chop plate in chartreuse, $50.00.

Tracy Irwin designed these "pumpkin bowls" for Bauer in the fifties. All have in-mold "Bauer" mark. Pumpkin bowl in matte pink, 5" x 8", $80.00; pumpkin bowl in matte beige, 4" x 6", $60.00; half pumpkin bowl in matte green, 3¼" x 7¾", $80.00.

Bauer bean pot in yellow ware with exceptional overglaze decoration, $500.00+.

Photo courtesy of Rena Bransten Gallery, San Francisco.

MARC BELLAIRE

The distinctive ceramic creations of Marc Bellaire have been attracting more and more collecting converts in recent years. Though Bellaire's work is often compared with colleague Sascha Brastoff, his individual flair for animated decoration and design merit a closer look.

Marc Bellaire was the professional name of Donald E. Fleischman, born in Toledo, Ohio, in 1925. Beginning his formal training in art at age 14 under the auspices of the Toledo Museum of Art, he later studied with noted watercolorist Ernest Spring. After a tour of duty with the United States Navy during World War II, during which he was stationed in Southern California, Bellaire enrolled at the Chicago Academy of Art. Before relocating to Southern California in 1950, he augmented his art education by attending classes at the Chicago Art Institute.

Bellaire pursued additional studies at the Los Angeles County Art Institute (now Otis Art Institute) and Immaculate Heart College prior to his employment in Sascha Brastoff's ceramic plant, located in West Los Angeles, in the early fifties. While working for Brastoff, Bellaire, inspired by his employer's blossoming enterprise, decided to decamp and establish his own ceramics business in nearby Culver City.

The Marc Bellaire Ceramics Studio was housed in a 10,000-square foot, fully-equipped building where coordinated ensembles for the modern home were produced to coincide with the semi-annual gift shows held in Los Angeles and elsewhere. Many of his popular lines featured exotic locales or activities, including Mardi Gras, Jamaica, Friendly Island, Beachcomber, and Polynesian Star. Some of these lines accommodated figures or figure groupings, some very large in scale, which have in recent years become some of the most sought after Bellaire items. As was the practice at the Brastoff factory, Bellaire had his trademark "signature" placed prominently on nearly every item completed. It is not known for certain, however, whether the full signature vis-à-vis a simple "Bellaire" indicates an original by Marc Bellaire rather than a decorator's example, but this is likely the case.

Recognizing his contribution to the industry, *Giftwares*, a leading trade publication at the time, included Marc Bellaire on its list of the ten top artware designers of the late fifties. During the sixties, as business began to ebb, Marc Bellaire devoted more time to teaching and writing about the art of ceramic design and decoration than to actual ceramic production. Articles by Bellaire routinely appeared in

Large Friendly Island free-form tray from the mid-fifties with hand-painted decoration and overglaze gold, signed "Marc Bellaire." $225.00.

magazines like *Popular Ceramics* and *Ceramics Monthly*, with the latter publication issuing two of his handbooks for budding ceramists, titled *Underglaze Decoration* and *Brush Decoration*. Also a talented painter and sculptor, Bellaire moved to Virginia after leaving the ceramics business, where he maintained both a private art studio and art gallery. He later returned to California, first locating in Marin County, north of San Francisco. From the early eighties until his death in 1994, Marc Bellaire's studio was located in Cathedral City, California.

Markings generally were freehand painted on the base and/or obverse side of objects, and incorporated the full or last name of Marc Bellaire, as shown. Signatures were often accomplished by means of a sgraffito technique. Printed marks were also used.

Marc Bellaire

Jamaica line candlesticks, both signed "Marc Bellaire." Candlestick on left is 10½". $125.00 – $175.00.

Jamaica line divided dish, 10", signed "Bellaire Calif./ Jamaica" in sgraffito fashion on underside, $150.00.

Decorative 10" plate with exotic pear-shaped floral spray, signed "Marc Bellaire," $150.00.

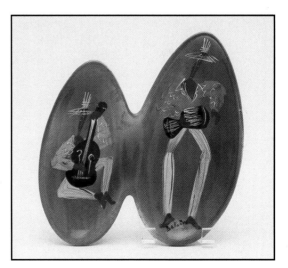

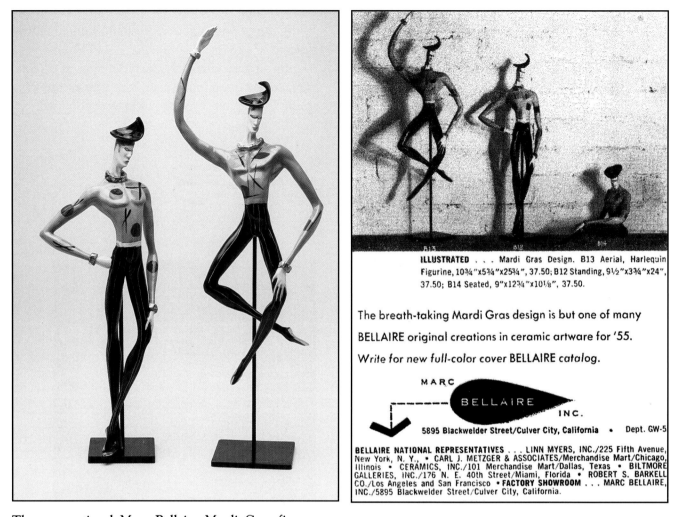

These sensational Marc Bellaire Mardi Gras figures are supported or held aloft by heavy metal stands. Figure at left measures 24" while the one at right rises to 30", including its metal support. Signed "Bellaire." 24", $1,200.00+; 30", $1,500.00+.

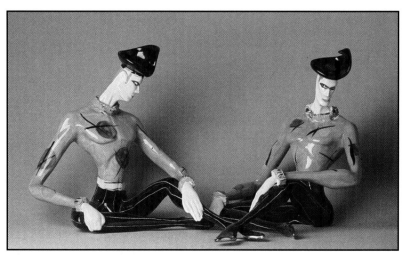

Large and imposing seated Mardi Gras figures by Marc Bellaire. Bellaire figures like these are very hard to find. $1,000.00–1,200.00+ each.

Pitcher-shaped vase, 18", from Bellaire's popular Mardi Gras line, $300.00.

This asymmetrical vase with Mardi Gras-like painted figure is 18" tall, $300.00.

This Jungle Dancer oval platter measures 18" x 13". Signed "Bellaire." $200.00.

Left: Magnificent Bali dancers by Marc Bellaire, figure on left stands 24". Above: Detail of Bali Dancer figures shown. $1,000.00 –1,500.00 each.

Two Bali figures. 8" seated figure, $1,000.00+; 13" dancing figure, $1,500.00+.

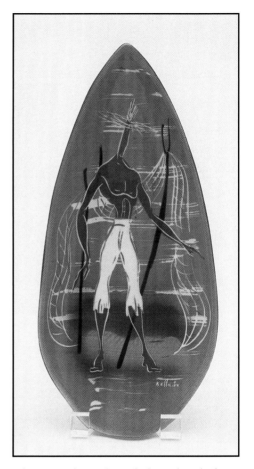

This teardrop-shaped low bowl from Marc Bellaire's Beachcomber line is 12" in length. Backstamped "Marc Bellaire California" with "Bellaire" signature on obverse. $100.00.

12" plate by Marc Bellaire with hand-painted native dancer in jungle setting, $200.00.

Oblong footed compote, 6" x 12", with decoration resembling a prehistoric cave painting, $125.00.

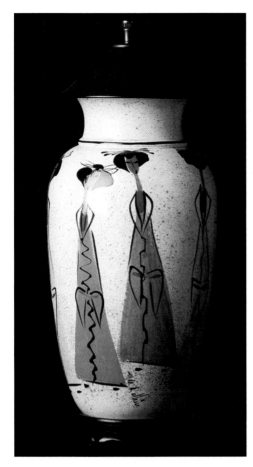

Large lamp base, 18" diameter, with simplified yet skillfully painted decoration of Japanese geishas, signed "Marc Bellaire," $250.00.

Egg-shaped platter, 14", with Oriental-style painted scene of sampans, signed "Marc Bellaire," $250.00.

Charger, 15", with highly stylized bird-on-branch motif, signed "Marc Bellaire" (post-Culver City), $200.00.

Cortillian free-form bowl, 13" x 9", hand-painted recessed figure by Marc Bellaire, $200.00.

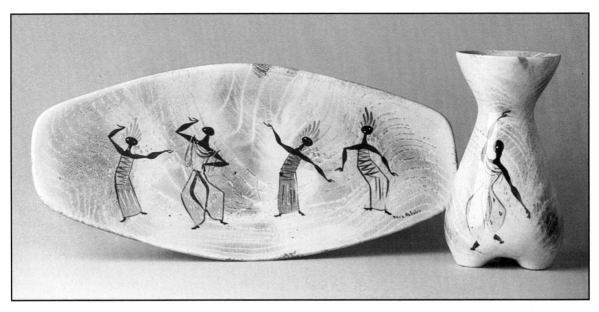

From the Bali line, footed compote, 8" x 17", signed "Marc Bellaire," $250.00, and 8" vase, $250.00.

Charger, 15", custom made by Marc Bellaire (post-Culver City). Surrealistic scene of trees with foliage in relief was achieved by using slip mixed with sand. $300.00+.

Stick People vase, 12", with irregular beak-like opening, $250.00.

Heavenly charger, 15", signed by Marc Bellaire (post-Culver City), $400.00+.

Marc Bellaire just beginning the process of decorating a vase, ca. 1963.

Black Bird Isle(?) ashtray, 9" x 8", with theme akin to Bellaire's Bird Isle line. Possibly a prototype, signed "Marc Bellaire," $200.00.

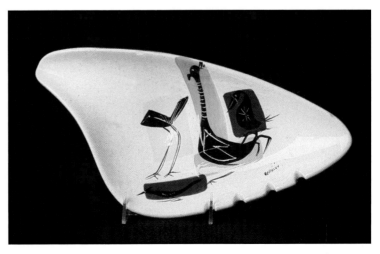

Bird Isle asymmetric ashtray, 7" x 14", signed "Bellaire," $85.00.

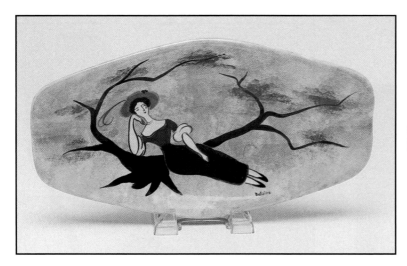

Oblong ashtray, 14¼", from Marc Bellaire's Pastorale line, signed "Bellaire," $150.00.

Pieces from the Pastorale line, all signed "Marc Bellaire" with underside marks in sgraffito style reading: "Marc Bellaire/Calif./Pastorale." Divided dish, 10", $200.00; sugar and creamer, $175.00 set.

Native American-style vase dated 1990. Pieces such as this were produced at Marc Bellaire's Cathedral City studio, $400.00+.

SASCHA BRASTOFF

The Sascha Brastoff saga is unique. His was the quintessential example of an artist's personal vision reaching an appreciative mass audience!

Sascha Brastoff was born to parents of Russian and Hungarian descent in Cleveland, Ohio, in 1918. After high school, he attended the Western Reserve School of Art in Cleveland before leaving home at age 17 to begin working on his own in New York. In Manhattan, Brastoff became a member of the Clay Club. Two of his terra cotta figures won the award for "Sculpture Showing Unusual Humor or Whimsy" at the National Ceramic Exhibition at the Syracuse (now Everson) Museum of Art in 1939. Two years later, a successful one-person show of his ceramic sculpture was sponsored by the Clay Club.

Participation in the U.S. Army Air Force's entertainment services during the war renewed a prior interest in show business which continued when Brastoff moved to Los Angeles in 1945 and was employed as a costume designer for 20th Century Fox. Through a publicist at Fox, his terra cotta sculpture came to the attention of Winthrop Rockefeller who expressed a willingness to finance Brastoff if he would agree to manufacture a prestigious line of American-made china.

In 1947, a ceramics business was established on a modest scale in West Los Angeles. Because Brastoff was basically untrained in ceramic production, a crew of skilled technicians was hired along with a salesman and decorating staff. The product at first was earthenware, the body and glazes worked out from scratch. Early designs included vases, bowls, ashtrays and dishes featuring fanciful fruit and leaf motifs. A series of decorative figures was also initiated early on. Nearly everything was hand painted, after Brastoff's artisans were thoroughly trained to duplicate his personal, flamboyant style of decoration. Overglaze gold trim was lavish and before long became one of the hallmarks of the business. Many new, often unorthodox, materials were tested and utilized to produce unique decorative effects.

Demand steadily grew for Sascha Brastoff's unusual creations, and in the early fifties Rockefeller's

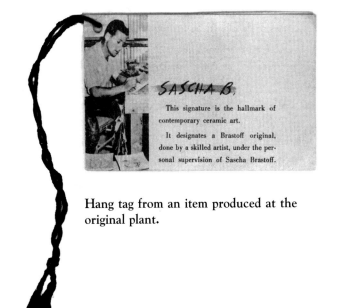

Hang tag from an item produced at the original plant.

friend E. E. (Ted) Campbell became president of Sascha Brastoff Products, Inc. With his urging and Rockefeller's backing, the business moved to a larger facility owned by Tom Hamilton of American Ceramic Products. The move proved ill-fated, however, when the building was destroyed by fire a few months later, in July of 1952. Resolution of the crisis came with construction of an all-new 35,000-square foot factory designed by noted architect A. Quincy Jones, at 11520 West Olympic Boulevard in Los Angeles. The new Brastoff plant was an elaborate ceramic studio and gallery and became a tourist attraction when it opened in 1953. Sascha Brastoff personally supervised his productive staff of 80 or more and was responsible for all shapes, decorative schemes, and glazes during the first 10 years of the business. Entire lines, encompassing 200 coordinated items at times, would emerge twice a year.

Winthrop Rockefeller's wish was finally fulfilled in 1954 when the first of 10 fine china dinnerware lines was marketed. Earthenware table settings were also produced, the most successful being Surf Ballet, a marbleized arabesque of gold or silver set against various background colors. Among the many decorative items produced at the Olympic Boulevard plant were flower arranging bowls, vases, figurines, lamps, wall plaques, and masks. Smoking accessories, including an astonishing variety of ashtrays, were the most popular of Brastoff's articles. An extensive output of enamel ware was also produced over the years.

Stricken with nervous exhaustion in 1963, Sascha Brastoff found it necessary to withdraw from his beloved business. The constant rigors of designing and decorating new lines, training and supervising artists, and personal promotion trips throughout the country finally took their toll. Even without his direct involvement, the Brastoff line of goods was sustained for another decade by plant manager Gerald Schwartz and art director Eddie Kourishima, although the operation was relocated to a smaller factory, at 12530 Yukon Street in Hawthorne. A few of Brastoff's protégés, notably Marc Bellaire and Matthew Adams, went on to form pottery businesses of their own.

After retiring from ceramics, Sascha Brastoff pursued successful careers in fine art, retailing, and free-lance design. The focus of his later years was custom jewelry, some of which incorporated holograms. He died in 1993, at age 75. Brastoff's work is contained in the collections of numerous museums including New York's Metropolitan Museum of Art and Guggenheim Museum of Art, the Los Angeles County Museum of Art, the Everson Museum of Art, and the Houston Art Museum.

An early Sascha Brastoff painted mark is shown (1). After relocation to the Olympic Boulevard plant, the chanticleer (rooster) trademark was incorporated into a backstamp (2) for use on both earthenware and china. These were often applied overglaze in gold or silver. Brastoff's success was partly the result of his personal celebrity which he augmented by having his "signature" appear on every piece produced. His trained decorators signed the name "Sascha B." (3), but only those pieces signed "Sascha Brastoff" (4, 5) were hand painted by Brastoff himself. A registration symbol was added after Brastoff's separation from the business in 1963 (see mark #2). Very few unmarked examples have been observed. The enamel ware was marked as described or with paper labels.

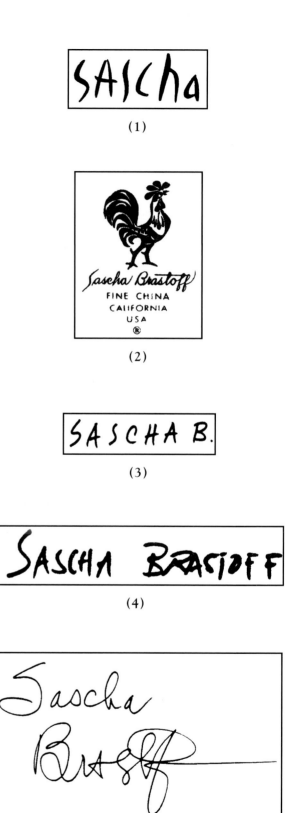

(1)

(2)

(3)

(4)

(5)

Archival image of completed ware photographed at the original Sascha Brastoff plant.

Native wall mask, 9½", one of a series, signed "Sascha B." $500.00+.

Sascha Brastoff Alaska line vase, 13½", signed "Sascha B.", $250.00.

Horse figure, 10½", platinum on matte pink, signed "Sascha B.", ca. 1957, $250.00.

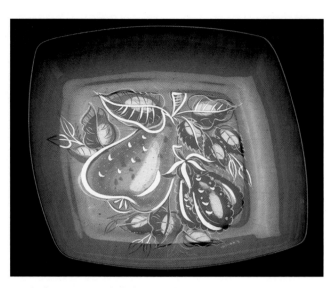

Left: Abstract design vase, 10", $150.00. Right: Minos design hooded ashtray, 8", $125.00. Both signed "Sascha B."

Early low square dish by Sascha Brastoff with fruit motif, 11¼", signed "Sascha B.", $100.00.

Exterior view of the Sascha Brastoff plant on Olympic in Los Angeles, designed by architect A. Quincy Jones. *Photo courtesy of Julius Shulman.*

Interior view of the Sascha Brastoff plant showing a section of the gallery. *Photo courtesy of Julius Shulman.*

Early period vase, 12½", with elaborate cut-outs and hand-decoration by Sascha Brastoff, signed "Sascha" on side, $1,000.00+.

Rooftops line. Free-form vase/planter, 5½" x 7½", $85.00; free-form server, 13", $65.00. Both signed "Sascha B." with rooster backstamp.

Three-footed bowl, 2¼" x 10", signed "Sascha B.", $125.00.

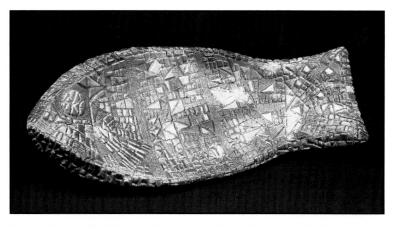

Sascha Brastoff's Mosaics line included this fish-shaped ashtray, 17",
signed "Sascha B." with rooster backstamp, $200.00.

Gravy bowl with attached under-plate, from Brastoff's earthenware
table service called Smoke Tree, $50.00.

This elaborately festooned ceramic
sculpture of Carmen Miranda by
Sascha Brastoff is 22½" in height and
has a shallow opening at the top for
flowers or a candle, full signature
inside hollow base, $4,000.00+.

Abstraction in gold, both signed "Sascha B."
Left: Patio lamp (candleholder), 9½", $175.00.
Right: Chalice-like vase, 6", $175.00.

Large Abstract Originals line by Sascha Brastoff included these floral containers, all signed "Sascha B." with rooster backstamp. Left to right: vase, 20", $250.00; free form vase, 10", $125.00; vase, 5½", $50.00; vase, 9", $100.00.

Hang tag from an item purchased at Sascha Brastoff's Olympic Boulevard plant. Back side shows exterior view of plant.

Left: Free-form ashtray, 8½", $35.00. Right: Round hooded ashtray, 3¼" x 5½", $35.00. Both signed "Sascha B."

Enamel ware ashtrays, both signed "Sascha B." Left: artichoke shape, 5½", $30.00; right: leaf shape, 6¼", $30.00.

Star Steed plate, 10½", hand decorated and signed "Sascha Brastoff," ca. 1959, $500.00+.

Footed free-form dish, 10", vaguely resembling a fish, was hand decorated by Sascha Brastoff in his characteristic whimsical style, $750.00+.

This ensemble in white foam finish came under the heading of Sculptural Accessories, both signed "Sascha B." "Merbaby" figure, $350.00; large shell candleholder, $200.00.

Sascha Brastoff's trademark rooster, 14", in sculptural form, from his Mosaics line of decorative household goods, signed "Sascha B.", $450.00.

Abstract line Sascha Brastoff ashtray, 15½" in length, "Sascha B." on obverse with rooster backstamp, $150.00.

Sascha Brastoff's extensive Alaska line included this square dish, 3½", $40.00, and oblong footed dish, 2¼" x 7½", $65.00. Both pieces signed "Sascha B."

Winrock porcelain dinner plate, 11", $50.00; Night Song porcelain salad plate, 9", $40.00, and cereal bowl, 6", $45.00. "Sascha Brastoff Fine China" stamped marks.

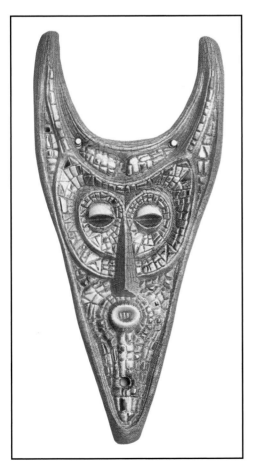

African style mask (#M32), 18½", from Sascha Brastoff's Mosaic line, signed "Sascha B.", $750.00+.

This 11½" plate has amusing hand-painted decoration of a tipsy elephant by Sascha Brastoff. Full signature on backside (see below). $1,000.00+.

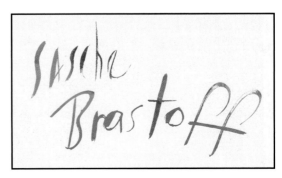

Close-up view of Surf Ballet cup and saucer in silver and pink on white glaze treatment, $25.00.

A teapot for a true tea lover, it measures 8¼" x 12", signed "Sascha B.", $150.00.

Americana line ashtray, 7", signed "Sascha B." on interior, plus rooster backstamp and "056A," $50.00.

This advertisement appeared in the February, 1958 issue of *House Beautiful*.

This very early charger, 16½", with hand-painted still life is signed "Sascha Brastoff," $1,500.00+.

Imaginative scene executed by Sascha Brastoff on matte finished 17" charger, signed "Sascha Brastoff" on front, $1,500.00+.

This 10" enamel ware pictorial tile was part of Sascha Brastoff's estate collection, $225.00.

The popular and enduring Star Steed line included these decorative items; all are signed "Sascha B." Vase, 9½", $100.00; ashtray, 4" x 5", $45.00; cigarette box, $65.00; individual ashtray, $25.00.

Paper tag from late period of the Brastoff business after plant was relocated to Hawthorne. Front and back shown.

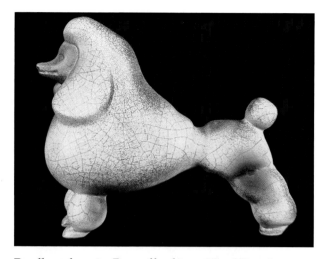

Poodle, a favorite Brastoff subject, 7" x 9", satin-matte crackle glaze, signed "Sascha B.", $250.00.

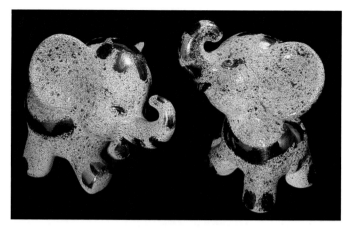

Circus elephant set, platinum on matte light blue, signed "Sascha B." Left: 7½", $250.00; right: 8", $250.00.

Horse head sculpture on wood base, 7½", satin-matte crackle glaze, signed "Sascha B.," $350.00+.

Sascha Brastoff working on metal wall sculpture made for the Winthrop Rockefeller estate know as Winrock, ca. 1955.

BRAYTON LAGUNA

In view of its innovations and influence, the Brayton Laguna Pottery ranks as one of the foremost companies in the history of Southern California pottery. The business was founded about 1927 by Durlin E. Brayton, a California native and alumnus of Hollywood High School. Brayton, who also attended the Chicago Art Institute, was self-employed as a carpenter before venturing into ceramics. At his residence on the Coast Highway in Laguna Beach, he built a modest kiln and workshop. With the help of his first wife, Durlin Brayton introduced a line of simple earthenware dishes in sets of mixed colors in the mid-to-late twenties, probably the first of their kind produced in the United States.

Brayton's pioneering colored pottery was press-molded by hand and then dipped in a remarkable series of opaque glazes including rose, strawberry pink, eggplant, jade green, lettuce green, chartreuse, old gold, burnt orange, lemon yellow, silky black, and white. Basic place settings were made along with accessory pieces such as teapots, pitchers and large serving bowls. The charming, unpretentious shapes perfectly accommodated the casual seaside lifestyle. Brayton also designed vases, flower pots, tea tiles, wall plates, and figurines, all of which were produced in limited quantities. The colorful display of goods in the Braytons' front yard attracted both Laguna residents and tourists and provided a sustaining occupation for a handful of assistants during the early Depression years.

Durlin met and married his second wife, Ellen Webster Grieve, in 1936. "Webb," as she was called, was an artist with a keen business sense, and through her efforts the Laguna Pottery changed from a small cottage shop to a significant commercial enterprise. Mrs. Brayton realized that a sizable market could be developed for mass-produced figurines designed and decorated by the abundance of artistic talent in the immediate area. This concept called for larger facilities which Durlin designed and constructed on a five-acre site between the Coast Highway and Gleneyre in 1938. The most modern production equipment, including two continuous tunnel kilns, was installed

Handpainted tile, 6", ca. 1929. These popular tiles are becoming rare. Below: Underglaze painted signature of Durlin Brayton on tile above. $600.00+.

on the premises along with ample work areas, offices, and a large showroom. Noted Swedish woodcarver H. S. "Andy" Anderson was the first outside designer hired. He modeled many whimsical figures and groupings including an English hunter with fox and hounds, a hillbilly shotgun wedding set, and one of Brayton Laguna's bestsellers, the purple cow, bull and calf family inspired by a popular Gelet Burgess poem.

Because of the company's reputation for quality figurines, it was the first pottery licensed by the Walt Disney Studios to produce ceramic likenesses of their famous animated characters. Among those marketed from 1938 to 1940 were Snow White and the Seven

Dwarfs, Pinocchio, Jiminy Cricket, Figaro, Ferdinand the Bull, Donald Duck, Mickey Mouse, and Pluto.

Hand-decorated figurines were so successful for the business that more than twenty-five designers were eventually employed. Among the early model makers were Lietta Ann Dowd and Frances Robinson, who each created a large number of figurines of children. A partial listing of the talented designers who added distinction to the Brayton Laguna line over the years includes Walter Bringhurst, Ruth Peabody, Charles Beauvais, Kay Kinney, Jules Erbitt, William Lyons, Carol Safholm, Jean Yves Mock, Peter Ganine, and Ferdinand Horvath. Most of these artists also maintained studios where they produced and marketed their own work.

Brayton Laguna's various sales representatives promoted the company's wares during World War II. By the end of the war, retail outlets had been secured in every major American city and in many foreign countries. This was the most productive period for the business, when overseas ceramic goods were unavailable to the giftware trade. The plant operated at capacity day and night, with over 150 people employed on two shifts.

Laguna Beach, well-known as an art colony and beach resort, was for a short time one of the major ceramics centers in California as a result of the operation's success. Over a dozen separate potteries had sprung up in the area by 1941, with the number exceeding 65 during the war. A cooperative organization known as the Laguna Beach Ceramic Society was established to help publicize the Laguna potters and foster better relations between them.

After the war the situation for Brayton and the other companies began to reverse. With Japanese and Italian companies flooding the domestic market with an abundance of cheaper wares, the extra help hired by the firm during the war had to be dismissed. Webb Brayton's untimely death in 1948 was a serious loss for the company. After 1951 and the passing of founder Durlin Brayton, the spark was gone and the business gradually declined. In 1968, a truly important chapter in California's ceramic history ended. Today, the buildings comprise the Laguna Art Center.

Brayton Laguna also produced what it termed sculpture — animals, birds, and human figures of moderate scale, usually offered in sets of two or more. Various finishes were used for these, including hand painting, airbrush decoration, monochrome and crackled glazes, woodtone (a stained textured bisque), and combinations of these. Vases, planters, ashtrays, candle holders, cookie jars, salt and pepper shakers, and other household items rounded out the line. Most of the ware was cast.

There was a definite evolution in Brayton Laguna's marking system. Knowledge of the time-frame of the various marks is a key to dating examples. The earliest mark (c.1927–1930) was "Laguna Pottery" (1) incised in Durlin Brayton's distinctive handwriting. From about 1930 to 1937, "Laguna Pottery by Brayton" (2) or "Brayton Laguna Pottery" (3) was incised. An early stamped mark (c.1938–1942) may be found on certain figurines, consisting of the silhouetted image of two pots and a gypsy walking his dog, with "Brayton/California/USA" centered below (not shown, but see trademark used in later years based on this image.) Other stamped marks of the forties were simpler, with the words "BRAYTON POTTERY" or "BRAYTON LAGUNA POTTERY" imprinted in block letters. Sometimes the name of a figurine appeared as part of the mark. The small foil-paper label shown (4) was used from the late thirties into the forties. A variation of this label was used on Disney character figurines of 1938–1940 (see color plate of Ferdinand the Bull on page 64.) A special stamped mark (5) appeared on the Pinocchio series. Another special mark appeared on the Webton line (named after designer Webb Brayton) during World War II, using the words "WEBTON WARE" in an arc with "BY BRAYTON LAGUNA/PEACE/CALIFORNIA/USA" centered below. An incised "Brayton's" mark (6), used from the mid-to-late forties, is shown. This mark, with some modifications, extended into the fifties. For most of the fifties through the sixties, recessed in-mold marks (7 & 8) were the norm, with the mark often including a catalog number. Much Brayton Laguna ware was not marked simply because there was no room for a mark. This holds especially true for the company's four-footed animal figures. One clue to their identity: an incised or painted decorator's initial is often present.

Early handmade decorative pottery by Durlin Brayton with incised marks. Left to right: Flower pot, $150.00; vase, 5½", $250.00+; bud vase with entwined snake, 8", $350.00+.

(1)   (2)

(3)

Handmade tiles by D. Brayton, incised marks, c. 1928. Left to right: Cats on roof, 4½", $500.00+; fanciful tree, 6½", $400.00+; mushrooms, 4½", $400.00+.

(4)   (5)

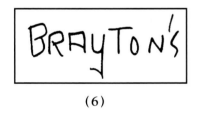

(6)

(7)

(8)

Early handmade items by Durlin Brayton, incised "Brayton Laguna Pottery." Vase, 5½", $400.00+; chamber stick, 3¼", $250.00+.

An assortment of the trailblazing colored pottery that was handmade by Durlin Brayton in the late twenties/early thirties. Cigarette holder and ashtray in foreground are especially scarce.

Chicken big and chicken little from Brayton Laguna, stamped marks. Hen cookie jar, 10", $350.00+; smaller candy jar, $175.00+.

Durlin Brayton's line of handmade colored pottery included pitcher, 5", $350.00+; teapot, 5½", $600.00+; pitcher, 5½", $300.00+; loop-handled pitcher, 7¼", $450.00+. All have incised marks.

Figures from the two Brayton Laguna childhood series, early forties. Left: Chinese boy and girl $100.00 each. Right: Black children $600.00+ single figure.

Popular Hillbilly Shotgun Wedding set designed by Andy Anderson, ca. 1938, stamped marks. Shotgun man stands 9". $1,500.00 set.

Homey facilities of the Brayton Laguna Pottery, ca. 1940.

Rarely seen Swedish peasant woman flower holder, 11½", incised mark, ca. 1939, $400.00+.

The kitchen of Durlin and Webb Brayton was featured in the August 1940 issue of *Better Homes & Gardens*. The legend, hand painted in Swedish over the windows, reads, "You are welcome in our home."

Christina (Swedish maid) cookie jar, 11", incised "Brayton Laguna Pottery," ca. 1941, $450.00+.

Mexican man, 9", $350.00+; mule, 7¼" x 10", $300.00+. Designed by A. Anderson.

Frances Robinson's childhood series included Pedro, 6½", $200.00, and Rosita, 5½", $100.00. Stamped marks.

This pair of Peruvian native figures designed by Carol Safholm was produced by Brayton Laguna in the fifties. Height of man is 9¼". $350.00.

The childhood series by Frances Robinson, heights range from 7" to 8", early forties. Dutch boy and girl, $200.00 pair; Eric and Inger (Swedish), $200.00 pair; Sambo and Petunia, $500.00 pair.

This powerful voodoo drummer by Carol Safholm combines areas of stained bisque, crackle glaze, and slip decoration, 13" in height, unmarked, $500.00+.

Brayton Laguna Fighting Pirates, 9", designed by Carol Safholm, ca. 1956, dark brown-stained bisque with colored and crackle glazes, $750.00+ pair.

Early Brayton Laguna storybook series of figurines, presumably by Durlin Brayton. Recognizable characters include Little Red Riding Hood and Little Boy Blue. $225.00–275.00 each.

Andy Anderson modeled this rarely seen 9" Brayton Laguna figure of a pirate sitting on his booty, $450.00+.

This ensemble is usually found incomplete. Maestro at piano (with small vase attached), $250.00+, and opera singer, $175.00, are from the early forties. Woman is 8½" and bears early stamped mark of gypsy walking his dog. Other pieces unmarked.

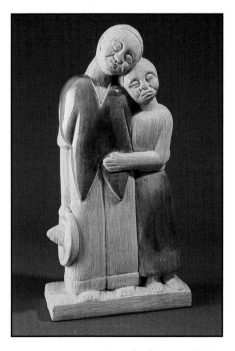

Mexican peasant couple figure, 12½", textured bisque with high glaze, in-mold mark, $225.00.

Figurines by Andy Anderson, late thirties. Fox (from English hunter with fox and hounds set), $125.00; St. Bernard, $150.00.

Toucan, 9", with different finishes, in-mold marks, fifties/sixties. Left: Woodtone with high glaze, $125.00. Right: Polychrome high glaze, $250.00.

From Brayton Laguna's Walt Disney line of figurines. Sniffing Pluto 3¼" x 6", $125.00; howling Pluto, 6", $150.00.

Most Brayton Laguna-made Disney items are very scarce and coveted by collectors. From the Disney film *Pinocchio*, Gepetto, 8", $800.00+; Pinocchio, 6", $500.00+; Jiminy Cricket, 3", $600.00+.

Two versions of Disney's Ferdinand the Bull by Brayton Laguna. Larger figure measures 7½" x 8" and has affixed paper label as shown, $500.00+; smaller figure, $300.00+.

Coachman candy jar from Walt Disney's animated film *Pinocchio*.
This extremely rare jar was produced about 1939 and is unmarked.
$3,000.00+.

These Alice in Wonderland figurines were not based on Walt Disney film characteri-
zations. They were produced prior to the Disney license and may have been modeled
by Durlin Brayton. Mad Hatter is 7" in height. No marks. $350.00 – 400.00+ each.

This gypsy woman head vase by Brayton Laguna, ca. 1939, is 9" in height, incised "Brayton Laguna Pottery," $450.00+.

Brayton Laguna's popular Gay Nineties series included this gent in top hat posing with a cigar store Indian. Copyright 1940 and measuring 9½", this figure is very rare. Incised and stamped marks, $750.00+.

The Gay Nineties series included this piece called "Lovers in Cab," 7½" x 11", incised mark, ca. 1941, $600.00+.

This hard-to-find lamp base of a little girl holding a doll is from a delightful series of children figurines and a favorite with collectors, early forties, $400.00+.

Equal parts remarkable and rare define this figure from Brayton Laguna's Gay Nineties series. Measures 11½", copyright 1940, $500.00+.

Walter Bringhurst designed this rather racy (for the early forties) figurine, 9½", incised "Brayton's" mark, $250.00.

Early, extraordinary, and very rare set of four musicians with maestro (11½", on right) presumably modeled by Durlin Brayton, no marks but unmistakable, $800.00+ each.

Popular hand-decorated Mammy cookie jar, $750.00+, with matching Chef and Jemima shakers, ca. 1945, $150.00 pair.

This pair of 18½" black princes feeding grapes to luxuriant tropical birds represents the zenith of the Blackamoor series, incised marks, very rare, $1,000.00+ each.

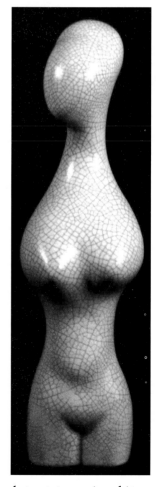

This striking head and shoulders sculpture in matte black glaze measures 12" x 13", late period in-mold mark reads "Brayton's Laguna Calif.", $350.00+.

This abstract torso, in white crackle glaze, dates from the fifties, $200.00.

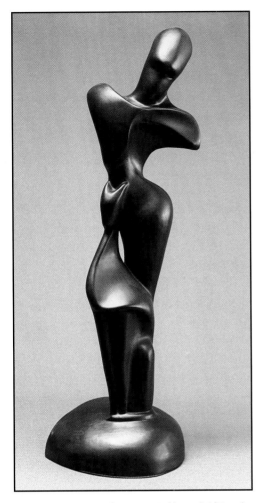

African native musical trio in combination stained bisque/white crackle glaze, fifties period in-mold marks. Left to right: 10½", $150.00; 8½", $150.00; and 11", $150.00.

Abstract man with cat, 21" (from M/F set), satin-matte black, in-mold mark, ca. 1957, $400.00+.

The elephant family, in woodtone/white crackle finish, by Brayton Laguna, ca. 1957. Left to right: 13½", $250.00; 7½", $150.00; 9½", $250.00.

Castle piece, 10½", from large-scale chess set designed for Brayton Laguna by Peter Ganine in 1946, in-mold mark, $250.00.

Logo used in later years of the business, note zip code.

CATALINA

The Catalina story is another fascinating chapter in the history of Southern California pottery. In operation just ten years, Catalina Clay Products, a project of the Santa Catalina Island Company, produced an extraordinary array of articles from materials indigenous to the picturesque island located twenty-five miles off the coast. It also provided a number of individuals with the necessary background to launch successful mainland potteries.

The Catalina venture began in 1927, shortly after discovery of the island's extensive clay and mineral deposits, with the establishment of a tile plant at Pebbly Beach, near the city of Avalon. The business was conceived by chewing gum tycoon William Wrigley, Jr., owner of the island, and his close business associate David Renton. Their idea was to serve two functions: give Catalina residents much needed year-round employment and provide economical building materials for the ongoing development of Avalon as a tourist resort. At its peak the operation was the cornerstone in an alliance of self-sufficient indigenous industries, including a furniture workshop and ornamental iron foundry, employing several hundred residents.

In the beginning, the principal product of the Catalina plant was tile. By 1929, a line of ornamental pottery was being turned out in vivid colored glazes to help meet the demands of civic improvement.

Artware of the early thirties. Back row: Handled vase, 8½", $350.00; vase, 9", $325.00; vase, 7½", $375.00; vase, 7¼", $500.00+. Front row: Covered dish, $250.00; bowl, 2" x 8", $300.00; tea tile, 6", $300.00+. *Photo courtesy C. L. McClanahan.*

Harold Johnson, who joined the business in 1928 after a long association with Pacific, contributed numerous pottery designs and glazes. Wrigley's most ambitious undertaking in Avalon was the huge multi-level Catalina Casino, which kept the factory operating at full capacity during its first three years. More than 100,000 pieces of roofing tile alone were used to complete the facility. Inside walls utilized hollow tile, while floors and promenade were paved with hand-made octagonal patio tile interspersed with colorful glazed inserts. When it was finished in 1929, the Catalina Casino received the Honor Award from the Southern California Chapter of the American Institute of Architects.

After completion of the monumental casino project, Catalina Clay Products began to diversify. Island souvenirs were stressed, but a complete line of vases, flower bowls, candle holders, lamps, and other decorative accessories for the home was produced and made available in island gift shops. Most of these slip-cast items were quite functional and original in design.

The clay used in production was a brown-burning type trucked in from a dry lake bed located a short distance from the plant. Pulverized rock (felsite) recovered from the Pebbly Beach rock quarry was also used. David Renton, who managed the pottery, hired ceramic engineer Virgil Haldeman after Harold Johnson's departure in 1930. The glazes of Johnson and Haldeman were developed from native oxides. When the glazes united with the island's brown clay, some remarkable effects were achieved. The company's press kit included the following description of one of the Catalina glazes:

"The yellow found in Catalina Pottery is one that has for centuries been the royal color of the reigning house of China, and therefore known as Mandarin or Manchu yellow. The exact hue has never before been duplicated outside the great wall of China, though chemists the world over have striven to achieve this one shade of yellow that can be best described as 'yellow-yellow' or the true gold of a California sun." [1]

Other standard glazes were Catalina blue, Descanso green, Toyon red, turquoise, pearly white, sea foam, and Monterey brown. Later colors, which Haldeman furnished, included beige, coral island, powder blue, and colonial yellow (all satin-matte finish).

The output of the Catalina pottery, which covered several acres and included twelve kilns of various size and type, averaged between 10,000 and 15,000 pieces per week. The wide range of clay products was well suited to the Spanish architecture seen throughout Southern California in the twenties.

The ware was further enhanced in this capacity by the addition of Spanish style wrought-iron frames and stands crafted by the island's foundry. Both the foundry and the furniture shop produced attractive tables that were fitted with scenic tile panels designed by a crew of Catalina artists. Motifs for these, and a related series of decorative wall plates, were suggestive of the island: undersea gardens, exotic birds of the Avalon Bird Park (now closed), flying fish, and Spanish galleons. Numerous hand-painted scenes were also rendered overglaze on plates of various size.

Tableware was introduced about 1930, with the entire spectrum of pottery glazes employed. Three basic dinnerware designs were offered along with many interchangeable serving pieces. In 1936, another complete service, with a raised rope border, was added in all satin-finish pastel colors. The pottery was popular with Catalina residents and tourists despite the Depression, and was shipped to many retail outlets on the mainland of California and elsewhere.

The only flaw in an otherwise successful operation was the native brown clay which proved to be brittle and easily damaged. William Wrigley insisted that Catalina pottery be manufactured only from indigenous materials. Even though it was less than satisfactory, the clay body could not be improved until after Wrigley's death in 1932. At this time, a tougher, white-burning clay was imported from Lincoln, California. The costly importation of clay to Avalon was ironically the major factor necessitating the sale of the Catalina line to mainland competitor Gladding-McBean in 1937.

Catalina Island ware can be distinguished from other Southern California lines of colored pottery by its remarkable series of glazes and, in the case of the pre-1932 ware, its brown clay body. Marks are also helpful. There were a few that were impressed into the leather-hard clay. The words "Catalina" or "Catalina Island" are the most common of these. Sometimes these words were incised by hand, with variations in handwriting. Certain early items were stamped underglaze "Catalina Island" in an oval, or similarly stamped overglaze. Variations on most of the marks exist, making it difficult to determine the dates that specific ones were in use. Paper labels were also used. The recessed or stamped mark "Catalina Pottery" was used by Gladding-McBean on its Catalina Pottery line and should not be confused with the earlier island production.

[1] A. Overholt, "Color To Order," from company publicity kit, c.1933.

Dinnerware designs. Back row: Coupe design plate, 11¼", $65.00; wide shoulder design dinner plate, 10", $50.00; and salad plate, 7½", $45.00; Rope design dinner plate, 10½", $40.00. Front row: Punch cup, $50.00; coffee/tea cup, $50.00; refrigerator jar, $60.00; cup and saucer, $85.00; Rope design cup and saucer, $50.00; hexagonal design creamer, $150.00+. *Photo courtesy C. L. McClanahan.*

Rhapsody in Catalina blue. Fluted vase, 6", $200.00; vase with handles, 9", $350.00.

Catalina glazes. Tumbler in Monterey brown, $70.00; demitasse cup in pearly white, $35.00; coffee mug in Catalina blue, $50.00; pitcher in Toyon red, $250.00+.

Plate, 11½", with hand-painted scene of old Mexico, impressed mark, ca. 1932, $500.00+.

Rolled edge design tray, 14½", turquoise glaze, in forged iron handle, ca. 1934. Tray, $200.00; handle, $300.00+.

Monk design bookend, 5" x 4", Descanso green glaze, ca. 1932, $500.00+.

With slight modification, a vase becomes a cream pitcher, both 6", with impressed "Catalina" mark. Cream pitcher in turquoise, $250.00; vase in Toyon red, $200.00.

Catalina mixing bowls are not easy to find in good condition. This one measures 11" in diameter, the largest of seven sizes, and is impressed "Catalina," $250.00+. Refrigerator jar with cover is 2¾" in height, unmarked, $150.00.

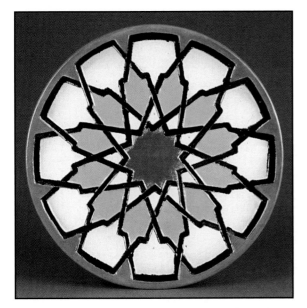

Decorative plate, 11", Moorish design, ca. 1932, $450.00.

"Rope" design items in powder blue matte glaze, ca. 1936. Covered sugar, $50.00; teapot, $200.00; creamer, $40.00.

Display of Catalina Pottery at a Los Angeles area gift show, ca. 1932. *Archival photo.*

Vase with handles, 7½", Mandarin yellow, $350.00; vase, 7", Monterey brown, $400.00. In-mold "Catalina."

This tile plaque depicting green macaws is inset in the exterior wall of a Spanish-style building in Avalon.

A Catalina classic known to collectors as the step vase, Monterey brown with early brown clay body showing through at edges, in-mold "Catalina." $375.00.

Muted and delicately commingled colored glazes distinguish this early example of Harold Johnson's wizardry. Vase measures 9" in height, marked in-mold "Catalina Island." $750.00+.

Catalina rarities. Vase, 10½", $500.00+; nude shot tumblers, 3¼", $300.00+ each; vase #325, 5", $300.00+.

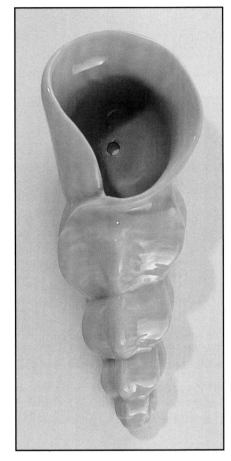

Page 25 of an undated Catalina Pottery catalog, showing three of the most elusive of the company's Catalina Island souvenirs.

Seashell wallpocket in turquoise, incised mark, $250.00.

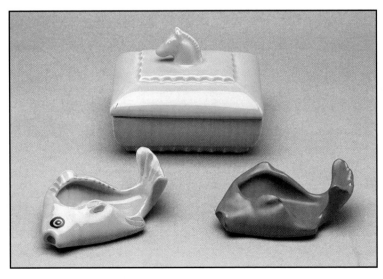

Souvenirs of Catalina Island. Cigarette box with horse's head on lid, $250.00; decorated and undecorated small fish ashtrays, 4½". $125.00 – 175.00 each.

"Cat-lina" cactus planter, in Descanso green with overglaze hand decoration, was a souvenir of Santa Catalina Island, made by the Catalina Pottery around 1936. $400.00+.

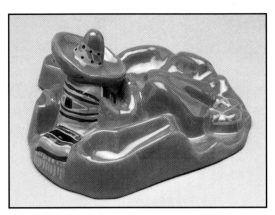

Toyon red glazed Catalina Island pottery: (left to right) vase, 8", $400.00; vase, 7½", $375.00; shell-shaped bowl, 8¾", $250.00; flower pot, 4½", $85.00; sombrero-style ashtray, 2½" x 4", $450.00+. All unmarked except vases; ashtray attributed to Catalina.

Catalina Clay Products called this Catalina Island souvenir "Mexican peon pipe holder, match holder, and ashtray." It measures 3½" x 7½" and was frequently decorated overglaze like this remarkably intact example, $450.00.

Submarine Garden decorative plate, 14", impressed mark, $1,500.00+.

Catalina Island souvenir items. Goat ashtray, 4", $400.00+; seal candelabra, 5" x 10½", $400.00+; bear ashtray, 3¼" x 5½", $500.00+.

Three late period flower containers with impressed and incised marks. Vase, 7", in coral island glaze (satin finish), $175.00; vase, 5¾", in powder blue glaze (satin finish), $150.00; vase, 5½", in Mandarin yellow, $135.00.

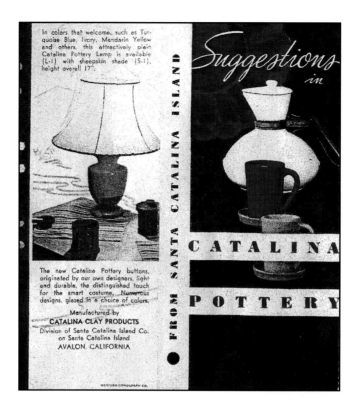

Detail of colorful fold-out promotional brochure produced by the Catalina Pottery and distributed by a gift shop located in the Catalina Casino of Avalon.

CLEMINSONS

Many of the smaller Southern California potteries had their beginnings in family garages. The suburban Monterey Park garage of George and Betty Cleminson witnessed the birth of one of the most successful husband and wife-owned giftware companies to emerge in the World War II period.

The enterprise began in 1941 as a hobby of Betty Cleminson. Betty's initial, tentative efforts were crude but charming and included a hand-painted pie bird. This modest item was greeted with such neighborly enthusiasm that a pastime was immediately turned into a full-time business. Originally calling it "Cleminson Clay," Betty enlisted the services of her husband George to manage the business affairs while she created.

Timing played a large part in the success of most of the garage-based potteries that appeared during the war in Southern California. With overseas goods virtually non-existent, the Cleminsons and others like them were able to sell most everything they could make in the way of ceramic giftware. Because of the popularity of the pie bird, Mrs. Cleminson con-

centrated her efforts at first on kitchen-related articles. She added spoon rests, cookie jars, canisters, salt and pepper shakers, butter dishes, and string holders over the two-year period the business remained in its original location. Much of the ware at this point was personally decorated by Betty Cleminson.

The pottery outgrew the confines of the garage in 1943, and a factory was constructed at 3336 East Grand Avenue in El Monte in which all the necessary equipment for mass-production was installed. Over fifty workers, many of them decorators, were hired at this time, and the name of the company was changed to The California Cleminsons.

One of the most successful products manufactured in the new plant was a line of tableware called Distlefink, featuring a bird motif in a style akin to Betty's Pennsylvania German ancestry. Numerous kitchen items were added during the many years this pattern was produced. In the mid-forties, the output of the business was broadened to embrace various giftware novelties — wall plaques, vases, figurines, hanging plates, cup and saucer sets, children's dishes,

Betty Cleminson at work decorating one of her Sprinkle Boy laundry sprinkler bottles.

The popular Cleminsons pie bird, 4½",
Betty Cleminson's initials in-mold, $60.00.

etc., many featuring homey, hand-lettered phrases. At the height of production just after the war, the Cleminsons pottery employed over 150 people.

After her own plant was destroyed by fire in 1958, Hedi Schoop worked with the Cleminsons on a new fifties modern line of household items employing a new dripped glaze technique that she had developed. This line utilized some of Hedi Schoop's molds and some of Barbara Willis' molds in addition to molds the Cleminsons provided. Other contemporary Cleminsons lines followed in the wake of this successful collaboration. Business in the fifties remained good for the company because most of the items in the line were inexpensive and could compete with the imported Japanese wares. By the early sixties, however, it was no longer possible to offer a competitive product of any quality due to the amount of hand

work involved. In 1963, rather than cheapen their merchandise, George and Betty Cleminson decided to close the pottery.

The regular stamped Cleminsons mark is shown. A variation, without the children on either side of the circular shield, was also used. Special lines, like Distlefink and Galagray, had individualized marks (also stamped). Betty Cleminson's incised monogram appeared on certain early items, including the pie bird.

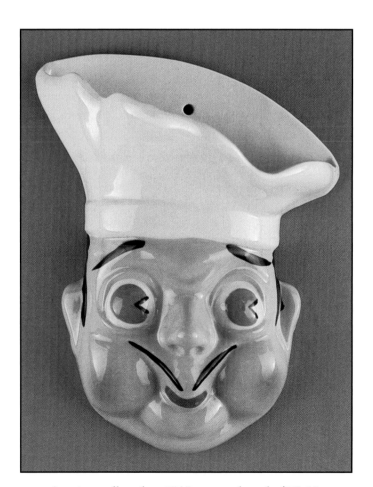

Antoine wall pocket, 7¼", stamped mark, $75.00.

Katrina cleanser shaker, 6¼", by the California Cleminsons, hand-decorated, stamped mark, $25.00.

Two of the multitude of Cleminsons wall pockets, both with stamped marks. Kettle, 7¼", with legend "...the kitchen is the Heart of the Home," $25.00; key, 7¼", with legend "Welcome Guest," $60.00.

Delightful artist salt and pepper shakers, 6¼", stamped Cleminsons mark, $75.00 pair.

Chinese man covered jar, stamped mark, $60.00. Shown with variations on an egg cup, $25.00 each. No marks.

Clever "Bobbie Guard" bobby pin holder with cover, $40.00; butler toothpick holder, $40.00. Both are 4½" with stamped marks.

Reverse side of egg cup in center at left revealing its hand-painted pun.

From the popular Cleminsons' Distlefink line. Bread tray, 12½" long, $25.00; gravy bowl with ladle, 5½" high, $50.00. Both have stamped marks.

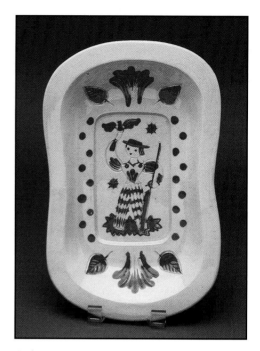

Galagray tray, 12", stamped mark (see below), $20.00.

Distlefink butter dish cover and base, $35.00.

This kettle-shaped wall decoration with verse is 9" high including detachable handle, stamped mark, $45.00.

Expertly rendered decorative plates, 7½", have hand-painted fruit and flowers as subjects, ca. 1948, stamped marks, $25.00 each.

Plate, 9½", decorated with crowing rooster, $60.00.

This Cleminsons' ad appeared in the August 1948 issue of the *Registered California Pictorial*, published monthly by Registered California, Inc.

This Cleminsons 8" decorative wall plate has holes for hanging, stamped mark, $25.00.

Little house on top of the world wall pocket, 8" wide, stamped mark, $150.00+.

Cleminsons wall pocket shaped like a fireplace bellows, 10½", stamped mark, $40.00.

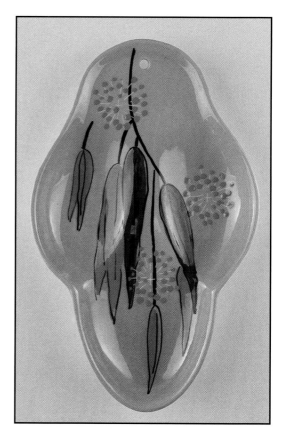

Spoon rest, 8½", $30.00.

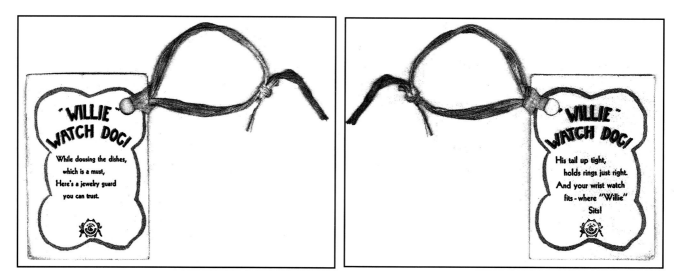

Two-sided hang tag from bulldog-shaped ring holder, with illuminating verse by Betty Cleminson.

Jumbo size cup and saucer, stamped marks, $25.00.

Wall-hanging string holder in the shape of a house, 6½", stamped mark, $125.00.

Left: Cleminson figurals with stamped marks: Egg timer, 3½", $60.00; razor blade bank, 3", $45.00. Right: Rear view of "egghead" showing glass timer.

ORDER FORM

THE CALIFORNIA CLEMINSONS
P. O. BOX 630
El Monte, California

SHIP TO ___ REP. ___
ADDRESS ___ DATE ___ TERMS: 2% 10 E.O.M., F.O.B. FACTORY
CITY ___ STATE ___ WHEN SHIP ___
BUYER ___ HOW SHIP ___
SALESMAN ___ ORDER NO. ___ DEPT. NO. ___
HOLD FOR CONFIRMATION — YES ☐ NO ☐

QUAN.	NO.	DESCRIPTION	PRICE PER DOZ.	AMT.
	102	OVAL	10.50	
	104	PIE BIRD	5.40	
	105	DARNER	9.00	
	107	LARGE HEART	15.00	
	108	SMALL HEART	10.50	
	203	DOILIE	10.50	
	210	RAZOR BANK	7.50	
	214	SWEETHEART FRAME	15.00	
	301	NOSEGAY	36.00	
	305	CANDY HEART	4.50	
	318	PUPPET	7.50	
	411	FANCI PANTS	15.00	
	412	WILLIE	7.50	
	414	MY OLD MAN C/S	22.50	
	415	MOM, POP, DAD C/S	14.00	
	416	MY BEST GAL C/S	22.50	
	417	CHATTER C/S	15.00	
	418	HIS & HER FIGURE C/S	22.50	
	504	DENTURE DISH	15.00	
	509	MATCH HOLDER	10.50	
	511	MATCH PLANTER	9.00	
	610	CALICO PRINTS	15.00	
	630	GAY BLADE	7.50	
	708	BOBBIE GUARD	9.00	
	709	PROUD PAPA	15.00	
	711	PLAID GINGHAM PLATE	15.00	
	760	SPRINKLE BOY	12.00	
	761	SPOON DRIP ASST.	9.00	
	770	A. FLOUR-CHERRY CANISTER	42.00	
		B. SUGAR-CHERRY CANISTER	30.00	
		C. COFFEE-CHERRY CANISTER	24.00	
		D. TEA-CHERRY CANISTER	18.00	
	771	COOKIE JAR-CHERRY	30.00	
	772	DRIPPINGS-CHERRY	15.00	
	773	EGG CUPS, FAMILY	9.00	
		B. GOOD EGG	9.00	
		C. BRIDE & GROOM	9.00	
	801	SPORTSMAN CUPS, ASST.	15.00	
	804	TABLE TILE, FLOWER—BXD.	12.00	
	806	FLUTED PLATE	15.00	
	808	HOPE CHEST BANK	7.50	
	809	HEART STRING HOLDER	12.00	
	810	JOLLY TIME CUPS	15.00	
	811	SALT & PEPPER CHERRY—PR.	15.00	
	850	KANGAROO SALT & PEPPER	15.00	
	854	DUCKY PIPE HOLDER	7.50	
	859	JAM POT	9.00	
	860	COOKIE HOUSE (BOXED)	30.00	
			TOTAL	

QUAN.	NO.	DESCRIPTION	PRICE PER DOZ.	AMT.
		BAL. CARRIED FORWARD		
	861	A. DISTLEFINK BREADBIRD	22.50	
		B. DISTLEFINK BREADBIRD	22.50	
	862	A. DISTLEFINK BUTTERBIRD	15.00	
		B. DISTLEFINK BUTTERBIRD	15.00	
	863	A. DISTLEFINK SALT & PEPPER	15.00	
		B. DISTLEFINK SALT & PEPPER	15.00	
	864	A. DISTLEFINK PITCHER	24.00	
		B. DISTLEFINK PITCHER	24.00	
	865	A. DISTLEFINK SAUCE & LADLE	24.00	
		B. DISTLEFINK SAUCE & LADLE	24.00	
	866	A. DISTLEFINK BUFFET SET	22.50	
		B. DISTLEFINK BUFFET SET	22.50	
	867	A. DISTLEFINK CREAM & SUGAR	18.00	
		B. DISTLEFINK CREAM & SUGAR	18.00	
	869	ASHES & SPLASHES	12.00	
	870	WEEK DAY PLATES (BOXED)	10.50	
	871	HEN & ROOSTER	15.00	
	900	PIERCED HEART, S & P SET, ASST.	15.00	
	902	PICTURE POCKET	18.00	
	903	EGG NEST SALT & PEPPER	15.00	
	905	GIFT BOX SALT & PEPPER	12.00	
	906	MORTGAGE BANK	9.00	
	907	BOND BANK	9.00	
	909	SERVICE CUPS & SAUCERS	15.00	
	910	SALT BOX	24.00	
	912	ANTOINE	12.00	
	913	NIGHT CAP	7.50	
	914	CALORIE COUNTER GRAVY BOAT	15.00	
	950	MARIE (WITH POT HOLDERS)	18.00	
	951	SAMPLER	27.50	
	952	MORTGAGED HOME	22.50	
	953	PICTURE PLANTER	24.00	
	954	CASTLE C/S	15.00	
	955	STAR PLATE, B & B OR WB	18.00	
	956	DAILY DOSE	15.00	
	957	SPECIALTY PITCHER	15.00	
	958	BLADE SAFE—RED OR GREEN	6.00	
	959	COTTON TOP	9.00	
	960	PIERRE	10.50	
	961	TELEBANK	7.50	
	962	PIN POCKET (PINK & BLUE)	7.50	
	963	LONGIES	9.00	
	964	TID BIT TRAYS, ASST.	9.00	
			TOTAL	

Cleminsons order form, ca. 1951, with list of prices for available items and names the company assigned to them.

Gay Blade razor blade bank, 4", stamped mark, $35.00.

Skillfully decorated pot-bellied stove cookie jar by the California Cleminsons, 9" high, unmarked, $150.00.

This heart-shaped cookie jar with "Mother's Best" legend by the Cleminsons is not easy to find, $375.00. Note: legends vary.

Fifties modern line that was a collaborative effort between Heidi Schoop and the Cleminsons. One of Schoop's molds was used to make the large crowing cock vase in center. *Archival photo.*

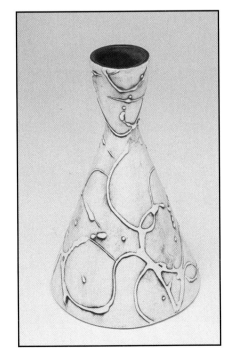

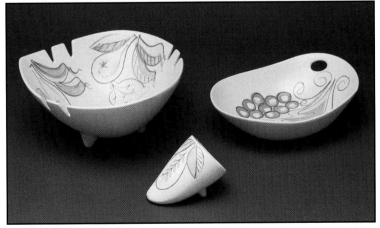

Above: Cleminsons' line of decorative convenience ware, ca. early sixties, stamped marks. Left to right: Ashtray, $25.00; cigarette holder, $20.00; candy/nut dish, $25.00.

Left: This unmarked 6" vase is from the Cleminsons line of late fifties featuring a distinctive glaze technique developed by Hedi Schoop, $45.00.

KAY FINCH

Kay Finch Ceramics was one of the most successful and respected of the California commercial artware studios of the forties and fifties. Its originator, Katherine (Kay) Finch, was born in El Paso, Texas, in 1903. An early interest in clay modeling led to formal instruction at Ward Belmont College in Nashville, Tennessee in 1920–21. While studying at the Memphis Academy of Arts, she met husband-to-be Braden Finch; they were married in 1922.

The Finches moved to California in 1929, with Kay continuing her art education in private lessons with noted Santa Barbara sculptor Andrew Simon. In 1937, they moved to Santa Ana, after Braden's acceptance of a position with the *Santa Ana Journal*. Kay attended Scripps College in Claremont at this time, studying with William Manker in the newly established ceramics department.

Kay's terra cotta sculpture so impressed Manker that he urged her to make art more than just a hobby. With added encouragement from Braden, she began producing clay models of horses and other animals for production in a ramshackle studio behind the Finch residence. But prior to establishing her business, the Finches took an around-the-world trip. This experience solidified Kay's determination to pursue pottery commercially, as she made a study of native ceramics in the various countries they visited.

The Kay Finch studio and showroom, Corona del Mar in 1947. *Archival photo.*

In 1939, after Braden resigned his newspaper job and purchased a house and adjoining acreage on a bluff overlooking the Pacific Ocean in Corona del Mar, the Finches launched their momentous enterprise. Braden wisely assumed all of the administrative duties, leaving Kay free to create. Their first commercial success came in 1940 with a series of pig figurines and banks hand decorated with fruit and flowers. An expanded studio and retail showroom, located at 3901 East Pacific Coast Highway, was inaugurated on December 7, 1941. With only ten employed in the beginning, the company quickly grew to over fifty full-time workers.

Kay Finch decorating staff of 1941. Kay Finch is third from left. *Archival photo.*

Kay personally trained the crew of female decorators in her own painting style, but performed much of the work herself. Animals of all kinds were her specialty, and she modeled and painted them with a genuine sense of self-expression. No competitors matched Kay's unique combination of animated form and hand-painted linear detail. Human subjects were somewhat limited; the most impressive being Oriental figures measuring up to twenty-five inches in height. The Finches' son George designed and modeled most of the non-figural items the company produced, including vases, bowls, planters, bath accessories, and ashtrays, in a restrained yet modern style which nicely complemented his mother's more flamboyant approach. Breakfast sets of dishes with hand-painted patterns were a collaborative effort.

In the forties, Kay Finch began a life-long interest in champion dog breeding. This led to her extensive line of ceramic dogs (some modeled after American Kennel Club champions), with wall plaques, ashtrays, tiles, steins, pins, and figurines of all sizes and breeds among her canine creations.

In 1950, a series of Christmas plates was initiated and continued through 1962. Measuring 6½", each was hand painted. Other seasonal items were offered and distributed to fine gift and department stores throughout the country, in South America and elsewhere. Although the business was affected by cheap foreign copies and other imports after World War II, the outcome was not as grim as was the case with most giftware manufacturers in California, a testament to the high quality of the Kay Finch line and the esteem it enjoyed. It was Braden's death in 1963 that ended the highly successful venture. Without his support, Kay ceased operations and devoted her full attention to breeding show dogs.

In the mid-seventies, the Freeman-McFarlin Potteries, which had earlier purchased some of her molds, commissioned Kay Finch to model a new set of animal figures. Production of these models was undertaken in Freeman-McFarlin's standard glazes and finishes until 1980.

The Kay Finch marking system ran the gamut from impressed and incised (in-mold) marks to ink-stamped and hand-painted ones. A cross-section is shown. Paper labels were also used. Very small figurines were usually not marked. It should be noted that certain Kay Finch models have entered the arena of molds-for-hobbyists, but resulting works are easily distinguished from the genuine article.

Kay Finch with some of her canine friends, ca. 1950.
Archival photo.

These figures are somewhat of a mystery. No names or dates have been assigned to them as yet. Figure on right measures 7½", while the other is slightly taller, at 8". Stamped "Kay Finch California." $150.00 each.

Kay Finch's Godey ladies. At left is the larger and more detailed model, at 9", while the smaller, more commonly found figure on the right measures 7½". Originally sold with proportional male counterparts, "K. Finch Calif." in-mold. 9", $85.00; 7½", $65.00.

Pair of circus monkeys, named Jocko and Socko, 4", ca. 1948, $400.00 each.

This monkey called "Happy" measures 11". He was introduced in 1949 and is stamped "Kay Finch," $1,200.00+.

Seashell low flower bowl, 2" x 12¾", with fish, 3¼" x 7", incised marks. Bowl, $50.00; fish, $100.00.

Girl figurine, 5¼", $75.00.

Kay Finch turkey, 5", first offered in 1948, no mark, $75.00.

Left: Two renderings of Toot, the 6" owl. Hand-decorated version on the left is from the Kay Finch studio, $65.00. The one on the right is later Freeman-McFarlin version in gold leaf, $45.00.

Right: Hoot is Toot's other half, measuring 9" in height, with stamped mark, $200.00.

Kay Finch was commissioned to design and produce the first "Missouri Mule" cups to celebrate the inauguration of President-elect Harry S. Truman in 1949. Subsequently, they were made open stock. Reverse side reads "Southern Comfort," paper labels inside. $250.00 each.

President Truman received the first presentation set of "Missouri Mule" beverage cups as a gift. Rare. $4,000.00+ set.

Kay Finch working on a clay model outside her oceanside studio in Corona del Mar in 1941. *Archival photo.*

Sassy pig, 3½", with strawberries, stamped mark, $100.00.

Prancing lamb, 10½", was one of Kay Finch's early designs and is not easy to find. The body cavity of this example has been partially filled with BBs for stability. Stamped mark, $1,200.00+.

Kay Finch Airedale, 5", $550.00; Jezebel, the contented cat, 6" x 9", $275.00; mini Jezzy, 2" x 2", $150.00. Stamped marks.

A Kay Finch stamped mark.

Skunks of a different color from Kay Finch. Skunk with tail down, 5", $250.00; skunk with tail up, 4½", $250.00.

Hannibal, the angry cat, 10¼", $850.00; Yorky pup, 5", $275.00.

Yorky Pup, 6¾", $275.00. (Pup in left photo completes the set.)

Cottontail, 2½", ca. 1946, $100.00.

Chanticleer, 10¾", in-mold mark, $500.00.

Hunting for Kay Finch's Papa Duck #471, 7½", may prove frustrating as he is hard to find, stamped mark, $300.00+.

Kay Finch Pomeranian called "Mitzi," 10", hand decorated, ca. 1944, $2,000.00+. *Archival photo.*

Cocker, named Vicki, 11", was one of the many canine models by Kay Finch, in-mold mark, $1,200.00+.

Pup and Puss shakers, 6½", were smaller versions of matching cookie jars by Kay Finch, $1,000.00+ pair.

Kay Finch poodle, "Doggie with Silver Bell," 7½", has two holes on either side of molded bells so actual bells can be attached, "Kay Finch California" mark, $750.00+.

Examples of the Kay Finch Dog Show. Yorkie, 2½", $450.00; Dachshund, 5", $500.00; Westie, 4", $500.00.

Dachshund pup, 8", in natural colors under-glaze, unmarked, $750.00.

This hard-to-find Kay Finch Afghan head named "Banu," 10", originally came with a detached base, 2", which is even harder to find, stamped mark, $1,500.00+.

Cigarette holder with Yorkie attached, 3½", "Kay Finch" in-mold mark, $350.00.

One of a series of dog head ashtrays, stamped mark, $65.00.

This elephant is likely a late period piece, ca. 1958, after decorators' salaries had climbed and cheaper Japanese wares were threatening the industry as a whole. Satin-matte black glaze sans decoration, 7" in height, incised "Kay Finch Calif.", $150.00.

Kay Finch ware designed by George Finch, incised marks. Low flower bowl, 12", $100.00; Song of the Sea ashtray, 5" x 7", $35.00; footed vase, 9", $50.00.

Santa Claus toby mug, 4¼", stamped mark, $75.00.

English village bank, 5½", dated 1944, $350.00+.

Santa sack holder, 10" x 10", $350.00+.

FLORENCE

The Florence Ceramics Company owed its existence to a tragic event in the life of founder Florence Ward. In 1939, after death had claimed one of her two youthful sons, Mrs. Ward began to dabble in clay as a means of overcoming personal grief.

Not surprisingly, her first pieces were of children, individually shaped and decorated in the garage at her residence in Pasadena. Florence Ward, who was basically untrained in art, decided to turn her engrossing hobby into a full-time occupation after attending a ceramics class in 1942. With her husband and other son away during the war, she boldly established the enterprise on her own. When it had outgrown the family garage, Florence Ceramics moved into a modest-sized plant on the east side of Pasadena in 1946.

Joining her at that time were her husband Clifford, her son Cliff Jr., and over forty employees. The Wards' company sold its output of hand-decorated figurines through a local jobber prior to 1946. After relocating, the firm began displaying its wares at the Los Angeles gift shows and selling directly to retailers throughout the United States, Hawaii, Canada, and South America. The volume of business increased rapidly with the addition of sales representatives in many major cities, and in 1949 a modern 10,000 square foot factory equipped with a continuous tunnel kiln was erected at 74 South San Gabriel Boulevard in Pasadena. The company was incorporated at this time with Clifford D. Ward, President; Florence Ward, Vice President; and Clifford Ward, Jr., Secretary-Treasurer. The latter was also sales manager. The work force totalled over one hundred in the new location.

Florence Ceramics produced some of America's finest semi-porcelain figurines. "The Florence Collection," as it was called, featured authentic and exquisitely detailed reproductions of historical couples in period costume. Fictional characters were also produced, such as Rhett and Scarlett from the motion picture *Gone With The Wind.* Figures of European royalty included Louis XV and Madame Pompadour, and Louis XVI and Marie Antoinette. Lawrence's "Pinkie" and Gainesborough's "Blue Boy" were faithfully reproduced and added to the line which featured

Florence Ward holding one of her creations.

an extensive offering of individually named ladies and gentlemen outfitted in the Godey fashions of the late nineteenth century. A less expensive line of figurine-vases was also produced, along with various small scale children. Other Florence articles included busts, wall plaques, wall pockets, candle holders, picture frames, clock frames, vases, smoking sets, and a large assortment of birds. Some of the more elaborate human figures were incorporated into lamps complete with custom shades.

Florence was one of the first potteries to utilize actual lace decoration on figurines. The lace was cut to size and then dipped in slip and applied to many of the cast pieces prior to decorating. In firing, the cloth burned away leaving a delicate ceramic replica. Clays used to manufacture the Florence artware came from Kentucky, Tennessee, and Florida. Body and glaze (with underglaze china-painted decoration) were matured in separate firings. Items with overglaze 22K gold trim received a third trip through the kiln. Imports had a limited effect on the business when they were reintroduced in the early fifties. By then the reputation of the Florence line was so firmly established that wholesale buyers eagerly awaited Mrs. Ward's latest creations when they were unveiled semi-annually.

In an attempt to broaden its scope, a separate offering of bisque-finished animal figures modeled by sculptor Betty Davenport Ford was added in 1956. These highly stylized sculptures, which required minimal airbrush decoration, included rabbits, doves, squirrels, dogs, and cats. Production on this series was continued for only two years.

Business slowed somewhat in the early sixties, and following the death of Clifford Ward, Sr. in 1964, the company was sold to the Scripto Corporation. The Florence trade name was retained by Scripto, but advertising specialty ware, i.e., mugs and ashtrays, was the extent of their production. The company ceased operations entirely in 1977. Florence Ward died in 1991 at the age of 93.

Florence diligently documented its product with stamped and incised marks where possible, or with paper labels. The top-of-the-line figurines were generally stamped with one or the other of the circular marks shown, (1) and (2). The second (2) mark was also used on less expensive figurine-vases. The finer figurines usually bore their designated name in-mold as well as the company name. Some items were stamped with the "Florence Ceramics Copyright" block lettered mark (3). Others were incised in-mold "Florence Ceramics" in script (4). The stamped "Floraline" mark (5) was used on a special offering of floral containers and accessories. Betty Davenport Ford's line sometimes bears her name in addition to the company name. The paper label shown (6) may also be found on a variety of ware.

Florence's Charmaine, 8½", Godey fashions, fancy version with lace and 22K gold trim, in-mold and stamped marks, $300.00.

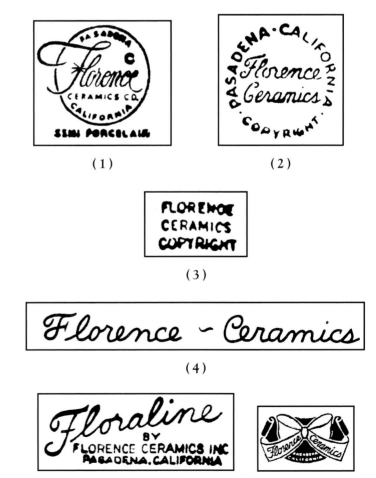

(1)   (2)

(3)

(4)

(5)   (6)

Shirley figurine, 8", hand-applied compact, rose, and fur trim, 22K gold, stamped mark, $350.00.

Cynthia figurine, 9¼", lace and fur trim, 22K gold, stamped mark with "Cynthia" in-mold, $750.00+.

Priscilla figurine, 7¾", John Alden figurine, 9¼", $325.00 each. Minimal gold, stamped marks.

Ballerina variations, stamped marks. Left: 7", lace trim, 22K gold. Right: 7¼", fur trim, 22K gold, $350.00+ each.

A tip of the hat from Suzanna and Stephen, who measure 8¾" in height. With lace and 22K gold trim, they sold for $9.00 each wholesale in the mid-fifties and could prove difficult to find today. $350.00+ each.

Ready for prom night. Don, 9½", and Judy, 8¾". Deluxe models with fine detailing. Don, $250.00+; Judy, $350.00+.

Relatively few Florence figurines were not created by Florence Ward. Three are shown, left to right: Taka, 13", Mikado, 14", and Karlo, 14". $200.00+ each.

Dainty Florence artware. Bud vase, 6¾", $65.00; Dresden picture frame, 5" x 7", $100.00.

Four views of early unnamed flower girl, 9", stamped marks along with paper labels, $150.00 each.

Florence Ward's most ambitious early works were inspired by illustrator Charles Dana Gibson's ideal American girl of the 1890s. These two very scarce figures are representative. Left to right: Gibson Girl, 11", with hollow body and painted mark "Florence Pasadena," $250.00+; Gibson Girl, 10½", with regular base and painted mark "Florence 'Original' Pasadena," $250.00+ each.

Dear Ruth, 9", usually labeled a TV lamp in the Florence Ceramics catalogs, but this example is not equipped as such. Rare in any form, $1,000.00+.

One of Florence Ward's most complex later models was called "Grandmother and I." It measures 9" x 7" and is hard to find, $2,000.00+.

Susann, a.k.a. Susan, 9", is not an easy find, especially in yellow gown. In-mold and stamped marks, $350.00+.

Florence CERAMICS CO., 74 South San Gabriel Boulevard
Pasadena, California

A page from a Florence Ceramics catalog (date unknown), picturing some hard-to-find models.

Florence ceramic royalty, stamped marks. Louis XVI figurine, 10", lace and fur trim, 22K gold, $350.00. Marie Antoinette figurine, 10", ruffled bodice, hair ornamentation, roses and lace trim, 22K gold, $400.00.

Victoria on divan (attached), 7" x 8¼", ribbon, roses, and lace trim, 22K gold, stamped mark "Victoria" in-mold, $600.00+.

Kay figurine, 6", fur trim, 22 K gold, $150.00; Florence dealer sign, 6¼" x 5", 22K gold, stamped mark, $500.00+.

Violet wall pocket, 7", 22K gold, stamped marks, $150.00.

The Florence Ceramics display sign without attached figurine is very hard to find, $700.00+.

A page from the Fall 1957 retail catalog showing some of Florence's more elaborate and expensive models.

A view of the Florence Ceramics plant located on San Gabriel Boulevard in Pasadena.

Unlisted Merrymaid, perhaps an early reject, by Florence Ceramics. Measuring 6½" in length, it is very rare. $400.00+.

Shell vase, 6" x 6½", in pink and grey lustre. Stamped "Florence Ceramics" mark, as shown below. $75.00.

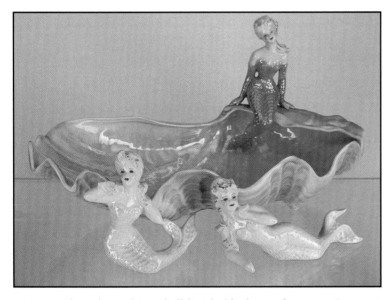

Merrymaids and matching shell bowl. Clockwise from top: Jane 7", $200.00; Rosie 3½" x 7", $200.00; Betty 4½", $200.00; bowl, 3¼" x 15¾", $150.00.

Florence figurines of children, ca. 1951. Left: Mary and John, $250.00+ each. Right: Blondie and Sandy, $250.00+ each. *Photo courtesy Tony Cuñha.*

Mockingbird #W4, 5¼", attached flowers on base, $200.00+.

Examples of the Betty Davenport Ford-designed porcelain bisque ware, like this dove, 6" x 9", are scarce. See stamped mark below. $225.00+.

Florence cockatoo, catalog #W24, 13¼", stamped mark, $275.00+.

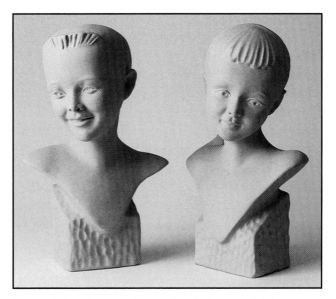

Small fry collection from Florence Ceramics included Bud and Dot, 7½", in full western regalia, $300.00+ each.

Boy and Girl busts in bisque finish from mid-fifties. Boy, 9¾", $200.00; girl, 9½", $200.00.

FREEMAN-McFARLIN

Freeman-McFarlin was a partnership between Maynard Anthony Freeman and Gerald H. McFarlin. The business was the last in a series of artware potteries that Gerald (Mac) McFarlin had successfully operated in the Los Angeles area since 1927. Freeman, upon his release from military duty after World War II, joined forces with McFarlin and immediately became the chief designer. The union of McFarlin the businessman and Freeman the creative spirit resulted in a long and rewarding business.

Success for the new partners came with the introduction of Maynard Anthony Freeman's distinctive line of slip-cast earthenware sculpture. Subjects for this ware ranged from wild and domesticated animals (including many unusual varieties), to common and exotic birds. Human figures were occasionally combined with an animal (usually a horse with rider). Freeman's output included both naturalistic and highly stylized models, all of which bore the trademark "Anthony." Favored designs were copyrighted.

Accounts were obtained with many fine department stores in California and elsewhere for the Anthony collection which included horses, dogs, cats, mice, rabbits, giraffes, elephants, llamas, owls, roadrunners, flamingos, parakeets, eagles, falcons, and many others. Most of these figurines remained in production until the business was sold and were produced in a variety of colored glazes and finishes. The Freeman-McFarlin Potteries utilized numerous non-glazed finishes over the years, such as woodtone and gold leaf, which were routinely juxtaposed with its staple of high-gloss glazes. The company also produced an extensive line of decorative household items. These included bowls, vases, compotes, candlesticks, ashtrays, and numerous related articles. Free-lance designers were responsible for some of this ware, as well as a line of unglazed stoneware planters cast in the shape of various animals. One of these free-lance designers was Jack White, who had been the chief model maker for the business prior to enlisting in the service in 1942. After the war he was responsible for modeling many of the aforementioned decorative accessories for the home.

After Kay Finch closed her pottery in Corona del Mar in 1963, Freeman-McFarlin purchased some of her molds. Selected figurines were reproduced in the Freeman-McFarlin glazes and finishes and were markedly different from Kay Finch's original hand-decorated models. At a later date, Kay was commissioned to create a series of new pieces. From the mid sixties to the late seventies, Kay Finch worked on a freelance basis, modeling numerous new animals for the business, including dogs, cats, lions, rabbits, ducks, and many others. These are currently the most collectible items made by the pottery.

In 1968 Freeman-McFarlin added a second plant in San Marcos (in San Diego County). The El Monte factory was closed about 1975, with operations subsequently consolidated at the San Marcos location. By this time the company was distributing its line worldwide and employed about 150 people.

Gerald McFarlin sold his interest in Freeman-McFarlin in the late sixties. Freeman and new partners Leland McKenzie and Pat Callahan sold the business to International Multifoods in 1972. Hagen-Renaker purchased the plant in 1980.

Maynard Anthony Freeman's sculpture line and most of the other articles he designed bore the incised in-mold "Anthony" designation. A copyright symbol often accompanied this trademark. Free-lance designed pieces were sometimes incised with the designer's name in-mold. The "Hetrick" mark is one of these. Most other items were impressed "F.McF.", aligned either horizontally or vertically. The example shown includes the words "Calif. USA" and the copyright date. At least two sizes of the Freeman-McFarlin paper label exist as shown.

Lions by Kay Finch in green glaze accented with gold, paper labels. Large lion, 6" x 7½", $225.00; small lion, 5" x 5½", $175.00.

Kay Finch produced this horse model for Freeman-McFarlin after closing her own business. It stands 13½" and is not marked. $450.00.

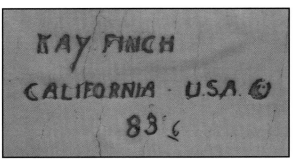

Left: Yorkshire terrier, 7" x 12", in Florentine white glaze was one of Freeman-McFarlin's Kay Finch models, $300.00. Right: Mark on Yorkshire terrier above.

Kay Finch-designed Yorkshire terrier #831, silverleaf finish, $500.00+.

Frog, 4½", in Freeman-McFarlin's rendition of the woodtone finish, in-mold "Anthony ©" mark and paper label, $50.00.

This imposing buffalo, 9" x 15", in gold leaf finish is unmarked, $175.00.

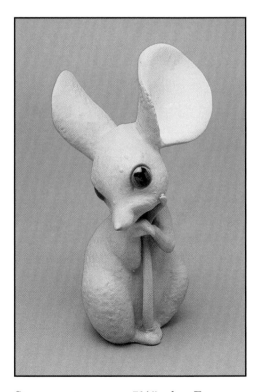

Seated coyote, 10", $60.00; owl about to take flight, 5", $40.00. Both in gold leaf and unmarked.

Stoneware mouse, 7½", by Freeman-McFarlin, marked in-mold "425 USA," $40.00.

Cat, 4½" x 12", $75.00; owl, 5" x 5", $35.00. Both in gold leaf, marked "Anthony."

Giraffes by Maynard Anthony Freeman, woodtone with white crackle high glaze, in-mold marks. Female, 11", $100.00; upright male, 21", $100.00.

Pair of amorous cats, woodtone, in-mold "Anthony" marks. Male, 12½", $65.00; female, 11¾", $65.00.

These small ducks in "fine arts" glaze treatment are unmarked. $25.00 each.

These early Freeman-McFarlin toddler miniatures with attached safety pins measure about 3". Small, round paper labels. $40.00 each.

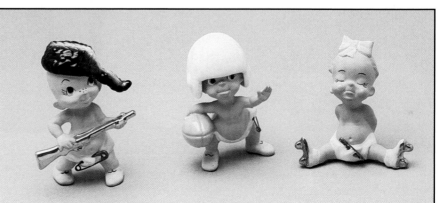

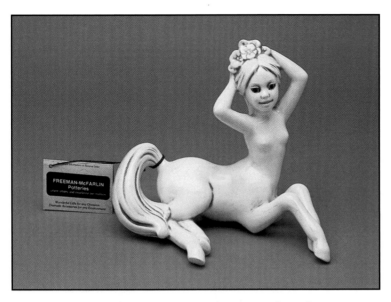

Freeman-McFarlin "centaurette" in Florentine white glaze, 7" x 8", "Rutledge" signature in-mold, attached paper tag, $100.00.

Extraordinary Freeman-McFarlin vase, 17", in woodtone finish with green glazed accents and interior. Marked in-mold "Anthony ©" and "#316," $150.00.

Mermaid holding shell dish, pink-tinted bisque with high glaze, ca. 1957, $65.00.

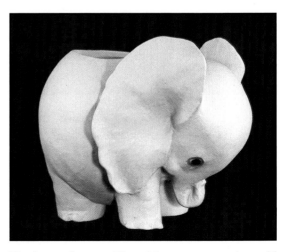

Elephant planter, 7" x 9", stoneware, in-mold "Anthony" mark, from sixties/seventies. $45.00.

Faun figurine in hand-painted bisque finish, 2½" x 3", unmarked, $35.00.

Freeman-McFarlin owls from sixties and seventies. Small owl, 6", $45.00; large owl, 9", $75.00.

Fox (#145), 9", with "Anthony Calif. USA" in-mold mark, $65.00.

Owl candle lamp, 6½" x 7½", in woodtone with glazed eye sockets, paper label shown below, $65.00.

Vase, 11¼", $45.00; stemmed vase, 10¾", $35.00; bud vase, 8", $30.00. All have in-mold marks and paper labels.

Kiwanis Club ashtray, 5½", by Freeman-McFarlin Potteries, design copyrighted 1958, $45.00.

Space age vase by Freeman-McFarlin, in variegated glaze, measures 2" x 7", in-mold mark reads "FMcF © USA /Calif /539" with additional paper label, $50.00.

GLADDING-McBEAN/ FRANCISCAN CERAMICS

The Franciscan plant of Gladding-McBean & Company was California's largest and most technically sophisticated. The substantial success the business experienced was commensurate with its contribution to the industry.

Gladding-McBean was originally founded in Lincoln (Placer County) in 1875 by Charles Gladding, Peter McBean, and George Chambers. Owing to the initial success and rapid expansion of its ornamental terra cotta and other building materials, it evolved into a diversified organization which, by 1926, was the largest clay products concern in the western United States.

The Southern Division of the business, after merging with the Los Angeles Pressed Brick Company in 1924, consisted of plants in Los Angeles, Santa Monica, Alberhill, and Glendale. The Glendale (later Los Angeles) plant, where Franciscan Ware was produced, started in 1902 as the Pacific Art Tile Company, the first factory of its kind on the West Coast. This plant, located at 2901 Los Feliz Boulevard, afterward became known as the Tropico Pottery, and was acquired by Gladding-McBean in 1923.

The patenting in 1928 of a one-fire talc body, designated Malinite, named after technician Andrew Malinovsky, led to Gladding-McBean's first dinnerware line in 1934 called El Patio. It was designed by Mary K. Grant, wife of Frederick J. Grant, who was hired in 1934 to head the new pottery division.

El Patio was introduced in eight brilliant glaze colors in order to make it competitive with the colored ware which Bauer originated in 1930. The trade name "Franciscan" was chosen to be symbolic of California. In 1936, the company conceived the starter set, consisting of four place settings packed in an individual carton. Both El Patio and Coronado, another successful line introduced in the early thirties, were included in these sets which were ideal for newlyweds and as such set an industry standard for marketing.

In 1937, Gladding-McBean produced its initial hand-painted Franciscan pattern (on the El Patio shape) called Padua. Following this came other decorated dinnerware lines including Del Mar and Mango in 1937, and Hawthorne in 1938. This progression culminated in 1940 with the Apple pattern. Apple's border design was embossed in-mold and hand-tinted

Early El Patio ware in flame orange, stamped marks #1 and #2. Water pitcher, $150.00; water tumbler, 3½", $25.00.

Dolphin vase, 5½" x 6", in coral, Catalina Art Pottery line, ca. 1938, unmarked, $200.00.

by a large and skilled staff of decorators and was one of its best sellers. The other two best-selling underglaze patterns introduced in the wake of Apple's success were Desert Rose (1942) and Ivy (1948.)

In 1937, the Catalina Clay Products line was purchased from the Santa Catalina Island Company. This major transaction included dinnerware and artware molds and the use of the trade name "Catalina." It added about 175 new items immediately, with additional artware designs created between 1937 and 1942. Catalina Rancho, a simple and graceful tableware in solid colors (satin-matte and high-gloss) was produced from Catalina Island molds between 1937 and 1941.

An extensive artware assortment, consisting mainly of vases and bowls, was marketed under the heading "Catalina Art Pottery" and included the following design groups: Angelino, Aurora, Avalon, Capistrano, Coronado, Encanto, Floral, Nautical, Polynesia, Reseda, and Saguaro.

The well-equipped and staffed lab developed some extraordinary glazes for the artware package, from monochromes and duotones (various gloss and matte color combinations) to attractively mottled finishes such as matrix blue, gold, agate, and verde green. But the firm's crowning achievement in glaze chemistry was the Ox Blood line perfected by ceramic engineer Max Compton using selenium under specially controlled kiln conditions. Many of the Chinese style shapes that hosted the Ox Blood glaze were utilized

Gladding-McBean's Coronado dinnerware line included this teapot, $100.00; covered sugar, $45.00; and creamer, $30.00.

for the Angelino ware which was produced in periwinkle blue, light bronze, and satin ivory. Dorr Bothwell's Samoan Woman & Child and Reclining Samoan Girl figurines and her popular Peasant Girl flower holder were included in the miscellaneous articles that rounded out the Catalina Art Pottery.

New York's Metropolitan Museum of Art commissioned Gladding-McBean in 1939 to produce a set of the prize-winning dinnerware design submitted to its 15th Exhibition of Contemporary American Industrial Art by Morris B. Sanders. Designer Sanders' prototypes for the competition proved to be so striking that they were purchased by the company and put into production the following year. The Metropolitan service, in a variety of monochrome and duotone satin-finish pastels, was nationally advertised as the first entirely square-shaped dinnerware made in America. The successful line was renamed Tiempo in 1949 when new high-gloss decorator colors were applied to the basic shapes.

The hotel china developed in 1939 for the Dohrman Hotel China Company of San Francisco provided the Gladding-McBean technicians with a trial run for a new vitrified body which was perfected and introduced the following year as Franciscan Fine china. Distinguished by its extreme thinness and formal elegance, the Masterpiece China line, produced from 1941 to 1979, included over 165 decorative patterns undertaken on nine basic shapes. Otto J.

This "Cat-lina" cactus planter was made using one of the molds obtained in the purchase of rival Catalina Clay Products Company in 1937. It measures 4½" x 7", is unmarked, and would not be an easy find. $275.00+.

Lund and George James designed most of the decorative patterns for the top-ranked Masterpiece China.

The patterns for the medium weight and informal china called Discovery (1958–1975) were created by a distinguished group of ceramic artists associated with the design department. The designers included Francis Chun, Dora DeLarios, Rupert Deese, Harrison McIntosh, Jerry Rothman, Henry Takemoto, and Helen Watson. Contours, a china artware collection of ultramodern free-form shapes designed by George James, was produced in the mid fifties. Numerous other china lines were offered to accommodate a wide range of tastes and incomes.

Fine quality, inexpensive Japanese china began to appear domestically in the fifties. The imported goods ultimately prevailed and the company's china production had to be terminated in 1979. The imports situation was not quite as devastating for the earthenware division. An overall decline in sales, however, was a factor in Gladding-McBean's decision to sell its Franciscan plant to the Lock Joint Pipe Company in 1962. This merger resulted in the formation of the International Pipe and Ceramics corporation, simplified to Interpace Corporation in 1968.

In the sixties and seventies, the firm's major expenditure of time and resources was put into generating competitive lines of dinnerware. Mary J. Winans supervised the design department after Mary K. Grant's retirement in 1952. The older Apple, Desert Rose, and Ivy lines were supplemented with Winan's new patterns, Tulip Time, Pebble Beach, Hacienda, and Madeira, among others. In 1968, due to a renewed interest among collectors in the colored pottery of the thirties, Franciscan created Kaleidoscope, a simple tableware design in monochrome glazes. The tile division (utilizing the trade name Hermosa Tile) continued to manufacture plain wall and floor tile as well as decorative tile, including tea tiles to match many of the dinnerware patterns, until 1982.

Because of the worsening imports problem, Interpace sold Franciscan Ceramics to Josiah Wedgwood and Sons, Ltd. of England in 1979. Determining that it could more profitably produce the successful Franciscan lines in its Stoke-on-Trent facility, Wedgwood ceased operations at the Los Angeles pottery in 1984. Two-hundred-eighty people were employed at the time of the plant's closing. The sprawling 45-acre site included 15 periodic kilns and

The Contour fine china artware designed by George James. Left to right: Shell tray in gray, $75.00+; bouquet vase in sandalwood, $250.00+; tube vase in sandalwood, $150.00+; covered candy jar in dawn, $150.00+; tall pitcher in gray, $165.00+. This line was produced for only one year, 1955–56. *Photo courtesy Shel Izen.*

36 tunnel kilns, many of which were idle in the later years.

A great many identification marks, labels, and backstamps were used over the years. Only a selection of these is shown. The earliest backstamp used on earthenware production was the abbreviated "GMcB" in an oval (1), sometimes with "Made in U.S.A." added. A considerable amount of early (and later) ware was stamped simply "Made in U.S.A." (2). The "Tropico Pottery" stamp (3) appeared on a limited line of artware and kitchenware in the mid thirties. Gladding-McBean's Catalina Pottery line bore a variety of impressed (4) and stamped (5) and (6) marks as well as the paper label shown (7). The first backstamp to indicate the Franciscan trade name was the letter "F" in a square (8). It replaced the early oval mark in 1938 and was in use less than a year. The first

Franciscan Ware backstamp, of 1938, (9) was followed by a circular stamp (10), with slight variations, used from 1939 to 1949. An arched backstamp (11) was used from 1949 to 1953. Another circular stamp (12) came into use between 1953 and 1958. A Franciscan Ware paper label (13) was affixed to various items during this period. Beginning in 1958 a backstamp resembling a TV screen was adopted. There were over 30 variations on this mark (14), including a paper label, which was used to identify both earthenware and china, with the appropriate wording included, such as "Masterpiece China as shown (15). Prior to 1958, oval backstamps were utilized on china (16). The Contours china artware had its own decal (17). More recent backstamps include the elaborate "California Craftsmen" mark adopted in 1974 (18) and a restyled "F" (19).

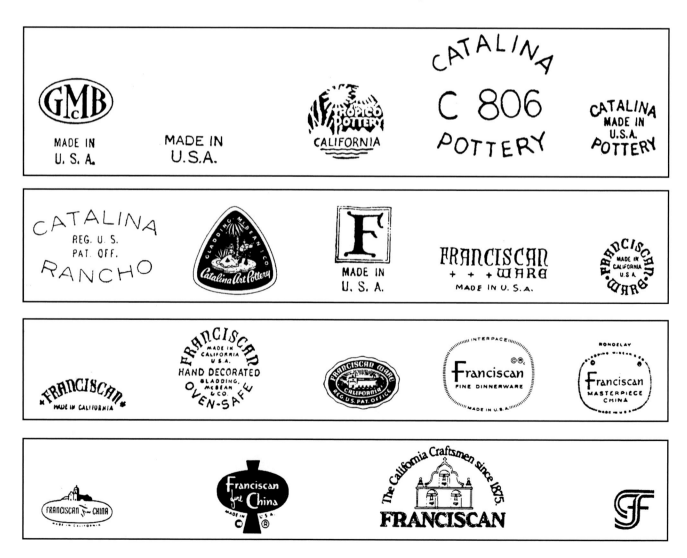

Two views of the sprawling Gladding-McBean plant, ca. 1940s.

Coronado place setting: service plate, 10½", $25.00; rim soup, $35.00; cup and saucer, $20.00; tumbler, $50.00+; salt and pepper shakers, $25.00; vase, 8½", $100.00.

Cocinero kitchenware of the thirties: batter bowl, $150.00, and custard cups, $35.00 each, in distinctive scalloped design.

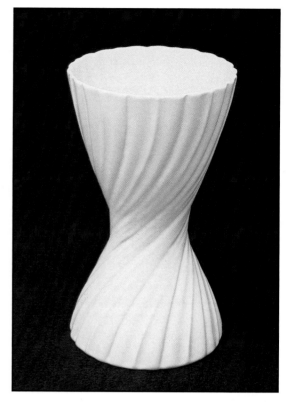

Gladding-McBean's Coronado artware line included this vase, 10", in satin ivory, mark #8, $100.00.

Shell vase, 6" x 10", in satin ivory lined with coral, in-mold and stamped marks read "Catalina Pottery C355" and "Made in USA" respectively, $75.00.

Popular peasant girl vase, 6¾", designed by Dorr Bothwell, was part of the Catalina Pottery package of the late thirties/early forties, $175.00.

SEMI-PORCELAIN POTTERY

A page from the Gladding-McBean catalog of 1932 picturing semi-porcelain vases. All very scarce today.

Is it Catalina Island or Catalina Pottery? Confused? This 6½" vase was called the "round vase with scroll foot." The turquoise version (left) was made on Catalina Island, ca. 1936, $150.00. The celadon green version, using identical master mold, was made in Los Angeles by Gladding-McBean, ca. 1938, $150.00 each. (See photos of marks below.)

Left: In-mold mark on turquoise Catalina Island vase above. Right: Stamped mark on green Catalina Pottery vase above by Gladding-McBean.

Dorr Bothwell designed these 13" Samoan women with child figures, ca. 1937. Figure on left in satin white glaze, $250.00+; figure on right in terra cotta finish, $350.00+.

This ad featuring El Patio appeared in the June 1938 issue of *House Beautiful*.

Apple pattern, 10½" dinner plate, stamped mark #12, $25.00.

Ivy pattern, 12" chop plate, stamped mark #10, $100.00.

Desert Rose pattern, 10½" dinner plate, stamped mark #12, $25.00.

FRANCISCAN
Desert Rose

You can have flowers on your table every day when DESERT ROSE blooms on your dinnerware. This hand-painted design is color-locked under a brilliant glaze that keeps it ever bright-as-new. Oven-safe—sturdily resistant to breakage.

Franciscan Ware by Gladding, McBean & Co., Los Angeles, Calif.

Leaf-shaped wall pocket, 7¾", in satin green, from the extensive Catalina Pottery line, $150.00.

Early Catalina Art Pottery items, stamped mark #2. Tropical leaf shaped vase, 12", $200.00; reclining Samoan woman figure, 5" x 8", $200.00+.

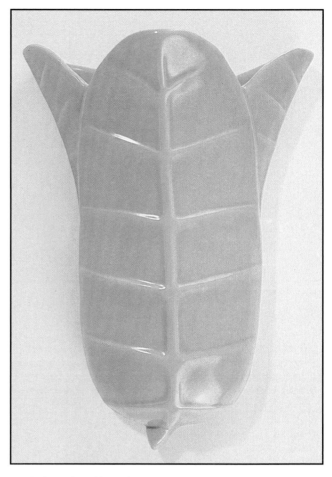

Gladding-McBean's Catalina Pottery, late thirties. Fish vase, 5", $175.00; vase from original Island mold, 8", $150.00; mermaid figurine, 9", $250.00+.

This Gladding-McBean teapot typifies the best of thirties period streamlining. Stamped mark "Made in USA." $200.00+.

Trumpet-shaped Catalina Pottery vase #C286, 11", in ox blood, stamped mark shown below, $1,000.00+.

Gladding-McBean's renowned ox blood glaze was used to best advantage on its Catalina Art Pottery line of the late thirties. Vase #C123, $1,000.00+; vase #C290, $750.00+. Both are 11" in height and have stamped marks.

The celebrated ox blood glazed artware, stamped "Catalina Pottery" or "GMcB" marks. Square vase, 4½", $275.00+; vase, 9½", $400.00+; trumpet-shaped vase, 6", $600.00+.

The highly acclaimed Metropolitan dinnerware. Dinner plate, 10", $25.00; cream soup, $50.00; after dinner coffee cup and saucer, $50.00; teapot, $125.00. Along with later Tiempo line tumbler, $50.00, and tea cup, $25.00.

Trio was another variation on the Metropolitan design. Coffee pot, $135.00, shakers, $30.00, and dinner plate, $30.00, from the line produced between 1954 and 1957.

Franciscan Fine China patterns: Debut teapot, $150.00; Mesa coupe soup bowl, $50.00; Westwood fruit bowl, $45.00; Brentwood oval vegetable bowl, $85.00; Cherokee Rose sauce boat, $100.00.

Peasant girl vase, 6¾", with hand decoration. This very popular design by Dorr Bothwell was patented. Stamped mark reads "Catalina Pottery/ Made in USA/C801." $250.00+.

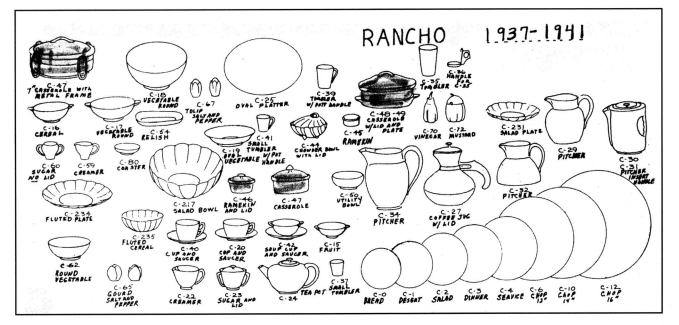

Line drawings of the Catalina Rancho ware of Gladding-McBean, made using Catalina Island master molds supplemented with numerous new designs. Only produced for a short time, 1937–1941. Most items are scarce and some are very rare.

Two very hard-to-find wall decorations in satin ivory by Gladding-McBean. Grapes (above) and pomegranates (below). Both designs measure 7" and are stamped "Made in USA." $250.00+ each.

Barely legible paper label on reverse of one of the wall decorations reads "G.G.I.E. (Golden Gate International Exposition) 1939/San Francisco/Barker Bros." and "Gladding, McBean & Co." These may have been made exclusively for Barker Bros. to issue at the 1939 World's Fair.

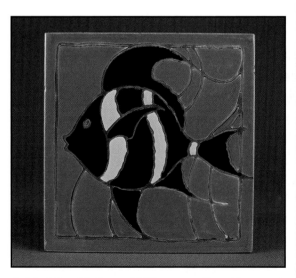

A Gladding-McBean 4" Hermosa tile with aquatic design, well suited for a bathroom wall, $75.00.

Ashtray, 4½", advertising the Franciscan Pottery trademark of 1937. In 1938, the mark was changed to the more familiar Franciscan Ware. $250.00+.

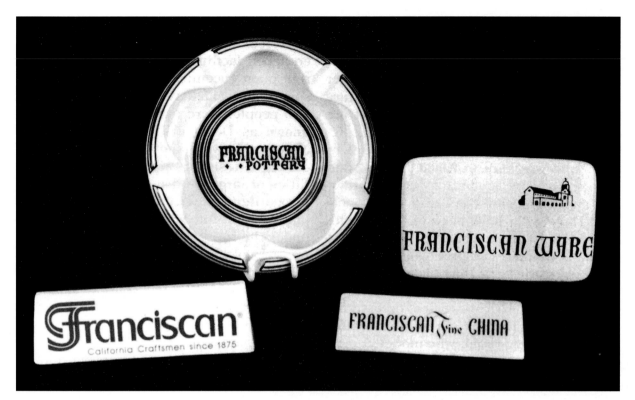

Franciscan Pottery ashtray of 1937, $250.00+; Franciscan Ware dealer sign of the fifties, $450.00+; Franciscan California Craftsmen since 1875 dealer sign of the seventies/eighties, $350.00+; Franciscan Fine China dealer sign, $400.00+.

Crown Renaissance 47.00

Royal Renaissance 50.00

Two of the many Franciscan Fine China patterns pictured in a promotional brochure in 1972.

This promotional dealer card dating from the 1980s features Desert Rose items intended for gift giving.

Franciscan Microwave Cookware

The first decorative ware designed for microwave use! Handpainted...hand-crafted...skillfully designed for oven-to-table use in some of America's most favorite patterns from Franciscan!

Desert Rose   Apple   Meadow Rose

Franciscan microwave cookware shown in a company brochure of the late seventies.

Franciscan® earthenware

		Apple*	Desert Rose*	Ivy*	Hacienda Hacienda Green Tulip Time	Nut Tree	Madeira	Pebble Beach
	5 pc. Place Setting, includes 1 each: dinner plate, salad plate, soup (cereal*), cup, saucer.	9.50 (12.55 Open stock value)	9.50 (12.55 Open stock value)	9.50 (12.55 Open stock value)	9.50 (12.55 Open stock value)	9.95 (13.75 Open stock value)	9.95 (13.75 Open stock value)	9.95 (13.75 Open stock value)
	16 pc. Set, includes 4 each: dinner plates, bread & butter plates, cups, saucers.	23.95 (35.40 Open stock value)	23.95 (35.40 Open stock value)	23.95 (35.40 Open stock value)	23.95 (35.40 Open stock value)	25.95 (40.00 Open stock value)	25.95 (40.00 Open stock value)	25.95 (40.00 Open stock value)
	20 pc. Set, includes 4 each: dinner plates, salad plates, cups, saucers, soups (cereals*).	35.95 (50.20 Open stock value)	35.95 (50.20 Open stock value)	35.95 (50.20 Open stock value)	35.95 (50.20 Open stock value)	38.95 (55.00 Open stock value)	38.95 (55.00 Open stock value)	38.95 (55.00 Open stock value)
	45 pc. Set for 8, includes 8 each: dinner plates, salad plates, cups, saucers, soups (cereals*), 1 each: creamer, sugar with lid, large vegetable, medium platter.	84.95 (121.10 Open stock value)	84.95 (121.10 Open stock value)	84.95 (121.10 Open stock value)	84.95 (121.10 Open stock value)	94.95 (132.30 Open stock value)	94.95 (132.30 Open stock value)	94.95 (132.30 Open stock value)
11	Plate, Dinner	3.50	3.50	3.50	3.50	3.75	3.75	3.75
08	Plate, Salad	2.65	2.65	2.65	2.65	2.80	2.80	2.80
06	Plate, B & B	1.60	1.60	1.60	1.60	1.85	1.85	1.85
20	Cup	2.30	2.30	2.30	2.30	2.65	2.65	2.65
21	Saucer	1.45	1.45	1.45	1.45	1.75	1.75	1.75
01	Fruit	1.95	1.95	1.95	1.95	2.15	2.15	2.15
02	Cereal	2.65	2.65	2.65	—	—	—	—
03	Rim Soup	2.75	2.75	2.75	—	—	—	—
03	Soup/Cereal	—	—	—	2.65	2.80	2.80	2.80
04	Handled Mug	2.75	2.75	2.75	2.75	—	2.75	2.75
05	Footed Soup/Cereal Bowl	2.65	2.65	2.65	—	—	—	—
07	Coupe Dessert Plate	—	2.65	—	—	—	—	—
10	Plate, Luncheon	2.75	2.75	2.75	2.75	—	—	—
12	Chop Plate, Medium	6.00	6.00	—	—	—	—	—
14	Chop Plate, Large	—	9.95	—	—	—	—	—
18	Side Salad	2.35	2.35	—	—	—	—	—
19	Beverage Mug	—	2.35	—	—	—	—	—
22	After Dinner Cup	1.95	1.95	—	—	—	—	—
23	After Dinner Saucer	1.40	1.40	—	—	—	—	—
28	Jumbo Cup	2.75	2.75	—	—	—	—	—
29	Jumbo Saucer	1.95	1.95	—	—	—	—	—
30	Tumbler, 10 oz.	2.00	2.00	2.00	—	—	—	—
31	Sherbet	2.50	2.50	2.50	—	—	—	—
33	Footed Egg Cup	2.10	2.10	—	—	—	—	—
34	Mug, 7 oz.	2.35	2.35	—	—	—	—	—
35	Compote, Footed	5.25	5.25	—	—	—	—	—
36	Chip & Dip Set (plate & bowl)	—	—	—	—	—	11.95	11.95
37	Tumbler, 6 oz.	1.75	1.75	—	—	—	—	—
40	Creamer	3.50	3.50	3.50	3.50	3.75	3.75	3.75
41	Sugar & Lid	4.60	4.60	4.60	4.60	4.75	4.75	4.75
47	Candleholder, Each	2.00	2.00	—	—	—	4.50	—
48	Candelabra	—	—	—	—	—	11.50	—
50	Teapot & Lid	9.95	9.95	9.95	9.95	—	—	—
51	Syrup Jug	3.25	3.25	—	—	—	—	—
52	Water Pitcher, 2½ Quart	8.95	8.95	8.95	8.95	—	—	—
53	Milk Pitcher, 1 Quart	5.50	5.50	—	5.50	6.50	6.50	6.50
55	Coffee Pot & Lid	9.95	9.95	9.95	9.95	11.95	11.95	11.95
56	Salt & Pepper Mill, Pair	9.95	9.95	—	—	—	—	—
58	Jumbo Salt & Pepper, Pair	4.50	4.50	—	—	—	—	—
60	Vegetable Dish, Medium	4.25	4.25	4.25	4.25	4.95	4.95	4.95
61	Vegetable Dish, Large	5.25	5.25	5.25	5.25	5.85	5.85	5.85
63	Divided Relish Dish	—	4.95	—	—	—	—	—
64	Divided Vegetable Dish	5.95	5.95	5.95	5.95	6.50	6.50	6.50
69	Platter, Small Oval	5.25	5.25	5.25	5.25	—	—	—
70	Platter, Medium Oval	7.35	7.35	7.35	7.35	7.95	7.95	7.95
71	Platter, Turkey	17.50	17.50	—	—	—	—	—
80	Salad Bowl	8.95	8.95	—	8.95	—	—	—
82	Casserole & Lid, Medium	9.95	9.95	9.95	—	—	—	—
84	Casserole & Lid, Large	—	—	—	10.95	13.95	13.95	13.95
90	Gravy Boat, Fast Stand	6.95	6.95	6.95	6.95	—	—	—
90S-A	Gravy Boat, Stand & Lid	—	—	—	—	8.95	8.95	8.95
92	Salt & Pepper, Small, Pair	3.25	3.25	3.25	3.25	3.50	3.50	3.50
94	Ash Tray, Individual	1.25	1.25	1.25	—	—	—	—
97	Relish Dish	4.25	4.25	—	—	—	—	—
99	Butter Dish & Lid	5.25	5.25	5.25	5.25	5.95	5.95	5.95
	Prices Subject To Change Without Notice							

Price list of Franciscan earthenware for 1972.

HAGEN-RENAKER

Specializing in miniatures has made Hagen-Renaker a stand-out among California potteries. The firm's continued prosperity is a testament to the dedication of the employees and to the high standards of design and workmanship that have been maintained.

The business formally began in 1946 in a facility of modest proportions in Monrovia. Maxine and John Renaker, with help from Mrs. Renaker's father Ole Hagen (hence the name Hagen-Renaker), built the plant, which was located on Chestnut Street, near the Walker Potteries where John had previously been employed.

Maxine's set of three tiny simplified ducks originated the miniatures, and the trend gained further momentum when a similar skunk family was added. Other ceramic items were produced in the early years but nothing succeeded as well as the hand-painted miniature animals.

Helen Perrin Farnlund joined the company as a decorator in 1947, but her talent for designing was soon discovered and encouraged. Over the years she has been responsible for modeling about 90% of the Hagen-Renaker miniatures. A second designer, Maureen Love Calvert, hired in 1951, has made an excep-tional contribution with her naturalistically modeled horses, both miniature and large scale. Both Farnlund and Calvert are currently associated with the business on a retainer basis, contributing new designs periodically.

Maxine, who was born in North Dakota, and John Renaker, a third generation native Californian, have made it a point to cultivate exceptional designers. Those who have been affiliated with them include: Tom Masterson, who was responsible for the acclaimed Pedigree Dogs line; Nell Bortells, creator of the Little Horribles series which depicted puns and popular expressions; Will Climes, who in collaboration with Masterson, created the highly stylized Black Bisque line; and Don Winton and Martha Armstrong Hand, who modeled most of the Walt Disney characters. From 1955 to 1960 the company produced, under license from the Disney Studios, miniatures and other figural items based on characters from the films *Alice in Wonderland, Snow White and The Seven Dwarfs, Sleeping Beauty, Cinderella, Bambi, Fantasia, Peter Pan, Lady and The Tramp,* and others. Mickey Mouse, Donald Duck, Pluto, and Goofy were also included in the line which was marketed mainly

Exterior view of the Hagen-Renaker plant in San Dimas.

through the gift shops at Disneyland in Anaheim.

A business related to Hagen-Renaker, known as Walker-Renaker, was organized by John Renaker and Joseph Walker in 1952. This offshoot, which was located across the street from the latter's Walker Potteries on Magnolia Street in Monrovia, produced a line of humorous porcelain miniatures and salt and pepper sets with clever titles like "Holy Cow," "Bum Steer," and "Pig O' My Heart." Also produced was a series of "Puti" figurines modeled by the noted Austrian ceramist Susi Singer. The Walker-Renaker operation closed in 1959.

In order to better facilitate their expanding miniatures trade, the Renakers constructed a larger Hagen-Renaker factory at the corner of Shamrock Avenue and Duarte Road in Monrovia in 1961. The business experienced some difficulty with foreign competition in the sixties, but through determined effort it emerged even stronger, moving to a better-equipped facility in San Dimas in 1966. The current plant encompasses an area of about 100,000 square feet on a seven-acre site and employs over 150 people. Here another facet of the business, known as Designers Workshop, was expanded. Maureen Calvert and Helen Farnlund were the exclusive designers of this collection begun in the fifties of larger and more detailed figures. After Hagen-Renaker purchased the Freeman-McFarlin plant in San Marcos in 1980, Designers Workshop, under the supervision of the Renaker's son John, was relocated there. The line was discontinued in 1986 and the plant was subsequently sold.

Hagen-Renaker, Inc. continues today as a successful family-owned corporation, although founders John and Maxine are now semi-retired and daughter Susan Nikas is in charge. Following in her parents' footsteps, Nikas is herself cultivating new talent. Bob McGuinness, whom she hired in 1990, is the latest designer discovery to join the illustrious Hagen-Renaker ranks. And once again, larger and more detailed models are being produced, which are now classified as "Specialties." Ninety percent of the company's current business is domestic-based, with gift shops, museum shops, pet shops, and zoos accounting for the bulk of its orders.

The clay used in production is a mixture of talc from California and ball clay from Kentucky and Tennessee. Every miniature undergoes more than a dozen steps from the casting and bisque firing stages through the hand decoration, final glazing, and labeling. The entire process, though streamlined to keep costs to a minimum, renders a lovingly hand-crafted appearance to the finished product. The company has experimented with a variety of supplemental (non-miniature) ware over the years, but with limited success. Hagen-Renaker's specialty has become its trademark.

Aside from their obvious characteristics, most Hagen-Renaker miniatures have been labeled where possible or attached to paper bases that include the name and address of the pottery. Some early models were incised with a conjoined "HR" plus a copyright symbol. Others were stamped with all or a portion of the words "Hagen-Renaker." About 20 different styles of paper label have been used through the years. Only a few are shown (in approximate chronological order.) Some of these include the designated name of a particular model or figure, and some include a copyright date. Supplemental ware was marked in a variety of ways with the company name.

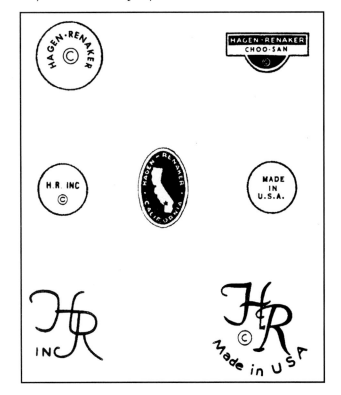

Worker attaching miniature animals to paper bases inside Hagen-Renaker's San Dimas plant.

Hagen-Renaker decorators at work inside the San Dimas plant.

These mini skunks by Maxine Renaker started it all and were in the line for many years. Skunk at left measures 2" in height, the one at right is just 1¾", $25.00 each. No marks.

Pedigree Dogs line by Tom Masterson included Carmencita, begging chihuahua puppy, 2". Label reads "Hagen-Renaker/ Carmencita/1953." $85.00.

Early Monrovia period forest critters. Squirrels measure 1¼". All unmarked. $20.00 – 30.00 each.

The Western horse, at left, was produced from 1979 to 1985, $15.00; draft colt and larger draft horse were early Monrovia models, $50.00 each; rearing stallion, 5½" x 5", was also a Monrovia model, issued in 1952–53, $150.00.

Seated puppy, Champ, in satin matte glaze is from the Pedigree Dogs line, 5", no mark, $150.00.

A pair of boxers from the Pedigree Dogs line. At left is Princess, 3½", $100.00, and on right is Duchess, 5", $100.00. Both satin matte glazed with paper name labels. Right: Paper name label on Dutchess.

Monrovia period miniatures by Hagen-Renaker. Calf, 1", $25.00; cow, 2", $35.00; black sheep, 1½", $45.00.

These sitting ducks are relatively early models. Both are 2" in length and unmarked, $35.00 each.

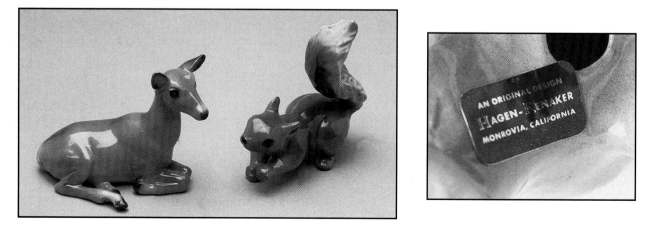

Somewhat larger models by Hagen-Renaker. Reclining deer, 3½" x 4½", $65.00; squirrel, 4½" x 4", $50.00. Photo of paper label on squirrel at right.

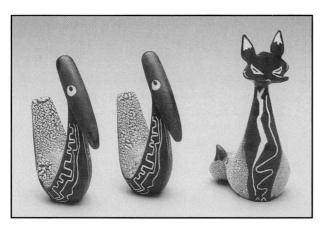

Black Bisque line dodo birds on left, $100.00+ each; flat face fox on right, $100.00+. Fox measures just under 4". Black toned bisque with turquoise high glaze.
Photo courtesy Tony Cuñha.

Black Bisque miniatures, no marks. Featherduster bird, 5" in height, $125.00+; goose, 5" in length, $100.00+.

The Three Bears, ca. 1950. Papa bear measures 2", $100.00 set. *Photo courtesy Tony Cuñha.*

Hagen-Renaker dealer sign, current design, along with early Monrovia period horse on left, $55.00, and current horses on right.

From the Designers Workshop. Left: Pasha, the baby elephant, 3½", label reads "Designers Workshop/Pasha/1955", $85.00. Right: Miss Pepper, reclining Morgan foal, 2¾" x 4½", ca. 1959, $125.00.

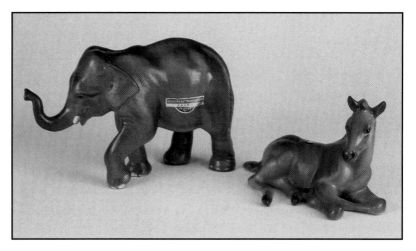

The Little Horribles line included this character called Pruneface (front and back views), 1½", complete with a 2" x 2" card reading, "Mix me another Martini Fred! The children have been Monsters." $65.00+ each.

#397

Sometimes you tickle me half to death

Little HORRIBLES
©
HAGEN-RENAKER POTTERIES

#407

not today, BOB .....
I'm nursing a HEAD

#400

what's my LINE ?

?

#419

Go ahead ....
SEARCH me !

#390

Please, MA .. can I have a FLATTOP?

#424

THIS.. is the story of my life ..

#389

I think I'm nearly over the hump

#405

Take me to your leader EARTHMAN

#422

BANG! BANG! gotcha with both barrels!

#404

are you sure the parade goes by here ?

One side of a fold-out sheet picturing the various bizarre images and witticisms connected with the Little Horribles miniatures line.

HAGEN-RENAKER POTTERIES

Monrovia, California

Your Order No. _____ Date _____

Date Wanted _____ Salesman _____

Shipping Instructions _____

B I L L T O _____

S H I P T O _____

May 1958

TERMS—2% 10 days, net 30 days. F.O.B. Monrovia. A service charge of 25¢ made on orders of less than $25.00. All orders subject to factory acceptance. Prices subject to change without notice.

TIA JUANA ROSIE
#400
$6⁰⁰ Doz. .20
Quant. Ext.

#399
$4²⁰ Doz.
Quant. Ext.

#389
$4⁸⁰ Doz. .20
Quant. Ext.

HAND
#396
$4⁸⁰ Doz.
Quant. Ext.

EYE SPIDER
#386
$6⁰⁰ Doz.
Quant. Ext.

TOOTHLESS
#401
$6⁰⁰ Doz.
Quant. Ext.

THREE ARMED PETE
#397
$6⁰⁰ Doz.
Quant Ext.

LITTLE OLD MAN
#383
$4⁸⁰ Doz.
Quant. Ext.

PRUNEFACE
#391
$6⁰⁰ Doz. .20
Quant. Ext.

LITTLE BLUE MAN
#390
$3⁶⁰ Doz.
Quant. Ext.

BAG IN A SACK
#398
$6⁰⁰ Doz. .20
Quant. Ext.

VULTURE
#394
$4⁸⁰ Doz
Quant. Ext.

CAVE
#392
$6⁰⁰ Doz.
Quant. Ext.

Hagen-Renker's Little Horribles series price list for the Spring 1958 season. All models are hard to find.

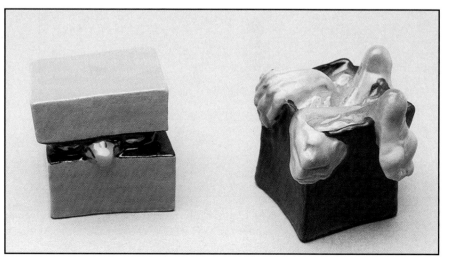

From the surreal Little Horribles series, created by Nell Bortells in 1958–59. FHA (left) and John and Marsha (right) are both about 1½", $65.00+ each.

Lady and Tramp from (you guessed it), *Lady and the Tramp*, released by Walt Disney in 1955. Tramp measures 2" in height, $200.00; Lady, $80.00.

Peter Pan, 2", from the Disney film of the same name, mid fifties, unmarked, $350.00.

The mini Duck family, fifties term and unmarked. Left to right: Walt Disney's Scrooge McDuck, $300.00; Huey, $150.00; Dewey, $150.00; Louie, $150.00; and Donald Duck, measures 1½", $250.00.

Snow White and the six dwarfs? As Doc was unavailable, this set of Disney's *Snow White and the Seven Dwarfs* figurines is incomplete. The little guys average 3½", $250.00+ each, while Snow White towers over them at 6", $600.00+. Mid fifties, paper labels. Paper label on back of Sleepy figure in right photo.

Hagen-Renaker miniature figurine of Malificent, 1½", from the Disney movie *Sleeping Beauty*," $1,200.00+. Designed by Martha Armstrong Hand, ca. 1954.

Cinderella, 2½", on original name card, from Walt Disney's *Cinderella*, mid fifties. Original paper base adds value to any Disney model by Hagen-Renaker. $500.00+.

Walt Disney line items from the movie *Fantasia*, fifties series. Baby Pegasus, $250.00+; unicorn, $250.00+; Pan on Greek column (two pieces), $350.00+ set, and Bacchus, $300.00+.

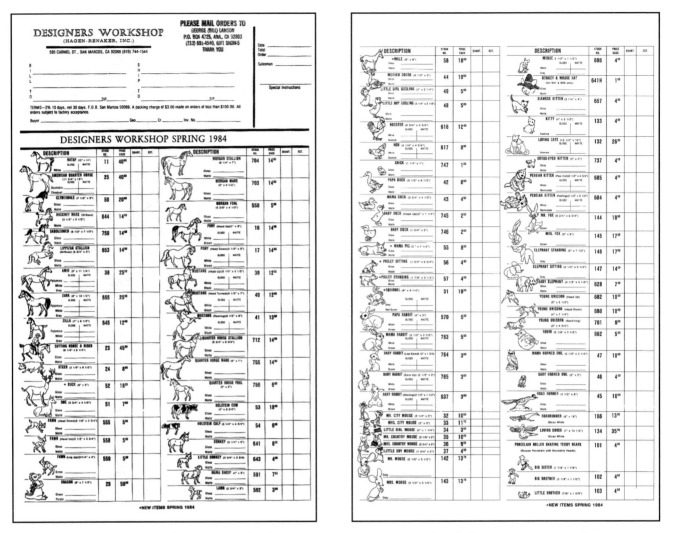

Designers Workshop price list for Spring 1984. New items introduced that season are starred.

Designers Workshop Arabian stallion, 9" x 11¼", $250.00, and colt, 6¾" x 6¼", $175.00. Modeled by Maureen Love Calvert.

Standing goose, 6½", $60.00, and baby rabbit, 2¼", $45.00, are Designers Workshop models produced in recent years.

Advertising sheet for Designers Workshop line, Spring 1984, picturing mule, 8", designed by Maureen Calvert. $150.00.

Designers Workshop line Mother Goose, 6½", $75.00; and goslings, $45.00 each, designed by Maureen Calvert, issued Spring 1984. *Photo courtesy Warren Faubel for Hagen-Renaker.*

Miniature macaw, 2½", $50.00, designed by Maureen Calvert, introduced Spring, 1988. *Photo courtesy Warren Faubel for Hagen-Renaker.*

143

This is an example of Walker-Renaker's line of porcelain bisque miniatures. Hen measures 3" and is unmarked, $30.00.

Jitterbugging cats, 2", designed by Maureen Calvert, reworked by Laurlyn Bursen, issued January, 1988. $30.00. *Photo courtesy Warren Faubel for Hagen-Renaker.*

The Triceratops is a very recent model. It measures 3½" x 6" and has conjoined "HR" stamped mark.

Wall plaque, 15" x 22", of prancing horses was produced in 1960, paper label, $250.00+.

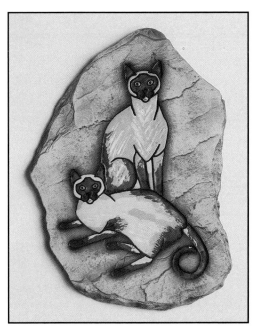

Rock-like wall decoration with Siamese cats, 16", no mark. These plaques were some of the largest items made by Hagen-Renaker. $225.00+.

This wall decoration with scary looking pompano, 7¼" x 12", is suggestive of a fossil, no mark, $225.00+.

Current production (1997) includes these miniature models: circus elephant on platform, 2", bison, 1½" (attached paper base includes price of $4.50), mare and colt on ceramic base, 2½".

HALDEMAN

Virgil K. Haldeman, along with his wife Anna, established the Haldeman Pottery in Burbank in 1933. Virgil Haldeman was a prominent figure during the time that he was active in the Southern California pottery industry. He was born in 1899 in Kansas and received his primary education there. Trained as a ceramic engineer at the University of Illinois, he graduated with honors in 1923.

After working briefly for a tile plant in Pennsylvania, Virgil moved to California. In 1927, he and a partner organized the Haldeman Tile Manufacturing Company in Los Angeles. This business was sold in 1930 when Haldeman went to work for the Catalina Clay Products Company on Catalina Island. He remained there as ceramic engineer and plant superintendent until leaving in 1933 to start his own business. That same year, the Haldeman Pottery began operations at 41 East San Jose Avenue in Burbank in a plant equipped with two large periodic kilns. Anna Haldeman worked closely with her husband from the beginning (they were married in 1931), processing the orders and supervising in his absence.

The designation "Caliente" was selected as the trade name of the company and was used on vases, low flower bowls, flower frogs, and figurines. Most of the designs were generated in-house, but some ware was created by freelance designers. Virgil, who specialized in glaze chemistry, created all the glazes. The variety was remarkable and included satin matte colors white, black, green, pink, and blue; and high-gloss colors turquoise, burnt orange, yellow, maroon, jade green, chartreuse, gold, light brown, and red brown. Blended colors included green-pink, blue-pink, turquoise-gold, and others.

During World War II, despite Virgil Haldeman's recruitment for defense work, the business experienced its greatest growth. A new line of "hand-made" low flower bowls with overlapped edges, introduced at the Los Angeles Gift & Art Show in 1941, was an immediate hit. This was followed by baskets with rope handles, hand-fashioned from twisted coils of clay, and bowls and vases with attached roses, poppies, dogwood, holly, or oak leaves. Other items in the

Haldeman Pottery's Virgil K. Haldeman.
Archival photo.

Caliente line were ewers, candle holders, ashtrays, planters, and numerous small figurines of animals and birds. An outstanding series of Art Deco dancing ladies was also produced.

In 1947, the Burbank factory was sold and the business was moved to Calabasas, in the outer reaches of the San Fernando Valley. Only about a half dozen of the twenty-five employees transferred to the new location, which was a cooperative involving several applied arts industries. Here Caliente ware was produced for six more years before the business closed in 1953.

At the same time he was operating the pottery, Virgil Haldeman was active in local ceramic organizations. He was president of the Southern California Chapter of the American Ceramic Society in 1947 and president of the Southern California Potters Guild in 1949. It was through the auspices of the latter group that Haldeman promoted Registered California as an attempt to uphold high technical standards in a mushrooming industry. During the war, when many essential ceramic materials were requisitioned by the government, Virgil aided several small potteries by helping them revise their glaze formulas and thus maintain their businesses.

After closing his own pottery, Haldeman worked for tile companies in Texas, New Mexico, and again in California before retiring in 1974 at age seventy-five. He died at Lake San Marcos, California, in 1979.

No consistent system was developed to mark the Caliente line. The earliest products bore raised numerals or "Made in California" in a semi-circle (1). Many of the later figurines were impressed "Made in California" in block letters (2). Numerous items were not marked; their only identification was the paper label as shown (3). An earlier version of this sticker exists without the Registered California logo. On later period low bowls, baskets, etc., a hit-or-miss method was used, with all or some of the following words: "Haldeman Potteries/Caliente/hand made/California"

(4). These were incised in-mold in a variety of handwriting styles. If a mold was overused, these markings will appear faint and almost unreadable.

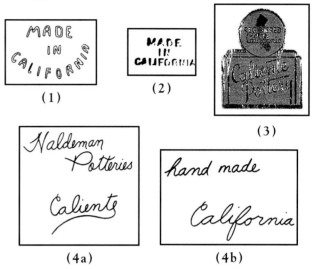

An assortment of Caliente Pottery low flower bowls, ca. 1946. *Archival photo.*

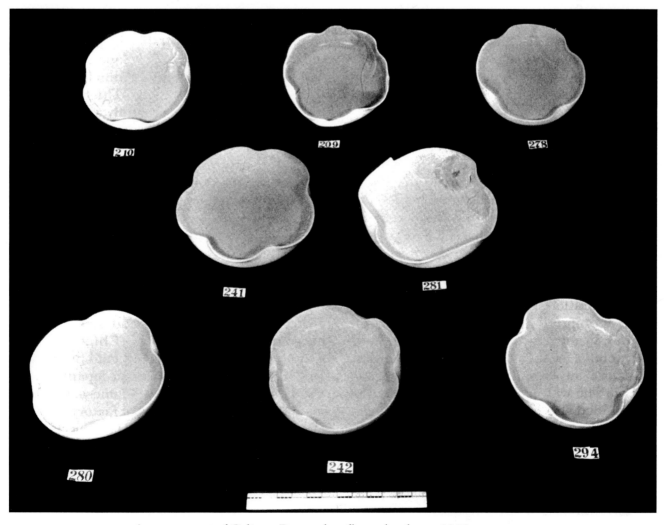

Floral Artware. Vase, 5¾", $50.00; vase, 7½", $45.00; ewer, 10", $40.00; triple bud vase, 6½", $45.00.

Caliente Pottery candleholders, incised marks. Left to right: Acorn-shaped double with raised oak leaves, 8¾" x 8", $40.00; lily-shaped single, 2" x 5", $30.00; rose-shaped single, 3", $25.00; bowl-shaped single with raised leaves, 2" x 4", $30.00.

Caliente dancing ladies of the late thirties, impressed marks. Row 1: Lady #408, 6½"; lady #412, 6"; lady #402, 7". Row 2: Lady #401, 7"; lady #403, 6½"; lady #405, 6½"; lady #407, 7". $100.00 – 125.00 each.

Graceful dancing lady figure, 6", by the Haldeman Potteries, $125.00. Marked as shown below.

Swan planter or candy dish, 5" x 7", in sand lined with turquoise, $40.00; shell planter, 5" x 9½", in pink, $40.00. Incised marks.

More Caliente ladies with satin matte glaze finishes, mark #2 with incised numbers. Left to right: 7" lady #404, in light green, $75.00; 7" lady #405, in green, $75.00; 7½" lady holding basket for flowers, #409, in white, $65.00; 7" lady flower holder, #414, in green and gold, $65.00.

Caliente lily-shaped vase, 8", in white with sand glaze color inside, incised mark "20 USA," $50.00.

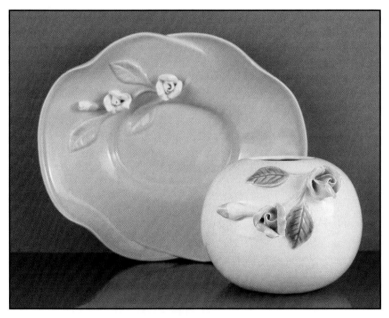

Artware with applied hand-made roses from the mid-forties. Low flower bowl, 9½" x 11¼", $35.00; rose bowl, 4¾", $45.00.

A *rose is...* Vase, 3½", in pink and white, $35.00; pitcher-shaped vase, 9½", in rare brown glaze, $75.00. Incised marks.

Early hand-decorated animal figurines. These and other decorated Caliente Pottery animals are rather scarce. Goose, 4½", $65.00+; deer, 4½" x 5", $65.00+; hen, 3", $65.00+ each. Mark #2 with incised numbers.

Hand-decorated frog figure, 3" x 4", mark #2 with incised "USA 354," $65.00+.

The Caliente clay menagerie, late thirties/early forties. Row 1: Deer, 5", $30.00; Caliente Pottery dealer sign, 3¼" x 9½", $350.00+; comic elephant, 5", $45.00. Row 2: Duck, 4", $30.00; sad hound, 2¼" x 4", $35.00; with fire hydrant, 3½", $35.00; pointer, 4" x 6¾", $45.00. Row 3: Goose, 1¾" x 4½", $30.00; seated deer, 3¼", $30.00; penguin, 3¼", $35.00.

Caliente monkey dressed as a bellhop, 2¾", unusual hand decoration, ca. 1943, $75.00+.

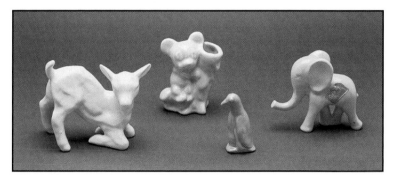

Various design styles are evident in this group of Caliente animals. Left to right: Naturalistic faun, 4", $45.00; comical koala bear in tree (bud vase), 4", $40.00; naive penguin, 3", $30.00; Art Deco elephant, 4", $60.00. Close-up of paper label on elephant shown below.

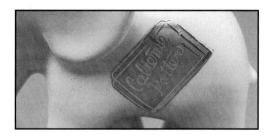

Caliente Pottery animals in white satin matte glaze, in-mold and incised marks. Left to right: Ostrich, 6", $50.00; monkey, 2½", $65.00; elephant, 7½" x 9", $75.00; zebra, 4", $50.00.

A choice selection of vases by the Haldeman Potteries, in-mold marks. Left to right: Vase #31, 6", in rare brown with sand glaze color inside, $65.00; vase #23, 9½", in orange, $65.00; vase #9, 7", in turquoise, $65.00; vase #1, 9", in turquoise and yellow, $100.00.

Decorative Caliente Pottery, incised marks. Row 1: Low flower bowl with applied dahlia and leaves, 3" x 10", $30.00; low flower bowl with applied dogwood and leaves, 3½" x 11¾", $30.00. Row 2: Low bowl with hand-coiled handles, 3" x 6¾", $30.00; candle holder, 1½" x 4½", $20.00.

Low flower bowls were, once upon a time, used to arrange flowers for centerpieces. A figurine was essential to complete the arrangement. Here are two examples. Low rose bowl, 9½", with figurine of birds on branch, 5½", $75.00; low bowl, 7", with figurine of egret, 4½", $70.00.

Chinese style flared bowl, 3½" x 10", in one of Haldeman's blended glazes, $50.00.

Caliente low flower bowl, 14", in white with turquoise inside, and sailboat flower frog, 6½", in maroon, incised marks. Bowl, $35.00; sailboat, $45.00.

Unusual slave woman at block figure, 7", with low bowl, 1½" x 10". Slave woman, $150.00+; bowl, $25.00.

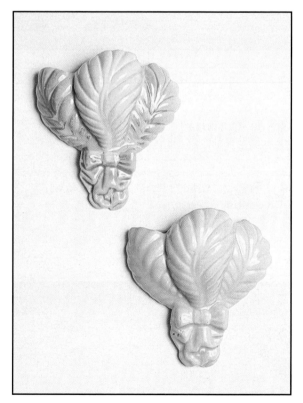

Glaze variations on Caliente Pottery plumes and bow wall pocket, 6½", in-mold marks read "California/USA/6" and "Calif. 6," $50.00 each.

BRAD KEELER

Bradley (Brad) Keeler was born in Lincoln, California, in 1913. He was the eldest of four children born to Mr. and Mrs. Rufus B. Keeler. At the time of Brad's birth, Rufus was employed as a ceramic engineer and designer at Gladding-McBean's Lincoln plant. He would later be instrumental in the founding of two Southern California tile businesses, California Clay Products (Calco) and the Malibu Potteries.

After graduation from Huntington Park High School in 1931, Brad enrolled in an evening painting class at the University of Southern California. This was the only formal art training he received prior to employment with the Philips Bronze and Brass Company of Los Angeles in the mid-thirties. While working for the firm that produced the Motion Picture Academy's Oscar award statuettes, the youthful Keeler perfected his natural skills as a clay modeler.

By 1939, a small ceramics studio had been established in the garage of the Keeler residence in Glendale. In 1940, a business relationship was formed between Keeler and James Webster, with a manufacturing facility leased on San Fernando Road in Los Angeles. The new venture, which was launched in 1941, was called Bradster Potteries, and it specialized in the production of artware, mainly figurines that were modeled by Keeler. Neighboring Shaw & Company was the sole distributor of the line. In 1943, owner Evan K. Shaw constructed a new ceramics plant in Los Angeles for himself in association with Keeler and a number of other giftware producers which Shaw handled. Shaw had obtained the exclusive license to manufacture Walt Disney character figurines, and Keeler and others had a hand in developing this very lucrative line for the newly established American Pottery.

The Keeler line of birds included several flamingo models which proved to be his bestsellers. Keeler's own hand-picked crew performed the duties of airbrush and hand decoration. Many other naturalistic birds and fowl were produced, including seagulls, swans, blue jays, ducks, chickens, cockatoos, pheasants, parrots, parakeets, canaries, and penguins. Many of these were created as male/female sets, or with two birds incorporated into a single unit.

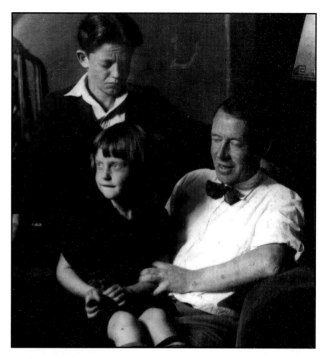

Cozy family scene shows young Brad Keeler with his younger sister, Jean, and father, Rufus B. Keeler. Ca. 1926. *Archival photo.*

Brad Keeler reorganized and relocated his prosperous business in 1946 after a fire completely destroyed the American Pottery plant. A new 15,000 square foot factory was erected at 2936 Delay Drive in Los Angeles (near Glendale) on land Keeler's father had bequeathed to him. Both tunnel and periodic kilns, including small batch-type kilns for experimental work, were installed in the new facility.

Produced at the new plant was a charming slate of florist ware — planters and figurines of children, animals, and baby-related articles known as Pryde & Joy. Especially nice were the models that resembled hand-stitched stuffed dolls. These items, the work of free-lance designers, were used to send greetings to new or expectant mothers. Many new items or lines were added to Brad Keeler's stock-in-trade by enlisting the services of designers who worked on a freelance basis. Fred Kaye was the most favored of these, and he modeled some of the birds the company was renowned for, including what was designated the Exotic Series.

In 1956, Keeler, assisted by glaze technician Andrew Malinovsky, Jr., developed a brilliant red glaze which he called Ming Dragon Blood. It was one of the first true reds to be successfully adapted to commercial production. An extensive array of household goods in the Chinese Modern mode was developed to utilize the new glaze in combination with black. The ensuing Ming line included vases, ginger jars, low bowls, planters, and smoking sets. In order to fully capitalize on the Ming Dragon Blood glaze, a successful line of buffet serving dishes featuring red lobster handles was produced. Other Keeler ware consisted of plain and decorated vases, flower bowls, and tea sets.

Representation of the Brad Keeler Artwares line was transferred to the China Dry Goods Company of San Francisco and Paul Straub of New York in the late forties. Although Japanese imports posed a serious post-war threat, Brad Keeler was constructing an even larger factory in San Juan Capistrano in 1952 when a heart attack claimed his life at age thirty-nine. The company, which employed nearly two hundred people at the time, did not survive the loss, and the new plant was sold in 1953.

Brad Keeler's ware was backstamped in two ways: "© BRAD KEELER" or "© B. B. K. /Made in USA" (1) in conjunction with a stamped model number or with an American Pottery paper label. After 1946, a new Brad Keeler Artwares paper label (2) was adopted. A recessed in-mold mark (3) was also used. A stamped mark reading "CATHERINE M. KEELER" or "© C. M. K. Made in USA" indicates items issued by Brad Keeler's wife, Catherine, after his death, during a short-lived attempt to continue the business.

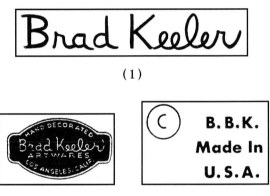

(1)

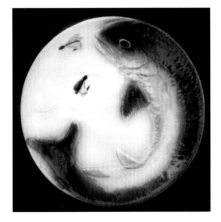

(2)   (3)

Brad Keeler
Archival photo.

Brad Keeler plate, 11", with trout and lure motif in low relief, from early period of business. Incised and stamped marks, including © symbol and "141." $45.00.

Brad Keeler pheasants, in-mold marks. Left to right: Male pheasant, 9" x 11" (missing female companion), $85.00; female pheasant, 6½" with male companion, 7", $125.00 set.

This seagull by Brad Keeler measures 10½", marked in-mold "Brad Keeler #29," $100.00.

The Exotic line from Brad Keeler included these models. Left: Peahen #715, 10½", $165.00. Right: Matching peacock #717, 11½", $165.00. Center: Peacock #701 (for size comparison), 16", $250.00+. In-mold marks.

The Brad Keeler Exotic line, modeled by Fred Kaye, included this pair. Peahen #702 and matching Peacock #701, both 16", in-mold marks, $500.00+ pair.

Stately crested heron #43, 15½", with in-mold recessed "Brad Keeler" mark, $225.00+.

Flamingo #903, 6", part of a male/female set, in-mold "Brad Keeler" with stamped "903," $85.00. Most Brad Keeler flamingo sets had male with head up and female with head down.

Swan #725, 9", with early stamped mark (see above), $100.00.

Two ducks on base, 6", with stamped mark reading "Brad Keeler 53," $50.00.

An egret or crane, 9½", with "Brad Keeler" in-mold, $85.00.

Pair of graceful flamingos, in-mold marks. Female (head down), 7¼", $125.00; male, 9½", $175.00.

Naturalistic blue jay, 9¼", marked in-mold "Brad Keeler #735," $85.00.

Pair of small-scale ducks, stamped marks, $45.00 set.

Canary set, female (tail down), 6"; male, 8¼", in-mold marks, $100.00 set.

This Siamese cat (#946) on Ming Dragon Blood red pillow measures 3" x 3", $45.00.

Divided dish with red lobster handle, 11½", stamped mark, $65.00.

Siamese cat with printed mark "Brad Keeler #798," $75.00.

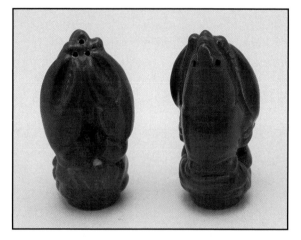

Brad Keeler red lobster-shaped salt and pepper shakers, paper labels, $45.00 set.

Begging cocker spaniel pup, 6", marked in-mold "Brad Keeler #735," $45.00.

From the Pryde & Joy line of Brad Keeler, circus elephant vase/planter, 8½", stamped mark "502" and Pryde & Joy paper label, $65.00.

WILLIAM MANKER

California's ceramic heritage has been enriched by the contributions of a number of exceptional potter instructors. William Manker is among those who helped shape the course of commercial studio pottery in Southern California.

A California native, born in Upland in 1902, Manker began his ceramics career in 1926 when he secured a position with the Batchelder-Wilson Tile Company in Los Angeles. He had been part of the inaugural student body at the Chouinard School of Art at the time, but eagerness for practical experience led him to accept an apprenticeship under Ernest A. Batchelder.

A young man with a keen interest in color and design, Manker found a creative outlet in the tile business where he advanced to the position of Batchelder's design assistant, a post he held until the plant closed in 1932. Undaunted by the economic uncertainties of the Depression, William Manker opened a studio in Pasadena the following year. Although just a one-man operation at first, his skillfully crafted earthenware vessels, celebrating the classic simplicity of Chinese ceramics, attracted the attention of Pasadena art dealer Grace Nicholson. Her prestigious gallery gave Manker his first commercial account and recognition. Due to this swift success, former associate Batchelder became interested in the enterprise. Through his efforts an exhibition was mounted at a local college with the intent of attracting financing for a Batchelder-Manker partnership. The attempt, although unsuccessful, prompted Batchelder to organize a competitive business in 1936.

Continuing to prosper, William Manker Ceramics was relocated in 1935 to larger quarters in the Padua Hills fine arts complex north of Claremont, where Manker had already accepted a teaching position at Scripps College. The business greatly expanded after Manker's line began to be featured in fine department

William Manker inspecting ware in his Claremont studio, ca. 1947. *Archival photo.*

Lobed vase, 14", by William Manker, pictured on teakwood stand, $500.00+.

stores throughout the country. Among the notable outlets were Bullock's Wilshire in Los Angeles, Gump's in San Francisco, J. L. Hudson in New York, and Maison Blanche in New Orleans. Manker's elegant vases and bowls were especially favored by those interested in flower arranging, a popular Depression-era diversion.

All of the vessel shapes were designed and modeled by Manker personally. The exceptional glazes he achieved and used as their only embellishment was a high point of the work. Usually a contrasting color was sprayed over the base color, later blending with it in the kiln. Two different colors, one outside, the other inside, were frequently employed with equally striking results. In addition to vases and bowls, the items produced at Padua Hills included cigarette boxes, ashtrays, candle holders, lamp bases, and a short set of tableware shaped like a stylized leaf. The latter was produced only during 1947–48.

In 1952, William Manker made a career change, assigning management of the pottery business to his son Courtney. By then he had resigned his teaching post at Scripps College and at the Claremont Graduate School. During his tenure at Scripps, he was responsible for founding the college's ceramics department and for initiating its popular ceramic annual,

one of the first such exhibitions held on the West Coast. Also during this period, he was active in pottery organizations, like the American Ceramic Society, and exhibited non-production pieces in major shows around the country. Many ceramic artists received support and encouragement from Manker through the years. Among the more prominent were Kay Finch, Howard Pierce, Jean Ames, and Betty Davenport Ford.

By the late fifties, the cost of labor had risen to the extent that the pottery was no longer viable and it was closed. At its height, just after World War II, about fourteen workers had been employed. Following a distinguished career in ceramics, William Manker became a successful interior color consultant. He was on the staff of *House Beautiful* for many years and more recently had been an independent design consultant. Manker died in 1994.

William Manker's work of the early thirties was hand incised (1). After the move to Padua Hills the familiar ink-stamped mark (2) was adopted. During the war a new stamped mark was used to stress that the product was made in California, USA (3). After 1952, when son Courtney took over the business, the stamped mark was changed a final time (4). A paper label (5) was also used at Padua Hills.

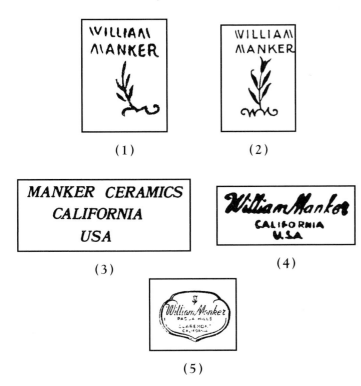

William Manker artware. Small egg-shaped bowl, 3¼", $85.00; cylinder vase, 8", $150.00; tall cylinder vase, 14", $300.00; stilted vase, 5½", $85.00.

Very early William Manker vase, 7½", ca. 1933, $250.00+. Below, hand incised signature of William Manker on vase.

Oblong bowl, 5" x 11", $85.00; potpourri jar, 5½", $200.00; footed egg shape bowl, 6½", $125.00. Stamped marks.

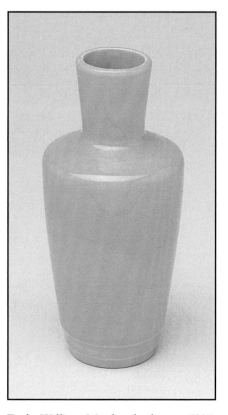

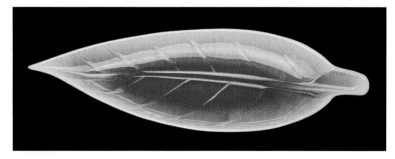

Leaf-shaped serving dish or centerpiece, 26", blended glaze, stamped mark #3, $200.00+.

Early William Manker bud vase, 5¾", in turquoise. Incised mark includes "William Manker" and his logo with "wm" under it. $150.00+.

Cylinder vase, 14", $300.00, and stilted vase, 5½", $85.00, in expertly blended glazes that were William Manker's hallmark. Stamped marks.

Elegant egg-shaped bowls, stamped mark #2. Small bowl, 3½", blended glaze, $85.00; large bowl, 5", duotone glaze combination of burgundy and pale turquoise, $100.00.

William Manker fluted vase, 6", in duotone combination powder blue and light rose, $150.00; flare bowl, 5", in blended glaze, $85.00. Stamped mark #2.

Covered jar, 6", in citron green, early stamped mark, $250.00+.

The standard William Manker logo (mark #2) close up.

Artfully blended glazes on 8" cylinder vases, early stamped marks. Left: Citron green and dove gray, $150.00. Right: Powder blue and light rose, $150.00.

Exceptional floral artware. Rectangular vase, 7½" x 6", $150.00; square vase, 7¼" x 3½", $150.00; fluted vase, 6", $150.00.

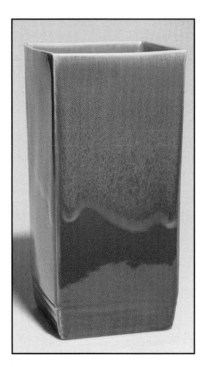

William Manker vase, 7¼", with characteristic drip glaze, early stamped mark, $150.00.

Rectangular vase, 7½", by William Manker, with stamped mark #2, $150.00.

Leaf-shaped luncheon set included bowl, 4" x 15", $135.00+; cup and saucer, $75.00+; and plate, 7½", $65.00+. Ca. 1947.

This 5½" three-piece potpourri jar was produced exclusively for a nursery in California, $200.00 complete. See photo of mark below.

Candle holders. Christmas design, 2¼" x 7½", $55.00; oblong design, 2½" x 6", $45.00; leaf design candle and flower holder, 2" x 6", $45.00.

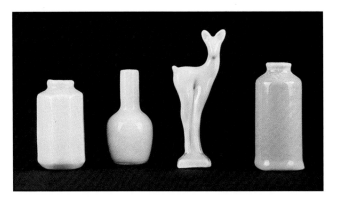

Miniatures by Manker. Six-sided vase, 2¼", $100.00; vase, 2½", $100.00; fawn figurine, 4", modeled by Howard Pierce, $150.00; vase, 2¾", $100.00.

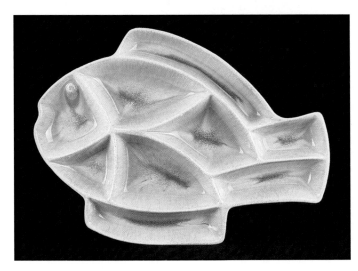

Fish design condiment tray, 11¾" x 16¾", stamped "William Manker/California/U.S.A," $200.00+.

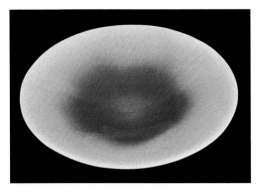

Low flower-arranging bowl, 16½", in burgundy and pale turquoise, stamped "Manker Ceramics" mark, $200.00.

METLOX

The history of Metlox Potteries is like no other in California. Proutyline Products, the business that preceded it, was founded in 1921 by T.C. Prouty and his son Willis. Organized as a California corporation, it specialized in the development and marketing of their numerous inventions.

Willis O. Prouty, who was born in Michigan in 1888, invented and patented at age 18 a tachometer used on aircraft during World War I. After moving to Southern California in 1919, he tested various local clays to determine their suitability for ceramic production. Finding that talc obtained from Death Valley was superior to ordinary clay, a tile body comprised of this material was formulated and patented in 1920. In 1922, a two-story tile plant was erected at 719 Pier Avenue in Hermosa Beach, the first manufacturing facility of the Proutyline Products Company. A year later, Prouty invented and installed a tunnel kiln especially suited for tile production. A patent was obtained for this kiln which utilized setters instead of saggers for maximum efficiency. The trade name Hermosa Tile was used to distinguish both decorative and standard wall and floor tile. The Hermosa Beach facility was sold to the American Encaustic Tiling Company of Ohio in 1926.

Metlox (a contraction of metallic oxide) was established by the Proutys in 1927 in a modern all-steel factory constructed on a four-acre tract at 1200 Morningside Drive in downtown Manhattan Beach. Initially, outdoor ceramic signs were produced at the new plant. These molded electrical advertising signs were devised for maximum day and night visibility and to withstand all types of weather conditions. Neon tubing was effectively used in one of the company's most impressive installations, the newly constructed Pantages Theatre in Hollywood (1928). Unfortunately, Metlox's innovative sign business dwindled with the onset of the Depression. Following the death of T. C. Prouty in 1931, the younger Prouty reorganized and converted the Manhattan Beach plant to dinnerware production.

In 1932, the first limited line of Metlox dishes, christened California Pottery, was produced in bright colored glazes similar to those popularized by Bauer. A more extensive line of table and kitchen ware called Poppytrail was introduced in 1934. The Poppytrail ensemble was even more understated in design than the initial dinnerware and was offered in fifteen different colors during its eight years of production. The "Poppytrail" designation was adopted in

Two advertising ashtrays produced by Metlox in the thirties. Large ashtray advertised "Poppytrail Pottery by Metlox," $65.00, small ashtray advertised "Globe A1 Flour/Ben Hur Coffee" at the San Diego Exposition of 1935, $45.00.

Poppytrail ice-lip jug in satin peach, ca. 1939, $75.00.

1936 as the trade name of the company as a way to emphasize California, the poppy being the state flower. Talc, the major component of the Metlox body, was mined in California, as were most of the metallic oxides that comprised the glazes.

From 1935 to 1938, Prouty's pottery produced an exclusive line of pastel-colored tableware and kitchen articles for Sears & Roebuck called Mission Bell. Yorkshire dinnerware, introduced about the same time and in the same glazes, was a swirled design similar to Gladding-McBean's Coronado line. The most striking and unusual set of dishes of this period was Pintoria. Based on an English Staffordshire design, its markedly geometric shapes (wide-bordered rectangular plates and bowls with circular depressions) were in production for only a few years, 1937–39. Some of these lines were modeled by Metlox designer George Skee, assisted by his son Stan who made the molds.

A talented sculptor by the name of Carl Romanelli was the first artware designer hired by Metlox. Soon after joining the business in the late thirties, he initiated the popular Metlox Miniatures, a collection of small-scale animal figurines and novelty items. Romanelli was also responsible for one of the company's most memorable artware lines. Called Modern Masterpieces, the series included figures, figural vases, busts, wall pockets, bookends, and vases with figures in relief. Most pieces bore the signature (in-mold) of "C. Romanelli" and many of the designs were patented.

During World War II, pottery manufacturing continued on a very limited basis as Metlox converted to 90% defense work. Full-scale production resumed after the war with the introduction of the company's first decorated dinnerware. Evan K. Shaw was the person most instrumental in steering Metlox onto this successful new course. Shaw, whose American Pottery in Los Angeles had recently been destroyed by fire, purchased the business from Willis O. Prouty in 1946. California Ivy, introduced the same year, was the first in a long succession of popular hand-painted patterns developed under the Shaw ownership. Others included California Provincial (1950), Homestead Provincial (1950), Red Rooster (1955), California Strawberry (1961), Sculptured Grape (1963), and Della Robbia (1965).

The fifties, a prosperous period for the business

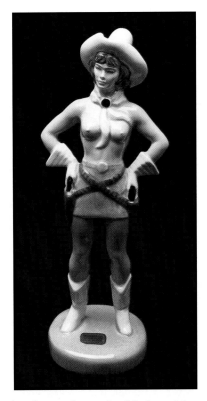

A popular figure from the Modern Masterpieces series is the 10" cowgirl #1819. This hand-decorated example has in-mold marks along with an erroneous Metlox Miniatures paper label. $300.00.

(with over 500 employed) yielded dynamic dinnerware lines Navajo, Aztec, California Mobile, California Free Form, and California Contempora. The shapes and decorative patterns for these were developed by art directors Bob Allen and Mel Shaw.

In 1958, Metlox purchased the trade name and selected dinnerware molds from Vernon Kilns after the latter ceased operations. A few of Vernon's best-selling lines were used to establish a separate Vernon Ware branch, which was headed by Doug Bothwell. Metlox's Vernon Ware division eventually rivaled the Poppytrail division in the number of shapes and patterns of dinnerware produced.

Artware, another Evan K. Shaw specialty, flourished in the fifties and sixties at Metlox. A line of contemporary vessels in earthy matte glazes, designed by well-known California ceramist Harrison McIntosh, was produced in the mid fifties. Concurrent was a series called American Royal Horses, finely detailed, hand-painted figurines of various equine breeds. This was complemented by Nostalgia, an offering of scale-model antique carriages and related articles inspired by Shaw's personal collection of actual carriages.

Shaw's ill-fated American Pottery was licensed to manufacture ceramic figurines based on the Walt Disney cartoon characters in 1943. The Metlox purchase in 1946 enabled him to continue production of this very successful line until 1956. Most of the famous Disney figurines were reproduced in both regular and miniature scale by the Metlox staff.

Poppets by Poppytrail, an extensive collection of doll-like stoneware flower holders and planters created by Helen Slater, were marketed in the sixties and seventies. Colorstax, a revival of dinnerware in solid colored glazes (1978) and Helen McIntosh's charming and novel cookie jars were best-sellers for the company in its last decade.

Kenneth Avery became president of Metlox Manufacturing Inc. following the death of Evan K. Shaw in 1980. In 1988, Shaw's daughter Melinda Avery became the guiding force. Metlox, the last survivor of the original "Big 5" manufacturers, ceased operations in 1989.

Metlox's Nostalgia artware line included this horse and carriage with young rider. Horse model is Large Hackney #644, 8¾", $200.00; Victorian Carriage #625 is equipped with lamp fixture, adapting it for use as a TV lamp, $125.00; rider is #564 Mary Jane, $65.00. All have paper labels.

There are nearly as many Metlox marks and labels as there are lines. The earliest mark was "California Pottery" (1) impressed in-mold on the first line of dinnerware produced in 1932. Beginning in 1934, the impressed "Poppytrail By Metlox" mark (2) came into use, followed slightly later by "Poppytrail Made in California, U.S.A." (3), which was used on dinnerware, and artware alike. "Mission Bell" (4) was impressed on a variety of ware made for Sears between 1935 and 1938. The "C. Romanelli" (5) designation was impressed on most of the artware created by Carl Romanelli in the late thirties and early forties. The Metlox Miniatures generally bore paper labels. The earliest one was shaped like an "M." Evan K. Shaw's Disney line carried an oval paper label reading "Walt Disney Productions/Evan K. Shaw Company Los Angeles" with the name of the depicted character in the center. In the fifties, the familiar ink-stamped logo with the word "Poppytrail" superimposed over an outline of the State of California (6) was adopted. The circular backstamp "Poppytrail by Metlox/Made in California" (7) was also used in the fifties and sixties, along with a similar "Vernon Ware by Metlox/Made in California" version. Two Vernon Ware backstamps that identify specific patterns are shown (8) and (9). Many other such marks were used on both Poppytrail and Vernon Ware dinnerware patterns. Country Side, an exclusive dinnerware line made for Sears in the 1950s, was stamped with their Harmony House trademark (10). Artware of the sixties and seventies bore the paper labels shown (11) and (12). A special circular paper label was used on the Poppets by Poppytrail series (13). Individual name tags have been found on some models.

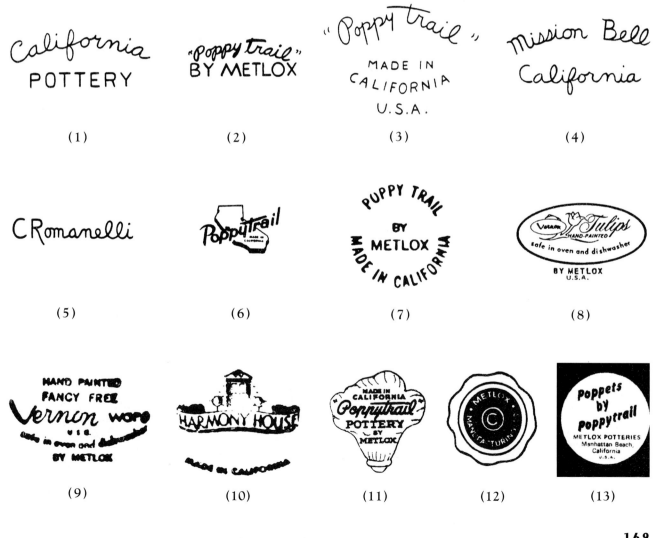

(1)   (2)   (3)   (4)

(5)   (6)   (7)   (8)

(9)   (10)   (11)   (12)   (13)

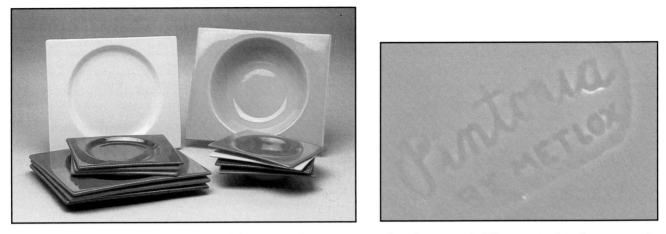

Metlox's Pintoria tableware was a radical departure when it was introduced, ca. 1936. All pieces in this short set are in short supply. Shown are 10½" dinner plates, $75.00+ each; 7¼" bread and butter plates, $60.00+ each; 7" service bowls, $75.00+ each; 11" large serving bowl, $200.00+. See in-mold mark on large serving bowl at right.

Two of the more elusive figures from the Metlox Modern Masterpieces series of the late thirties/early forties. In-mold marks include "C. Romanelli." Left: #1825 dancing girl and doves, 11", $250.00. Right: #1832 dancing girl, 9", $275.00.

Aquarius and Pisces vases, 8", from the Zodiac series by Carl Romanelli. Satin ivory and polychrome glaze treatments, in-mold and stamped marks. $175.00 – 200.00 each. Pisces vase markings are shown at right.

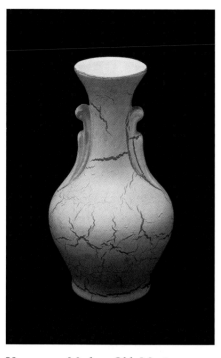

Very rare Metlox Old Mexico vase, 8½", ca. 1937, stamped mark, $100.00+.

Figurine-flower holder, 8¾", designed by Carl Romanelli, satin ivory glaze, ca. 1940, $200.00.

Carl Romanelli's double angelfish vase, 14", is not an easy catch, $275.00.

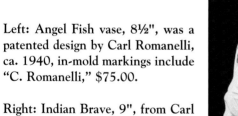

Left: Angel Fish vase, 8½", was a patented design by Carl Romanelli, ca. 1940, in-mold markings include "C. Romanelli," $75.00.

Right: Indian Brave, 9", from Carl Romanelli's "Modern Masterpieces" series of the late thirties/early forties, in-mold mark, $400.00+.

"Oddities of the Animal Kingdom" is how Metlox advertised the miniature scaled figurines of Carl Romanelli, some of the best miniatures ever produced. Left to right: alligator, $300.00+; armadillo, $200.00+; aardvark, $200.00+; thoughtful chimpanzee, $100.00; chimpanzee on all fours, $250.00+. Alligator is 8½" long.

Two of the rarest of the Oddities of the Animal Kingdom series of Metlox Miniatures are the prehistoric plated lizard, 3", $350.00+, and the dinosaur, 4½", $300.00+.

Tags were attached to the Oddities series of miniatures with a description of the individual animal inside, very rare.

One of the finest and hardest to find of the Metlox Miniatures is the elephant on ball, 6½", shown here in polychrome treatment, $375.00+.

Carl Romanelli's Hawaiian head vase #1833, 10½", with exceptional hand decoration, ca. 1942, in-mold marks, $400.00+.

Poppytrail

POTTERY

"ODDITIES IN THE ANIMAL KINGDOM"

89-G

82-G

93-G

88-G

83-G

86-G

84-G

92-G

76-G

75-G

A page from an undated Metlox catalog, ca. 1940, showing some of the Oddities in the Metlox Miniatures series designed and modeled by Carl Romanelli.

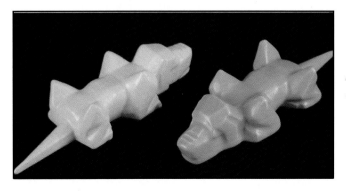

These cubistic dog figurines, 5", are from the extensive "Metlox Miniatures" line, late thirties, $150.00 each.

Front and back covers of promotional brochure issued by Metlox, ca. 1936, picturing the #200 Poppytrail dinnerware line.

These distinctive Metlox spiral candleholders, 7½", in satin turquoise and powder blue, date to the late thirties or early forties, $50.00 each.

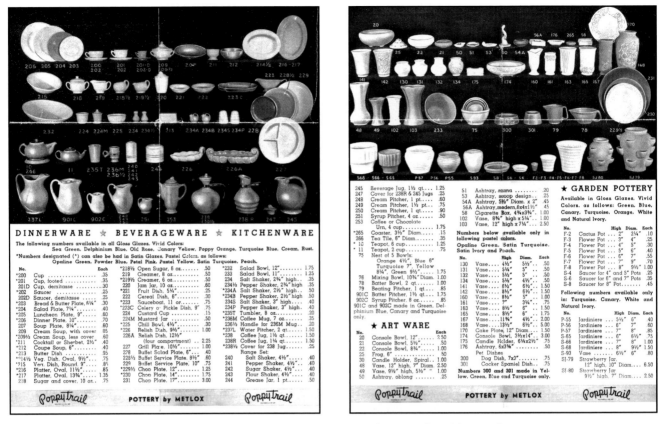

Inside pages of undated fold-out brochure picturing lines produced by Metlox, ca. 1936.
Note Bauer look-alike garden pottery.

Water pitcher from Metlox's popular Red Rooster Provincial line of dinner and kitchen ware, $85.00.

Red Rooster Provincial dinner plate, 10", stamped mark, $15.00.

Ultra-modern fifties styling by Metlox designers Bob Allen and Mel Shaw. Row 1: California Contempora tumbler, $70.00; California Free Form platter, $85.00. Row 2: California Mobile coaster, $40.00; covered butter dish, $175.00; jam and jelly, $95.00+. Stamped marks.

California Mobile dinner plate, 10", $35.00, and cup and saucer, $35.00. Stamped mark.

California Aztec twin vegetable, $250.00; covered vegetable, $375.00+; Stamped mark.

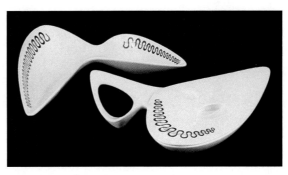

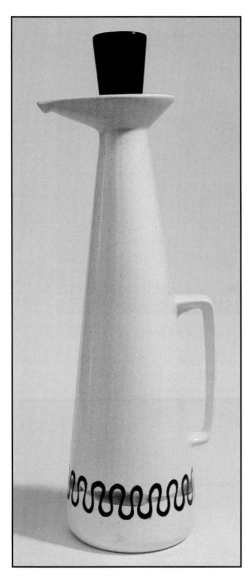

The California Aztec dinnerware line included this unusually tall coffee pot, ca. 1960, $300.00.

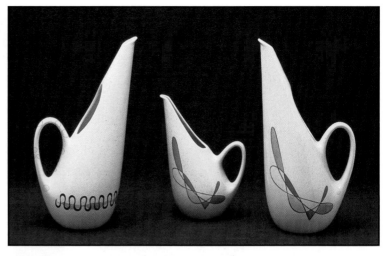

The design team of Bob Allen and Mel Shaw cooked up these extraordinary items for Metlox in the mid fifties. Left to right: California Aztec water pitcher, 14", $300.00; California Mobile milk pitcher, 9½", $275.00, and California Free Form water pitcher, 14", $300.00. Stamped marks.

More sensational Allen and Shaw mid-century design from Metlox. California Mobile covered sugar and creamer, $100.00, California Contempora jawbone, $200.00, California Mobile twin vegetable, $250.00. The Contempora finish is matte; Mobile is gloss.

Marvelous mid-century Metlox: Pepper Tree beverage server (juice cup-cover missing), $95.00; Tropicana (fish motif) low bowl, 12", $120.00; Mosaic bud vase, 6", $80.00; Tropicana (pineapple motif) teardrop vase, 17", $175.00.

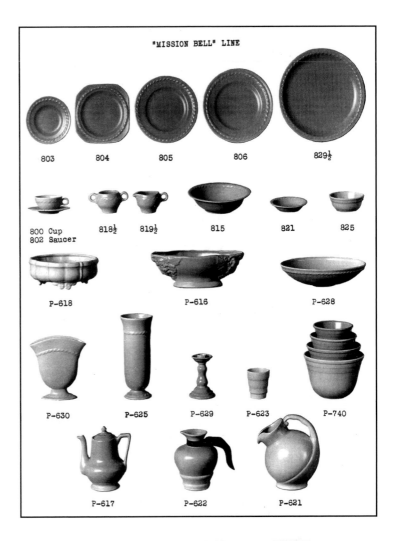

"MISSION BELL" LINE

803   804   805   806   829½

800 Cup
802 Saucer   818½   819½   815   821   825

P-618   P-616   P-628

P-630   P-625   P-629   P-623   P-740

P-617   P-622   P-621

The Ceramic Art Traditions line designed by ceramist Harrison McIntosh included this compote, 4½" x 12", $225.00+, and bottle vase, 12½", $250.00+. Speckled matte glazes, ca. 1956.

Peach Blossom dinner plate, $20.00, and Golden Blossom cup and saucer, $20.00. Early sixties, stamped marks.

More Poppets by Poppytrail. Left to right: Conchita, $60.00; Nancy, $45.00; Barney, $50.00; Sally, $45.00. Conchita measures 9". Note name tag attached to Sally figure.

Poppets by Poppytrail "Tina," 8½", partially glazed stoneware, modeled by Helen Slater, ca. 1970, $65.00.

Helen Slater's popular Poppets line included this Victorian age merchant named Schultz, 9", unmarked, $65.00.

The extensive Poppets assortment included Mike, 5", $45.00, Nellie, 8¾", $55.00, and Sam, 6", $45.00.

Complete set of Disney's *Alice in Wonderland* characters produced at Metlox under license obtained by Evan K. Shaw. All have paper labels (shown at right). Alice measures 6". $2,200.00+ set.

Paper label on back of Tweedledee figure.

Though these cute little mice seem identical at first glance, they appeared in two separate Walt Disney animated films. At left is the baby mouse from *Cinderella*; at right is the doormouse from *Alice in Wonderland*. Both 2½" and unmarked, $350.00 each.

Archival 8" x 10" glossy sheet issued by Evan K. Shaw shows various Walt Disney line items made by Metlox. Note Poppytrail dealer sign.

Cinderella and Prince Charming from Walt Disney's *Cinderella*. Both are 7½" with paper labels. Cinderella, $500.00+; Prince, $375.00+.

Metlox squirrel on pine cone cookie jar, ca. 1960, stamped "Made in USA," $100.00.

Vincent Martinez created three dinosaur cookie jars in the mid eighties, including Mona, at left, and Rex, on the right. Dina completed the set. In-mold marks, as shown on Rex, below. $150.00 each.

Metlox's Mrs. Bunny with carrot cookie jar, 13", debuted in 1985, in-mold mark, $125.00.

Lamb cookie jar has a "crier" in its hat that sounds off when lifted. Designed by Allen and Shaw, unmarked, $150.00.

Strawberry and Grape cookie jars by Metlox's design team of Allen and Shaw. Strawberry is 9" with in-mold mark reading "Metlox/Calif./USA," $85.00. Grapes is 8" with in-mold mark reading "Made in USA," $250.00.

Left: Metlox Pescado line 2-quart covered casserole from the eighties, $200.00. Right: Red fish canister/cookie jar from the sixties, note paper label, $250.00. See Pescado mark below.

BETTY LOU NICHOLS

Betty Lou Nichols was the archetypal head vase producer. Her vases, which generally took the form of a lady's head and shoulders, are justifiably attracting a growing legion of admirers.

Betty Lou Nichols was born Betty Lou Renken in Fullerton, California, in 1922. She also grew up there and attended Fullerton Junior College, where she got her first introduction to ceramics. Always interested in art, she immediately recognized the expressive possibilities that clay working represented after enrolling in Mary Hodgedon's pottery class. During World War II

Betty Lou Nichols in 1962, the year she closed her business.

while her husband John Nichols was overseas, she began to experiment with clay modeling in her parents' La Habra home. At war's end she decided to venture into ceramic production and began by producing a series of figurines of young ladies outfitted in fashionable period attire.

Imports from Europe and Asia were still unavailable to the gift trade, so it was still relatively easy to succeed with a well-made line that was strictly decorative. By 1949, Nichols had established a successful ceramics business in La Habra, located at 639 West Central, with thirty people employed full time. By that time her extraordinary hand-decorated head vases had become the principal product, with many of these models also outfitted in elaborate period attire. Much attention to detail set her head vases apart from the many others that would eventually follow her lead. Especially noteworthy were the handmade and hand-applied details like ruffled bodices, lace, hat bows, curled tresses, and the ever-present demure yet luxuriant eyelashes.

Calling her larger head vases "Floradorables," Betty Lou Nichols also produced miniature versions of some models dubbed "Demidorables." These models were not nearly as elaborate or festooned and were considerably

less costly. Also produced were full-figure floral containers of peasant men and women called "Pleasant Peasants" along with other figurines and figural flower holders. Complex and seldom-made three-quarter figure vases, from just below the waist up, were some of her most expensive items at the time they were produced. Nodders were another feature of the line, and included whimsical human and animal twosomes, usually with one head nodding "yes" and the other "no." Ruth Sloan, with a well-appointed wholesale showroom at the famous Brack Shops in downtown Los Angeles, was the sales representative for the business. Among her numerous customers nationwide were florists who used Betty Lou head vases to create seasonal arrangements (Mr. & Mrs. S. Claus was a perennial favorite) and other unusual floral displays.

As the fifties moved forward, many competitors both domestic and foreign flooded the market with inferior versions of the head vases popularized by Nichols. The Japanese-made head vases were budget priced compared to the labor-intensive original and put a serious dent in the business. In 1962, Betty Lou Nichols decided to call it quits and turned her attentions to painting and raising her two children.

Betty Lou Nichols' signature was her mark, usually painted by hand underglaze. Her name was also included in various block-lettered stamped marks in later years. Three variations of the painted marks are shown. Paper labels were also used.

This head vase named Nancy measures 8½". Painted mark reads "Nancy by Betty Lou Nichols," $650.00.

Hand-detailed head vase, 8", with painted mark reading, "Mary Lou by Betty Lou Nichols," $450.00.

These chic head vases represent subtle variations on a theme by Betty Lou Nichols. *Archival photo.*

Flower holder figurine named Margot, 10½", by Betty Lou Nichols, painted mark shown below, $200.00.

The two sizes of Betty Lou Nichols' Ermintrude head vase, painted marks. Registered California label on larger size head vase. Left: 6" size, $350.00. Right: 8" size (this example measures nearly 9"), $650.00.

Left: Betty Lou Nichols' Betty Lou (self portrait?) head vase, 6", $325.00. Right: Valerie head vase, 8", $650.00. Smaller size vase has separate openings on top for easy flower arranging.

Olga planter, 8" x 11½", with painted mark including copyright symbol, $250.00.

Only the Young Adorables series of head vases had open eyes. Left to right: Becky, Judy, and Kathy, each measures 5½", painted marks (see mark below on Kathy vase). $250.00 each.

Betty Lou Nichols' Demidorables series included these two smartly dressed models. $100.00 each. *Archival photo.*

Egg Heads by Betty Lou Nichols. Left to right: Girl, 4", $150.00; lady (Henrietta), 8½", $1,800.00+; man (Henry), 9", $1,800.00+; boy, 4", $150.00. Stamped marks.

The Egg Heads by Betty Lou Nichols came in two sizes. *Archival photo.*

Don't fence her in! Fence planter measures 4" x 9½"; Lisa flower holder figurine stands 11". Stamped mark on fence, painted mark on figurine. Planter, $175.00; Lisa, $275.00.

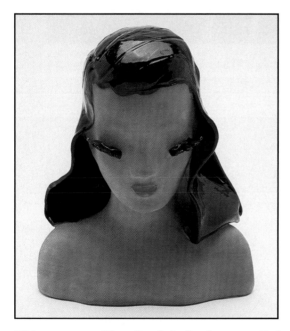

This very rare Hawaiian lady head vase, called Princess Aloha, measures 7½". Combination matte/gloss finish, with painted mark reading "By Betty Lou Nichols." $2,500.00+.

Anna and Fritz figurines by Betty Lou Nichols. Fritz, 9½", holds barrel for flowers. Stamped marks. $250.00 each.

These three Christmas angels are named Tom, Dick and Holly. Holly, checking her wish list, stands 6½". Stamped marks read "Betty Lou Nichols ©." $175.00 each.

These peasant girl figurines by Betty Lou Nichols double as flower holders. $175.00 each. *Archival photo.*

Nodder kids by Betty Lou Nichols. Boy, 7½", nods "yes;" girl, 7", nods "no." Stamped marks, $400.00+ set.

Betty Lou Nichols' amusing cat and mouse nodders (cat nods "yes;" mouse nods "no") are 7" and 4½", respectively. $400.00+ set.

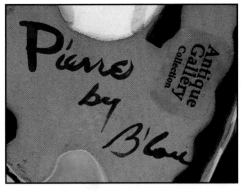

The Bunnydorables were flower holders well-suited for festive Easter Sunday tables. Pierre and Flossie each stand 8½", $275.00 each. See mark (above) on Pierre showing abbreviated "B-Lou."

Betty Lou Nichols' Duckydorables are all set for that big Easter parade. *Archival photo.*

This 7" Vicky by Betty Lou Nichols has a small hole in back so it can be used as a wall vase. No mark, $650.00+.

Hand-decorated and trimmed powder jar by Betty Lou Nichols, with stamped mark reading "Betty Lou Nichols/La Habra, California," $150.00.

Betty Lou Nichols' stamped mark.

PACIFIC

The Pacific Clay Products Company came into existence when William Lacy consolidated several local potteries in the early twenties. Included in this union were some of the oldest ceramic companies in California. Lacy's principal plant was situated in the Lincoln Heights district of Los Angeles, at 306 West Avenue 26. The Los Angeles Stoneware Company was the original business at this location and was built in 1890 to make kitchen stoneware, ollas, and similar ware. It was the first plant in Southern California to manufacture these products and one of the first to make clay products of any kind in the state. Architectural terra cotta, brick, and roofing tile were among the varied items produced there after the name change and formation of the consolidated Pacific Company.

Pacific's stoneware line was a quality product that enjoyed an excellent reputation throughout the Southwest during the twenties. The clays used in its production and later pottery were obtained from California deposits owned by the company. Among the numerous stoneware staples that Pacific provided were butter jars, yellow ware mixing bowls, and bean pots. Representative samples were displayed in the showroom of the Lincoln Heights plant where visitors were "always cordially welcome."

Harold Johnson, who was the son of plant foreman Fred Johnson (no relation to the Fred Johnson who worked for Bauer), joined his father at Pacific in 1917. Before leaving in 1928, he became highly skilled in many aspects of pottery production and had modeled numerous garden pots and vases that were added to the general stoneware line. His distinctive polychrome glazes were used to good and sometimes stunning effect on a variety of articles pictured in the company's stoneware catalogs of the late twenties.

Like many other manufacturers in the area, Pacific Clay Products prospered during the twenties building boom in Southern California, with its numerous structural clay products. When the boom period ended in the early thirties, the outlook was rather dismal. The new and promising colored ware of the nearby Bauer Pottery offered a solution to the Depression slump, and Pacific was one of the first companies to follow their lead. Not long after Bauer's introduction of its popular California Colored Pottery in 1930, a rival set of dishes and kitchen articles called "Hostessware" debuted. More than a quickie imitation of Bauer's prototype, Pacific's line was actually more extensive, more fully considered, and gave its neighbor some potent competition. Although following

The Pacific Clay Products crew of Plant #4 (Lincoln Heights) in 1935.

the general makeup of its rival, Pacific's glazes were distinctive, varying in density, texture, and tone. The seven original colors were Apache red (red-orange), Pacific Blue (cobalt), Sierra White, lemon yellow, jade green, delphinium blue, and desert brown. (Many of these were later reformulated and renamed.) John Lathrop, a ceramic engineering graduate of the University of Illinois, is credited with development of at least some of the Pacific Pottery glazes.

Quality consciousness embraced most aspects of production (seconds were discarded), but the outstanding glazes and streamlined styling are what ultimately set Pacific's colored pottery apart. In the line's May 1, 1935 price list, almost two hundred separate items were offered for sale, including an ample assortment of complementary artware. As an alternative to the monochrome glazes, the art department devised a series of accommodating underglaze decorations such as contrasting colored bands, spirals, and cross-hatching. These were joined by more complex patterns

with names like Dimity, Chrysanthemum, Wheat, and Willow. All "free hand fused decorations," as the company called them, were obtainable in complete sets of dishes.

In 1937, a lighter weight, pastel colored tableware called Coralitos was introduced. It, unlike its predecessor, was designed for the consumer seeking a more conventional product. A similar set of dishes, named Arcadia, was produced about the same time.

The art department of the pottery division of Pacific Clay Products created an extensive and impressive array of slip-cast artware. Unfortunately, the names of individual designers have been difficult to ascertain. The only ones known at present are Bernita Lundy and Robert E. Haynes. The variety of decorative articles, initiated about 1932, included vases (some hand-thrown vases presage this date), planters, candle holders, figurines, flower bowls, and flower frogs. Some of this production was also hand decorated. Large architectural vases, sand jars, and flower pots round out the distinguished but short-lived Pacific Pottery line.

Some of the many hand-painted patterns available on Pacific ware in the mid thirties. Front to back: "Spiral" salad plate, $95.00; "Plaid" dinner plate, $65.00; "Wave" dinner plate, $125.00; "Spoke" dinner plate, $125.00. (Author's names.)

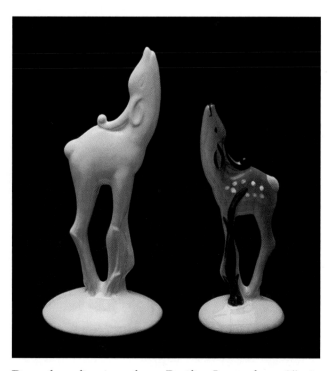

Deco deer figurines from Pacific. Large deer, 9", in white, $50.00. Small deer, 7", with hand decoration, $65.00.

In 1942, just as the business was beginning to experiment with new lines of dinnerware, the Lincoln Heights plant committed to full-time defense work and all pottery manufacturing ceased. The Pacific Clay Products Company presently operates out of its Corona plant, but no pottery is produced there.

In the twenties (or possibly earlier), the company adopted a logo consisting of the name PACIFIC enclosed in a rounded, diamond-shaped outline. In the thirties, this logo was modified (edges sharpened) and the paper label shown (1) was used extensively.

Many articles found unmarked today once carried this sole identification. The earliest pottery back-stamp used was the impressed (in-mold) PACIFIC (2) in block letters. In the late thirties, a raised circular mark (3) was developed for use on most ware. Some Pacific pottery, perhaps premiums, bore only the bottom half of this mark, minus the company name. Small items may be found today with the abbreviated PAC USA (4) in-mold mark. Additionally, stamped marks were devised for a few specific Pacific lines.

(1)

(2)

(3)

(4)

Blended glazed stoneware vessels of the late twenties are favored by collectors. Left to right: 12" rose vase, #523, $350.00+; 7" rose vase, #520, $250.00+; vase, 10½", $350.00+. See photo of stamped mark at right.

Stamped mark frequently used on blended glazed stoneware items.

This full-page Pacific Clay Products ad, ca. 1937, touted its boxed set of Coralitos as the ideal Christmas gift.

Examples of rare hand-thrown pottery produced by Pacific, ca. 1930. Vase, 10", $500.00+; vase, 8", $500.00+. Below: Painted marks seen on unglazed bottoms of hand-thrown pottery are believed to designate glazes.

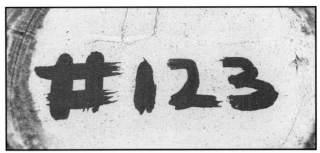

Floral containers of the early thirties from Pacific. Left to right: Vase (#19), 6", in Apache red, $175.00; vase with mock handles, 8½", in unusual matte cobalt blue, $300.00+; bowl vase with mock handles (#28), 5", in Apache red, $200.00.

Pacific ware, in-mold marks. Row 1: Early design egg cup, $50.00; later design egg cup, $40.00; 4" tumbler, $15.00; tumbler (has matching pitcher), $50.00. Row 2: goblet, $150.00+; cocktail cup, $40.00; covered jar, 5", $250.00+; early design custard cups, $50.00+ each.

Divided baby plate, 9", with bunny design border, ca. 1934, $200.00+.

Early ball jug , $80.00, with matching 5" tumblers, $25.00 each.

Pacific rivalled Bauer's Ring line with what was initially called Hostessware. Clockwise from top: Tray, 15", $75.00; 2-quart pitcher, $200.00; coffee/tea cup and saucer, $25.00; large coffee cups, $75.00 each; coaster, 4", $10.00; shaker, $10.00; small open sugar and creamer, $40.00 set.

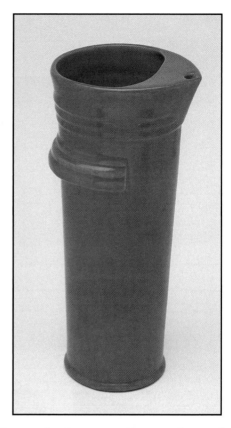

Rare cocktail mixer, 10½", complete with a long-handled chrome-plated spoon for mixing cocktails, was introduced shortly after the repeal of Prohibition in the early thirties. Raised mark, "630." $500.00+.

Streamlining with style from Pacific. Left to right: Hostessware 1-pint syrup pitcher in lemon yellow, $300.00+; batter pitcher in apricot (on glass block), $175.00; early design 2-cup teapot in Apache red, $125.00; later design 4-cup teapot in jade green, $125.00; after-dinner coffee pot in Sierra white, $400.00+.

Left: Hostessware cookie/pretzel jar in jade green is very hard to find, $600.00+. Right: Covered soup tureen, 9½", in delphinium blue is equally scarce, $600.00+.

A series of attenuated Pacific advertisements like this appeared in *House & Garden* in 1935.

Pacific Hostessware. Clockwise from top: Early design pitcher, 8½", $200.00; #24 mixing bowl, $45.00; divided salad dressing dish, 6", $60.00; early plain design #18 mixing bowl, $60.00.

Pacific 14" footed punch bowl in Pacific blue, $400.00+; 9" footed salad bowl in Apache red, $150.00. No marks.

Floral artware of the early thirties. Handled low vase, 5", $150.00; vase, 11½", $200.00; vase, 8¼", $100.00; vase, 7", $150.00.

Pacific advertised extensively in the late thirties in an effort to broaden its consumer acceptance. This full-page, full-color ad appeared in the April 1935 issue of *House and Garden*.

The clip-on wood handles on these kitchen items were patented. Baking dish, 8¾", $75.00, and pie plate, 11", $75.00, in delphinium blue; baking dish, 6¼", in jade green, $60.00; pie plate, 11", in Pacific blue, $75.00. Early in-mold "Pacific" marks.

Note: Handles add $35.00 each to these prices.

Artware with satin matte glazes designed by Bernita Lundy in the mid thirties. Left to right: Jack planter (#907), 5", in ivory, $45.00; Madonna bust (#902), 8", in pastel green, $80.00; Jill planter (#906), 5", in pastel green, $45.00.

Hand-decorated bird motif vase, 8¼", stamped mark, ca. 1939, $125.00.

Candle holders, no marks. Three-branch candelabra, 10", $75.00; square candlestick, 3", $45.00; flared candlestick, 4½", $35.00.

Choice Pacific artware, ca. late thirties. Left to right: Vase, #3603, 12", in blue and white, $200.00; vase with handles, #3309, 8", in white, $65.00; deco vase, #3107, 7", in yellow, $75.00. Raised circular mark #3.

PACIFIC

More late-thirties artware by Pacific. Left to right: Ovoid vase, #3602, 10", in white and maroon, $150.00; flared vase, #3600, 10", in white and maroon, $100.00; fluted shell vase, #3349, 8", in unusual deep purple lined with turquoise, $60.00. In-mold marks (right photo).

This unique 15" oval fish platter is a highlight of the extensive Hostessware line of Pacific Clay Products, raised circular mark #3, $250.00.

Hand-decorated ware like this is highly sought by Pacific collectors. Left to right, front: Individual melted butter dish, 4", in royal blue, $75.00+; teacup and saucer in royal blue, $150.00+; teacup and saucer in Apache red, $85.00+; sauce dishes in silver green, 5½", $100.00+. Left to right, back: 12" oval vegetable bowl in royal blue, $200.00+; 15" low coupe salad bowl in Apache red, $250.00+. Raised circular in-mold marks.

Pacific Hostessware 14" cake plate in Apache red with very unusual hand decoration, $300.00+; cockatoo flower holder, #3802, in canary yellow, $150.00.

Rare Hostessware flat salad server, 17", in Sierra white, with hand-decorated Dutch figures, $450.00+.

Pacific Hostessware 17" low coupe salad bowl with extraordinary hand decoration, no mark, $400.00+.

Pacific's Coralitos dinnerware was lighter in weight, and the colors were more restrained. Clockwise from top right: Covered coffee server with wood handle, $45.00; nappie, $10.00; demitasse cup and saucer, $25.00; 8" salad plate, $20.00; 7" pie plate, $10.00; tea cup and saucer, $10.00; 10" dinner plate, $15.00; covered butter dish, $60.00; handled soup bowl, $15.00.

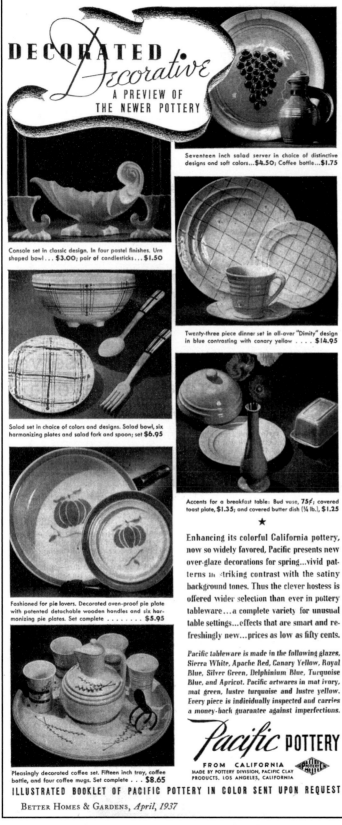

This Pacific ad featuring its new line of hand-decorated ware appeared in the April, 1937, issue of *Better Homes & Gardens*.

Stately hand-decorated egret flower arranger, 13½", stamped mark, $150.00.

Pacific porch pot, 14" x 18", in canary yellow, $750.00+.

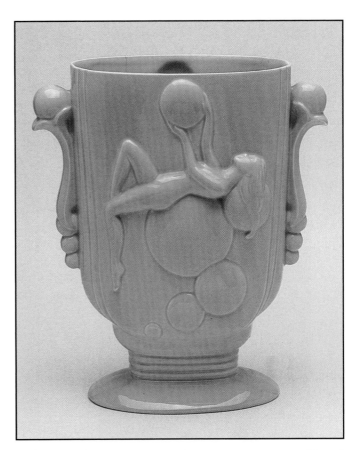

Dazzling and very rare vase, 15" x 13", in turquoise. Raised circular mark with #4600 in center indicates it was a late addition to the Pacific artware catalog. $600.00+.

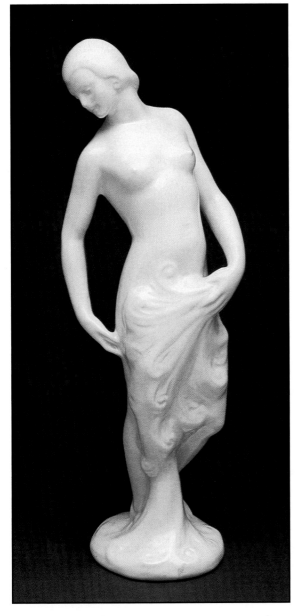

Statuesque fan dancer, 15½", may represent burlesque star Sally Rand, stamped mark (below), $600.00+.

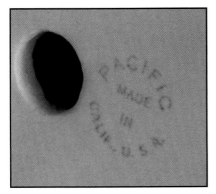

Pacific sand jar, 20½", in Apache Red, stamped circular mark reads "1100," $750.00.

Large stylized bird figurine in satin white, circular in-mold mark, $50.00.

Pacific vase (#4000), 13½", in pink, depicting the ornamented prow of a sailing ship, raised circular mark #3, $300.00+.

An example of one of the many lines of decorated dinnerware Pacific was developing in the early forties, before the pottery division switched to full-time defense work. Dinner plate, 10½", stamped mark (below), $35.00.

HOWARD PIERCE

Howard Pierce was one of the most original of the Southern California ceramists working commercially. Born in Chicago, Illinois in 1912, Pierce attended the University of Illinois and the Chicago Art Institute before moving to California in 1935. Locating in Claremont, he enrolled at Pomona College for further art instruction. In 1936, a miniature fawn that Pierce had modeled was purchased by William Manker and added to the line of ceramics the latter produced in Claremont. A job offer from Manker was also accepted at this time, an association which continued for three years.

Gaining a thorough education in ceramic production in Manker's plant along with the motivation to start his own business, Howard Pierce established a studio in nearby La Verne in 1941. So not to create direct competition for his former employer, he began producing small animal figures in pewter. In 1945, after a three-year hiatus in defense work in Long Beach, Howard returned to Claremont and the ceramics business by leasing a small building on 6th Street and outfitting it with one gas-fired kiln. With assistance from his wife Ellen, whom he had married in 1941, Howard began production of a very contemporary line of figurines in a porcelain material known as nepheline syenite, to which was added china clay from Florida and ball clay from Kentucky and Tennessee. He formulated the clay body and glazes, did the modeling, made the molds, and supervised every step of production, most of which he performed himself. A local florist provided the business with its initial account. Good public response led to additional accounts, and in 1950, the N.S. Gustin Company became Howard Pierce's national sales representative. During the fifties, which was the peak period, two ten-foot gas-fired kilns were added to the Claremont facility along with extra help.

Pierce's distinctively styled porcelain sculptures of animal, bird, and human subjects retailed in the finest gift shops and department stores in the country. Most items were designed and sold in sets of two or three, a feature which enhanced their decorative and sales appeal. The earliest glaze used was a satin-matte white.

Howard Pierce at work in his Claremont studio, ca. 1952. *Archival photo.*

Soon after, a satin-matte brown on white combination was added, and it became the favored finish for almost fifteen years. Other satin colors of this period included black on white, all black, and all gray. Standard high-gloss colors were brown agate, slate gray, and sandstone. Many experimental or special colors and combinations were produced over the years as a salient aspect of the work. Both body and glaze were matured in a single firing at 2150°F.

In 1956, Pierce developed his own version of Wedgwood's Jasperware in which the raised cameos were cast as an integral part of each of the various objects. Background colors were brown, green, and blue. Limited public acceptance resulted in a brief production. Somewhat more successful was a separate line of high-glazed vases and lamps with open centers containing miniature animals and plant forms in white porcelain bisque.

The business returned to a more relaxed pace after the Gustin representation ended in 1966. With their extra help no longer needed, the Pierces carried on as they had in the pre-fifties period until 1968, when they moved to Joshua Tree, a desert community near Palm Springs, and semi-retirement. In addition to his familiar small-scaled output, Howard Pierce produced life-sized and larger-than-life-sized sculptures for various sites in and around this desert outpost, including its community hospital. Pierce died in 1994.

Howard Pierce used the same stamped mark of his full name in block letters for most of his ceramics career. Occasionally, he marked a piece with only his last name. During the fifties, "Howard Pierce Porcelain" or "Pierce Porcelain" was used to call attention to this high-grade material. Pierce's incised signature (full name or last name) appears on numerous items, with "Claremont, Calif." occasionally added during the years the business remained there. Smaller items in a set were often left unmarked.

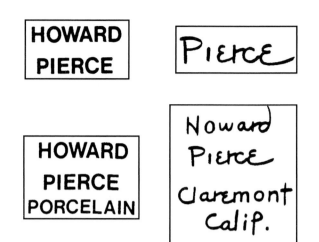

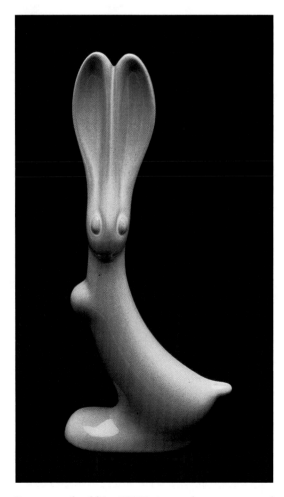

Long-eared rabbit, 10½", in sandstone, recessed in-mold "Howard Pierce 102-P," ca. 1953, $125.00.

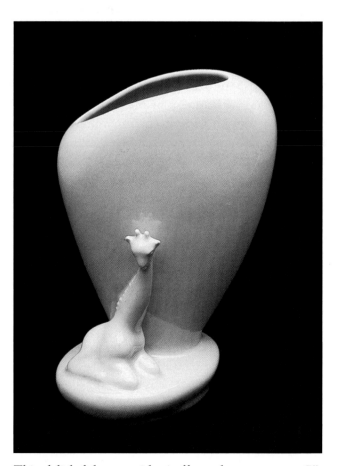

This delightful vase with giraffe on base measures 7", recessed in-mold mark "Howard Pierce 250-P," $125.00.

Howard Pierce penguins in matte black/white combination, stamped marks. Large, 4¾", $65.00; small, 3½", $45.00.

These brown on white glazed chickens by Howard Pierce measure 9" and 6", fifties period, stamped marks, $95.00 set.

Striking wind-blown horse in matte black with speckled mane and tail measures 8" x 7", stamped "Howard Pierce," $200.00+.

Cat, 9", with kitten, 4", in brown on white. Cat has stamped Howard Pierce mark; kitten is not marked. $150.00 set.

This impressive Howard Pierce sculpture of squirrels on forest stump, 11½" x 7", incidentally doubles as a floral container. Stamped mark. $250.00+.

Penguin, 7", black on white, stamped "Howard Pierce," ca. 1953, $150.00.

Two recumbent cats from slightly different time periods. The Siamese cat at right is not marked. The cat with no face measures 3" x 4" and is stamped "Howard Pierce." $50.00 each.

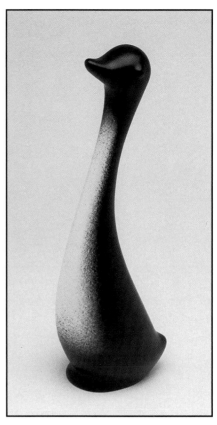

Howard Pierce native pair, brown on white, ca. 1957. Woman, 7"; man, 7½". $175.00 pair.

A high-rise bird by Howard Pierce. A goose, perhaps, it measures 11". Howard Pierce Porcelain mark, $100.00.

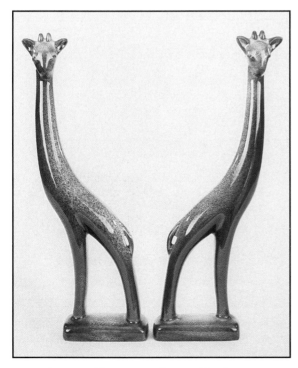

Animals with special glazes. Hippo and monkey, each 6", stamped "Howard Pierce." $95.00 each.

Pair of Howard Pierce giraffes, 10½", brown agate, in-mold marks, mid fifties, $350.00+ pair.

Parakeets in background measure 5" and are stamped "Howard Pierce Porcelain." $60.00 each. Bird in foreground is 4" and unmarked, $50.00.

Howard Pierce water bird, 14", $65.00; pigeon, 7½", one of two, $45.00. Fifties period, stamped marks.

Mismatched ducks (from two different sets.) Decoy-like duck at left is 6" in length. Matte glazes, stamped marks. $65.00 each.

Popular quail family of the fifties period. Large quail, 5½", stamped "Howard Pierce." $45.00 set.

Different bear models of the fifties: bear (has matching cub), 6", special glaze, $95.00; polar bear, 6½" brown on white, $150.00.

PORCELAIN FIGURINES

howard pierce

NO.	DESCRIPTION		COLOR	DOZEN PRICE
112-P	Madonna	7-1/2"	Matte White	9.00
212-P	Madonna	13-1/2"	Matte White	24.00
129-P	Bears	Set of 2	Gray, Brown	15.00
130-P	Quail	Set of 3	Gray, Brown	24.00
131-P	Chipmunks	Set of 2	Gray, Brown	18.00
133-P	Decoy Duck	Single	Gray, Brown	18.00
138-P	Seals	Set of 2	Gray	18.00
140-P	Monkeys	Set of 2	Gray, Brown	18.00
141-P	Honkers	Set of 2	Gray, Brown	18.00
142-P	Kittens	Set of 2	Gray, Brown	18.00
143-P	Dachshund	Single	Brown	12.00
149-P	Polar Bear	Single	Matte White, Brown	18.00
209-P	Pigeons	Set of 2	Gray, Brown	24.00
210-P	Water Bird	Single	Gray, Brown	24.00
211-P	Fawns	Set of 2	Brown	24.00
250-P	Geese	Set of 3	Gray, Brown	30.00
252-P	Cats	Set of 2	Gray, Brown	30.00
300-P	Ducks	Set of 2	Gray, Brown	30.00
350-P	Racoons	Set of 2	Gray, Brown	36.00

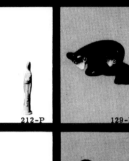

112-P 212-P 129-P 130-P

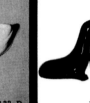

131-P 133-P 138-P

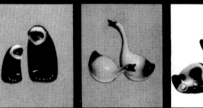
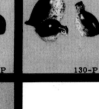

143-P 149-P 209-P

210-P 211-P 250-P

252-P 300-P 350-P

An unusually fine line of contemporary figurines....original sculptures by California artist Howard Pierce. These charming, whimsical birds and animals have been designed in sets of two or three....a feature which gives them unique decorative value and added sales appeal. Soft shades of matte gray on white and matte brown on white.

ALL PRICES F.O.B. FACTORY
CLAREMONT, CALIFORNIA
TERMS: 2% 10 DAYS, NET 30 DAYS

N. S. GUSTIN COMPANY
712 SOUTH OLIVE STREET • LOS ANGELES 14, CALIFORNIA
NEW YORK: 225 FIFTH AVE. • CHICAGO: 1583 MERCH. MART

Howard Pierce wholesale brochure prepared by his representative, the N. S. Gustin Company, ca. 1955.

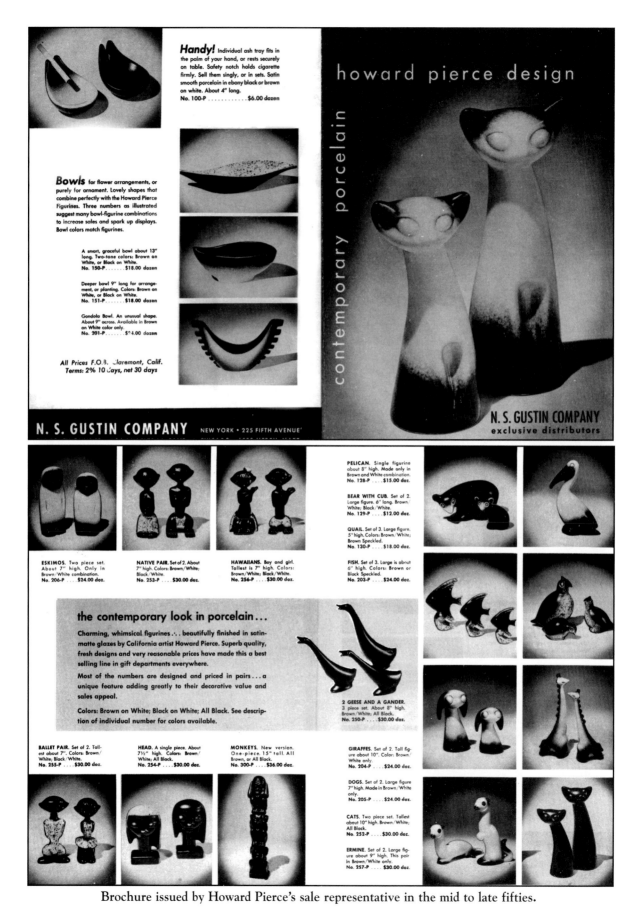

Brochure issued by Howard Pierce's sale representative in the mid to late fifties.

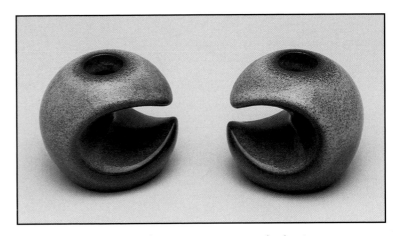

These candleholders in brown agate seem to be having a conversation. They measure 2½" in height and have Howard Pierce Porcelain mark. $75.00 pair.

Speckled green vase with silken white giraffe and palm tree in open center, 9". Claremont period in-mold mark below. $125.00.

A couple of unrelated Howard Pierce pieces finished in gold leaf, no visible marks. Angel candleholder, 8", $65.00; wild goose about to take flight, 6", $45.00.

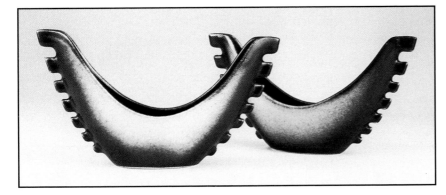

Pair of gondola bowls, 5" x 9½", brown on white, $100.00 pair.

Howard Pierce high-style ashtray with light gray lava glaze outside and cobalt blue high glaze inside, $65.00.

Two roadrunner models from later Joshua Tree studio. Roadrunners at rest, 8¾" in height, stamped "Howard Pierce," $150.00. Road-runner in motion, 8" in length, stamped "Pierce," $85.00.

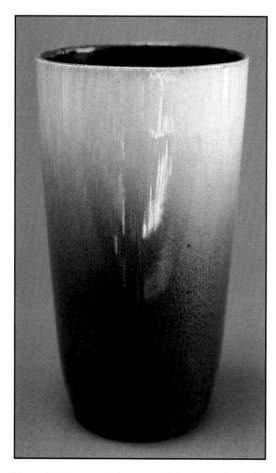

Vase, 7¼", mottled green high glaze, in-mold mark, $100.00.

Joshua Tree period howling coyote, 5¾", in unusual granite-like glaze, stamped mark, $175.00.

ROSELANE

The Roselane Pottery was a husband and wife operation owned by William "Doc" Fields and his wife Georgia. Roselane was established at the Fields' residence in Pasadena with the firing of the first kiln in February 1938.

Although Doc Fields was basically untrained in ceramic production, the business overcame many obstacles and by 1939 was selling its attractive figurines to local florists. At first, Doc sculpted all of the models while Georgia took charge of production with the help of a part-time technician.

With continued good fortune, the business outgrew its first location and was moved in 1940 to a newly constructed factory at 249 Mary Street in Pasadena. By the mid forties, twenty-five people were employed. Joining the firm as salesman was Doc Fields' brother Robert. Roselane was displaying its line at this time at the semi-annual gift shows in Los Angeles and San Francisco and shipping to all parts of the country plus Alaska and South America.

The most extensive offering of the forties was Chinese Modern and included vases, bowls, figurines, candle holders, and wall pockets produced in various high-gloss colors and combinations, such as black and white, cherry and dove gray, citron yellow and sage green, and bitter green and cocoa. From about 1945 to 1952, a successful buffet serving line called Aqua Marine was manufactured. It featured a stylized, sgraffito-like outline of swirling black fish against an aqua or pink background. In the mid fifties, Fields designed a striking series of small abstract ceramic sculptures of animals that were mounted on walnut bases. Unfortunately, these were deemed too advanced by the gift buyers and had to be modified with attached eyes to make them appear more naturalistic.

The impending construction of the #210 freeway through Pasadena forced Roselane's relocation to 5107 Calmview Avenue in Baldwin Park in 1968 where it remained until 1974. Begun in the fifties, the very popular Sparklers series in airbrush decorated semi-porcelain was continued in the new location. The line featured stylized, sometimes whimsical figurines of animals and birds, each complete with colored rhinestone (later plastic) eyes.

After the death of William Fields in 1973, Mrs. Fields sold the business to Prather Engineering Corporation and operations were moved to Long Beach. Roselane production ceased entirely in 1977.

In addition to the items already mentioned, Roselane produced flower bowls, vases, ashtrays, covered boxes, and other decorative housewares, much of which reflected the fifties' modern design trend.

Roselane employed a variety of incised (in-mold) and stamped marks, a sampling of which is shown. Prior to the move to Baldwin Park, the word "Roselane" was sometimes followed by "Pasadena, Calif." rather than simply "Calif." Paper labels were also used.

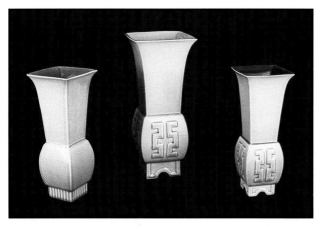

Chinese style vase, 8", $35.00; vase with raised Chinese Key design, 9¾", $45.00; vase with Chinese Key raised design, 8", $35.00.

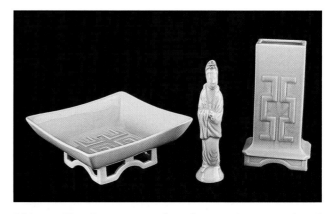

Chinese Key housewares, late forties. Square pedestal bowl, 2½" x 6¼", $25.00; figurine, 6", $25.00; vase, 6¼", $30.00.

Roselane child figurines with in-mold "Roselane" marks. Boy with dog, 5½", $35.00; sitting boy, $35.00; girl with hat, $35.00; girl with bouquet, $35.00.

Roselane angel fish, 7½", $150.00. See in-mold mark on underside of angel fish below.

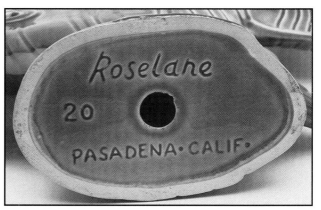

Roselane dealer sign, 3" x 12½", in deep aqua high glaze, $350.00.+

Pair of Roselane Bali dancers, male is 11"; female is 11¼". In-mold marks. $125.00 pair.

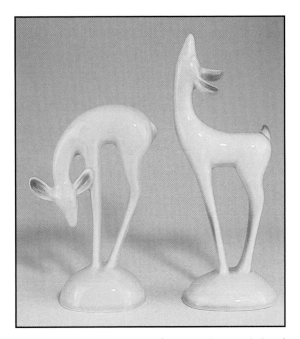

Deer with head down, 6", $40.00; deer with head up, 8", $40.00. Late fifties/early sixties.

Left: Fox, in bronze glaze, on wood base, 9", Roselane logo is burned into bottom of wood base (below), $175.00+. Right: Jackrabbit, 8", unmarked, $125.00.

Two more dramatic models from Roselane's series of animal sculptures mounted on wood bases. Mid fifties, burned-in marks. Horse, 9", $175.00+; dog, 7", $175.00+.

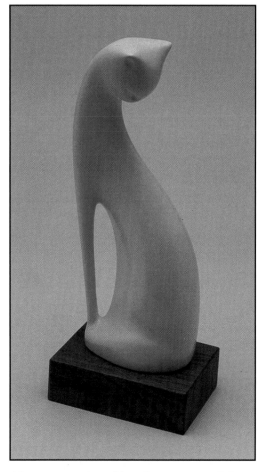

Modern elephant sculpture on wood base, 8", brown luster glaze, "Roselane" logo burned into bottom of wood base, rare, $200.00+.

Abstract cat, in white glaze, on wood base, 10", mid fifties, burned-in logo, $175.00+.

Roselane stylized pheasants in Howard Pierce-like brown on white matte glaze. Note ceramic seed pearl eyes. Female (tail up), 7¾". $65.00 pair.

This small scale raccoon with plastic eyes is marked in-mold "USA," $30.00.

Roselane Sparklers, no marks. Twin kittens, 2", $25.00; cat, 4", $35.00.

Popular Sparkler series owls with plastic eyes, sixties/seventies. Modern owl, 5¼", $20.00; baby owl, 2¼", $10.00; large owl, 7", $25.00; small owl, 3½", $15.00.

Giraffe figurine, 5½", light gray high glaze, ca. 1960, $50.00.

Small-scale Sparkler deer, 4" x 3½", with fawn, satin-matte brown on white, plastic eyes, ca. 1965. Deer, $25.00; fawn, $25.00.

HEDI SCHOOP

Hedi Schoop's trend-setting career in clay came about after her dislocation from formative theatrical pursuits in Europe. Born in Switzerland in 1906, Ms. Schoop received a wide-ranging education in the arts, including painting, sculpture, architecture, and fashion design at Vienna's Kunstgewerbeschule and Berlin's Reimann Institute, before joining her dancer sister, Trudi Schoop, on the German stage in the early thirties. Any thoughts of a professional career in the theatre, however, were cut short by the existent political turmoil.

Fleeing Nazi Germany with her husband, the well-known composer Frederick Hollander, Hedi Schoop emigrated to the States and settled in Hollywood in 1933. In 1938, a group of hand-painted plaster of Paris dolls which she outfitted in contemporary fashions was "discovered" by the Barker

Brothers department store in Los Angeles. Advised to adapt her designs to the more durable ceramic medium, Hedi immediately established a workshop in a rented building near her home. The unexpected success of her deftly painted slip-cast figures necessitated construction of a much larger facility in 1940.

The Hedi Schoop plant, located at 10852 Burbank Boulevard in North Hollywood, was financed by Hedi's mother and contained two general-purpose gas-fired kilns and a smaller electric kiln for overglaze gold and platinum decoration. Beginning with a crew of about twenty, the workforce of the business had more than doubled by the end of World War II. Several European actors, dancers, and musicians, their careers also interrupted by Hitler's rise to power, found temporary employment in this country as

Hedi Schoop sculpting in clay in her studio, ca. 1948. *Archival photo.*

Ms. Schoop's decorators. Most of these refugees were friends or acquaintances prior to the war. One of them, Sylvester Schaffers, a leading German painter, was allowed to initiate hand-painted pictorial motifs for plates and ashtrays in addition to his regular decorating duties.

With few exceptions, the figurines produced were personally designed and modeled by Hedi Schoop, and ranged from European and Asian couples in native attire to American debutantes and Hawaiian hula dancers. Many of the figures doubled as flower containers, a concept that Hedi Schoop popularized. Another innovation was her development of sharply incised texture on areas of the greenware prior to decoration and firing. Besides her animated human figures, Hedi produced animals (as figurines, flower holders, and candle holders), vases, wall plaques, planters, candlesticks, covered boxes, and ashtrays. Often, entire lines would be created with all the above listed articles included in a single coordinated decorative scheme or motif.

The company was incorporated as Hedi Schoop Art Creations in 1942, just as California's giftware business was beginning to intensify. The post-war years were the most productive, with an average of 30,000 hand-painted items turned out annually. To keep pace with the latest development in home entertainment, Hedi Schoop began a charming series of TV lamps in the mid fifties. Unfortunately, this line was cut short by a disastrous fire that leveled her plant in 1958.

Rather than rebuild, Schoop opted to withdraw from full-time production and sold some of her molds to local manufacturer and distributor, Lou Honig. She also helped develop a contemporary line for the California Cleminsons using some of her molds in conjunction with an inventive dripped glaze technique. She retired from the pottery business permanently in the early sixties and was active as a painter for an extended period prior to her death in 1996.

Hedi Schoop was one of the most imitated of the California giftware artists. One of her former associates, Katherine Schueftan, operating under the fictitious name Kim Ward, produced such obvious copies that a successful industry-supported lawsuit resulted in 1942. Two former employees, Max and Yona Lippin, established a separate and highly derivative business in the forties known as Yona Ceramics. These unauthorized Hedi Schoop spin-offs were only the beginning of what ultimately became an endemic California trend.

A variety of marks were used. These included both stamped and incised versions of Hedi Schoop's signature. The words "Hollywood, Cal." or just "California" were added in some instances. Unmarked examples would be very uncommon.

The King and Queen cookie jars of 1941 are on the want lists of most cookie jar and Hedi Schoop collectors. King is 12", $750.00+; Queen is 12½", $500.00+. Painted marks.

Hedi Schoop
HOLLYWOOD CAL.

Hedi
Schoop

HEDI SCHOOP
CALIFORNIA

This "love boat" by Hedi Schoop is an early piece (1939) that reveals her capricious side. Measuring 6" x 10½", it is incised "Hedi Schoop 40." $250.00+.

Hedi Schoop's dancing girls flower frog, 8", is an infrequently seen example of her early line, unmarked, $250.00+.

Hedi Schoop inspecting finished ware in her North Hollywood factory, ca. mid forties.

Hungarian man and woman figures were #57 and #58 in her inventory for 1940. Man is 10½" and unmarked, $100.00; woman is 10" with painted mark (below), $100.00.

Hedi Schoop's demure Debutante, 12½", introduced in 1943, has added handmade flowers and painted mark, $165.00.

Two Hedi Schoop figures of the early forties that were also flower holders. Gardening girl, 7" x 6", $85.00; lady of hearts, 7", $85.00. Painted marks.

Hedi Schoop's popular Tyrolean girl flower holder, 11½", was introduced in 1940 and stayed in her line for many seasons. $125.00.

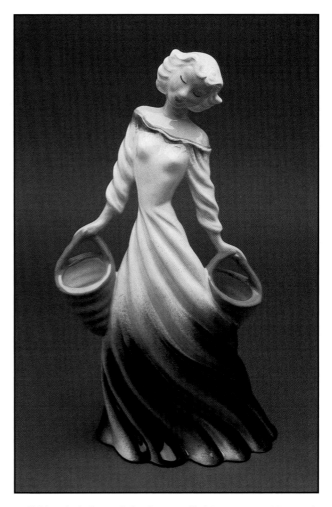

Tall blonde lady with baskets, called Vienna, 13½", with painted mark reading "Hedi Schoop Hollywood, Cal." $175.00.

Two variations on Marguerita, 12½", one of Hedi Schoop's most popular figurine-flower holders, painted marks. $125.00–145.00.

Boy angel, 8", is missing his angel girl companion (also 8"). Painted mark. $85.00.

Hedi Schoop's Colbert (modeled after Claudette Colbert) flower holder/lamp base, 11½", underglaze painted mark, ca. 1940, $150.00.

Josephine, 13", holds bowl suitable for small flowers or plants, stamped mark, ca. 1943, $250.00.

Dutch boy and girl combo, called "My Sister & I," is incomplete without small hanging buckets. The great popularity of this and other Dutch themed sets evidently resulted in Hedi Schoop becoming "Heidi" Schoop in the public consciousness. Painted marks. $225.00 set.

Hedi Schoop inspecting ware in her plant, mid forties. *Archival photo.*

Chinese musicians (Young China), 11", were introduced in 1946, stamped marks, $225.00 pair.

Chinese girl with lantern, 7", $85.00, and Chinese-style jardiniere with generous gold trim, 7½", $100.00. Stamped marks.

Figurine of clown playing cello, 12½", overglaze platinum, stamped mark, ca. 1955, $250.00+.

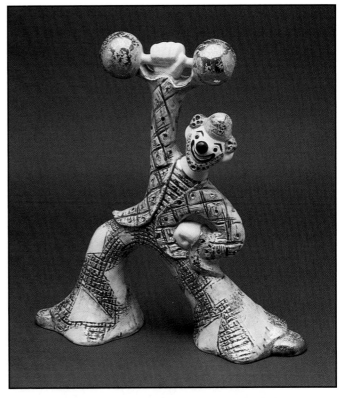

"The Strongman" is what Hedi Schoop called this creation of 1955. Measuring 12" x 12", he was part of a superb series of circus clowns and harlequins produced that year. Stamped mark. $250.00+.

Hedi Schoop's Conchita, 12½", is another fine example of her successful combining of art and function. Stamped mark below. $175.00.

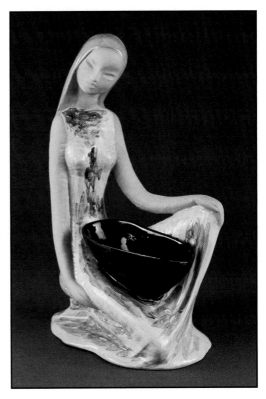

Hedi Schoop called this 1949 female figure holding bowl "Repose." Tinted bisque with high glaze. Stamped mark. $175.00.

Hedi Schoop crew enjoying a lunch break outside plant during World War II. *Archival photo.*

Variations on Hedi Schoop's popular Hawaiian hula dancer, 11", painted marks, $250.00 – 300.00 each.

Hedi Schoop's underglaze painted signature.

Pair of Siamese dancers introduced in 1947. Man, 14½"; woman, 14". Tinted bisque with high glaze and overglaze gold, stamped mark, $300.00 pair.

Rare Mermaid candle holder, 13½", stamped mark, ca. 1950, $750.00+.

Girl walking collie, 9½", $150.00, and girl with poodle, 9", $150.00, ca. 1954. Stamped and in-mold marks.

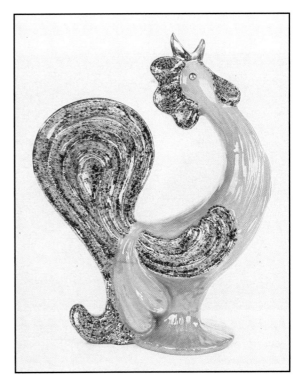

Crowing cock vase, 12", tinted clay body with transparent high glaze and overglaze gold, stamped mark, ca. 1949, $125.00.

Hedi Schoop's large Phantasy line of the mid fifties included this pair of figurine-flower holders, 12", with stamped marks, $300.00 pair.

King of Diamonds tray, in-mold mark, $100.00.

Two fish-shaped candy/nut dishes, $65.00 – 85.00 each, and one butterfly-shaped ashtray, $45.00. Overglaze silver and gold, stamped marks.

Queen of Hearts tray, in-mold mark, $100.00.

Pair of Chinese heads, male and female, from the fifties, $250.00 pair.

The Comedy & Tragedy TV lamp by Hedi Schoop seems to be the least troublesome to find of the series of four, $400.00+.

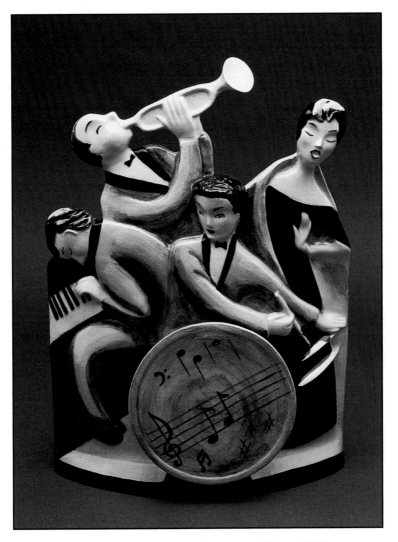

The Orchestra, 15" x 10½", one of a series of four TV lamps completed in 1954, is extremely hard to find. $600.00+.

Old Crow tray by Hedi Schoop, measuring 11" x 7½", is marked as shown below. $200.00.

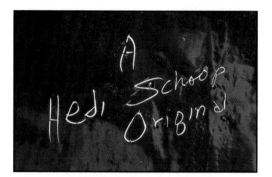

Department store window display, ca. 1948, featuring Hedi Schoop lamps. *Archival photo.*

TWIN WINTON

Twin Winton Ceramics was started by twin brothers Don and Ross Winton in Pasadena in 1936. The Winton twins were born in Canada in 1919. The family moved to Pasadena in the late twenties, with Don, Ross, and older brother Bruce attending high school and junior college there.

The Depression and its attendant hardships prompted the establishment of the business, which had its beginnings in a rented cottage at Busch Gardens in Pasadena. Initially, Twin Winton was known as Burke-Winton, a partnership between the twins and Helen Burke, who hand-decorated and sold the ware in a display room attached to the pottery. Don was responsible for modeling the stock-in-trade — small slip-cast figurines which drew inspiration from Walt Disney's cartoon characters. Ross made all of the molds and helped manage the financial affairs. The enchanting series of animals that Don Winton created and Helen Burke decorated proved to be a big hit with locals and tourists alike.

In 1939, the youthful Winton brothers withdrew from the partnership with Burke and leased a modest workshop of their own in Tujunga, just north of Pasadena. Continuing along the same lines as before, the Wintons soon outgrew the Tujunga shop and moved back to Pasadena (on Hill Street near Washington) in 1942. Don and Ross enlisted for military service the following year, and all operations were suspended for the duration of World War II.

In 1946, the Twin Winton business was re-established in a 2,000 square foot factory on Mission Street in South Pasadena. Older brother Bruce joined forces with Don and Ross and about eight others at this time, eventually becoming their business manager.

The very successful Hillbilly line inspired by the Paul Webb cartoon series was introduced in 1947. This consisted of pitcher and mug sets, pretzel bowls, salt and pepper shakers, lamps, ashtrays, and other novelty items. The various articles featured humorous hand-painted figures of the Ozark Mountain boys set against a simulated wood-grain effect under glaze.

The popularity of the Hillbilly line made a larger factory with additional workers necessary, so the Wintons relocated to Pasadena once again (1190 North Fair Oaks).

Don and Ross remained in the new facility only two years. In 1952, they sold their interest in Twin Winton to Bruce and began designing for various local firms on a freelance basis.

Bruce Winton, as sole owner, moved the pottery to El Monte (11654 McBean Drive). At the new location in 1953, the popular series of cookie jars in woodtone finish was begun with a winsome squirrel that Don designed and modeled. Produced in a brown-stained bisque with colored glaze accents, the cookie jar line ultimately included over fifty figural models. Don Winton, working in a freelance capacity, designed the entire collection and the matching salt and pepper sets and related household accessories, such as spoon rests, wall pockets, planters, ice buckets, napkin holders, and lamps.

In 1964, Twin Winton made its final move to the plant that Brad Keeler had built in San Juan

Twins Ross and Don Winton, late fifties. *Archival photo.*

Capistrano in the early fifties. The business remained active there, with about eighty employees, until its sale in 1975. Don continues to design and model ware for various concerns, and creates portrait busts and statuary commissions at his Corona del Mar studio. Ross died in 1980; Bruce died in 1991.

The earliest marks used were the slip-painted "Burke Winton" (1), sometimes abbreviated "B-W," and the impressed "Burke Winton" (2). A number of variations on the painted (3) and incised in-mold (4) marks as shown appeared on the ware until 1952. After this date the incised in-mold "Twin Winton Calif. USA" mark (5), with some variations, was used to identify the product.

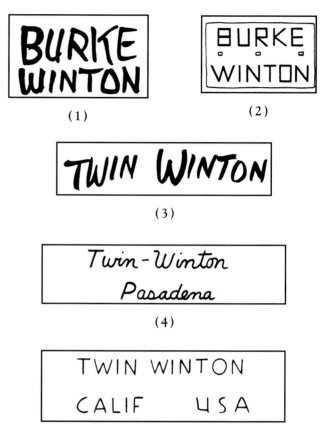

Early Twin Winton miniature animals. Skunk, 2½", $30.00; bear, 2", $45.00.

The Second World War inspired these skunk caricatures by Twin Winton of Italy's Benito Mussolini and Germany's Adolf Hitler. Hitler skunk is 3½". Painted marks. $250.00 – 300.00+ each.

This winking lion, 3¼", is unmarked but has been authenticated by Don Winton, $50.00.

Early, small scale animal figures modeled by Don Winton. Painted marks. Bear, 3", $25.00; skunk, 3", $30.00; squirrel holding box, 4", $45.00. Note: Bear may be Rio Hondo model by Don Winton.

Early Burke-Winton figures with underglaze painted "Burke Winton" marks. Bashful boy elf, 3¼"; little girl with pigtails, 4"; sitting elf, 2¾", $100.00+ each.

The Hillbilly line included this large table lamp, ca. 1949, $250.00+.

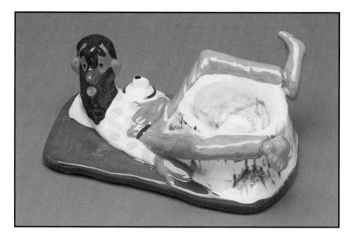

Hillbilly line ashtray, 7½" in length, with in-mold mark that includes "Clem." $60.00.

Hillbilly line stein, $35.00, and early (partially unglazed) mug, $50.00.

Twin Winton Hillbilly salt and pepper shakers, $20.00 set.

Figural-handled pitcher and mugs from the popular Hillbilly line of Twin Winton. Pitcher, $85.00; mugs, $35.00 each.

Steins, 7½", and mugs, 4", from the Twin Winton Hillbilly line. Note mugs have been personalized. In-mold marks (right). Steins, $35.00 each; mugs, $35.00 each.

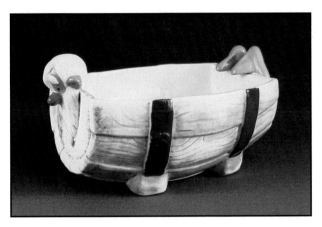

Hillbilly pretzel bowl, in-mold mark, $50.00.

The Bronco line included this pitcher and mugs, late forties. Pitcher, $200.00; mugs, $50.00 each.

Friar bank and Butler cookie jar in woodtone finish. In-mold marks of the sixties/seventies period. Bank, $40.00; cookie jar, $300.00.

Bear, 6", and squirrel, 5", salt and pepper shaker sets by Twin Winton. Bear set, $40.00; squirrel set, $40.00.

Left: "Thou Shalt Not Steal" admonition on front side of friar, 8½", with unknown purpose. $85.00. Right: Backside of Twin Winton friar showing opening. Is it a syrup dispenser? In-mold mark.

Robin Hood porcelain liquor decanter modeled by Don Winton and manufactured by Winfield, $55.00.

Modeled by Don Winton in California, the hand-painted Twinton series of children was produced in Japan. Black girl holding toy elephant, 3½", stamped mark (above right). $100.00.

Elf bank, 8", in wood finish, in-mold mark, $40.00.

Twin Winton cop cookie jar in wood finish measures 12½" x 7", $125.00.

VERNON

Vernon Kilns, which was known as Vernon Potteries prior to 1936, was an industry leader. Especially noteworthy was the company's creative association with various well-known artists.

In 1931, Faye G. Bennison, an Iowa-born entrepreneur who had previously owned a glass manufacturing business, purchased the former Poxon China plant located at 2300 East 52nd Street in Vernon. Seemingly fearless in the face of the Great Depression, Bennison added nearly one hundred new workers to the payroll almost immediately. This, in combination with a farsighted business policy, eventually transformed the struggling enterprise known as Vernon Potteries into one of the most successful in California.

For a short time, the new management utilized existing molds, with a few new underglaze patterns gracing the conventional shapes. But in 1934, a progression of original dinnerware designs was begun. The Montecito shape, first produced as white ware decorated with various decals, was transformed into a popular premium line called Coronado after it was manufactured in the standard array of California glaze colors. Capitalizing on this success, a more stylish and extensive line of solid-color ware called Early California was introduced the following year. A big factor setting the new Vernonware apart from the colored pottery made by other Los Angeles firms was its light weight.

Early California's sales appeal turned out to be strong and enduring, with some items still in production as late as the fifties. Modern California followed in 1938 in satiny pastel colored glazes. With extensive national advertising, it and later Vernon Kilns dinnerware lines achieved widespread consumer acceptance.

In the mid thirties, the Vernon plant established an art department headed by Gale Turnbull. First to join the new endeavor was artist Harry Bird. Using a unique process he patented and called Inlaid Glaze, Bird embellished unfinished plates obtained from the dinnerware section. Full sets of Bird's colorful dishes backstamped with his distinctive trademark were ultimately produced.

For a brief period beginning in 1936, noted ceramists May and Vieve Hamilton designed and modeled an exceptional body of artware for Vernon Kilns, including figures, busts, vases, flower bowls, and candleholders. The Hamilton sisters also created two original dinnerware designs, Rhythmic and Rippled, in their characteristic art moderne style. While majoring in art at USC, Jane Bennison, the owner's talented daughter, made a significant contribution to the art line. But dinnerware outsold decorative pottery by a wide margin, and in 1939, Faye Bennison decided to discontinue the latter. He concluded that the economic realities did not lend support to the less profitable artware. Instead, the business invested all its energies into transfer-printed dinnerware, with an impressive succession of noted artists creating the decorative patterns.

President of the United States Potters Association, Frederick H. Rhead, commented on this development in his annual report of January 1939:

"One of our group, Vernon Potteries of Los Angeles, has made a most interesting experiment in this direction (underglaze printing). With Gale Turnbull as Art Director they turn up at this year's Pittsburgh show with two tableware decorations by Rockwell Kent and two more by Don Blanding. Three of the patterns are underglaze prints in one color, the fourth, also underglaze, is in outline and beautifully hand-tinted by well-trained art students. It is enough to state without reservation that it is the greatest and most inspiring development since the production of Wedgwood's Queensware and the old Staffordshire underglaze prints. It is so far above anything that has been done in any country by any potter since that time that comparison would be idiotic." [1]

Don Blanding, known as the Hawaiian poet, was the first commissioned artist in 1938. Four tropical motifs similar to those he had created to illustrate his popular poetry books were produced. The number was eventually expanded to ten with the use of different color prints and corresponding pattern names. The most successful was Lei Lani, one of the company's best sellers.

Rockwell Kent, the famous painter, illustrator, and author, designed three patterns: Salamina, Our America (comprising thirty pictorial scenes), and Moby Dick. The latter was somewhat successful, but Kent's designs as a whole were not appreciated by the general public. Kent placed the blame on the Ultra California shapes designed by Turnbull that hosted the patterns, the "upside down" handles eliciting the most criticism.

In 1940, the firm contracted with Walt Disney for a number of dinnerware patterns based on the film *Fantasia*. Various figurines from *Fantasia*, *Dumbo*, and *The Reluctant Dragon* were also produced under a license granted to Vernon Kilns by the Disney Studios. The figurines required considerable hand painting, and were made in very limited quantities due to the added expense. In addition, vases and flower bowls with figures in high relief were produced from Walt Disney's own models.

Acclaimed ceramic designer Royal Hickman worked for Vernon Kilns in the late forties and early fifties, designing three dinnerware shapes: Melinda, San Marino, and Lotus. The war years saw the business barely able to meet the demand for its popular dishes. The hand-painted patterns, Organdie and Brown Eyed Susan, by Gale Turnbull, were very well received during this period. Numerous variations on Organdie's simple plaid decoration were marketed in later years.

A devastating fire leveled the thirty-year-old wood and sheet metal plant in 1947. Bennison, at the urging of his employees and associates, erected a new 130,000 square foot factory of steel-reinforced concrete, that was a model of efficiency with tunnel kilns replacing the old beehives. After rebuilding, Vernon expanded the transfer-printed specialty ware it had originated in the late thirties. Manufactured in regular stock patterns and on special order, these colorful plates commemorated famous and not-so-famous people, places, and events. Most of the artists on salary created designs for the specialty ware, including Orpha Klinker, Paul Davidson, Bill Cavett, Mary Petty, Margaret Pearson Joyner, and Ralph Schepe.

Elliot House replaced Gale Turnbull as art director in 1953 and was responsible for Anytime, one of Vernon Kilns' last dinnerware shapes, introduced in 1955. Nine different patterns were united with this shape, the most unusual being Imperial. Other notable lines of the fifties were Sharon Merrill's Chatelaine and Jean Ames' Sun Garden, both produced in 1953.

As the decade moved forward, Vernon Kilns felt the combined effects of mounting labor costs and increased competition from abroad. Despite valiant efforts by an efficient sales department and its advertising agent, Vernon succumbed in 1958. Faye G. Bennison had already retired as president of the firm in 1955. He died in 1974 at age ninety-one. After purchasing the molds, Metlox Potteries continued production of some of Vernon Kilns' best-selling dinnerware lines in its newly established Vernon Ware division.

Vernon Kilns created an individual backstamp for nearly every pattern it produced. A sampling is included here. The stamped mark with mission bells (1) was used on decal decorated ware of the early thirties. "Vernon Kilns/Made in USA/California" (2) was stamped on certain early colored ware. The "Early California" backstamp (3) is shown. Similar Modern California and Ultra California marks were used. "Authentic/Vernonware/Made in USA" (4) came into general use during World War II. The fifties had its version of this all-purpose mark (5). The trademarks of the various artists associated with the company included "Bird Pottery" (6), "May & Vieve Hamilton" (7), "Jane F. Bennison" (8), "Gale Turnbull" (9), "Don Blanding" (10), "Rockwell Kent" (11), and "Walt Disney" (12 and 13). Lines of the forties and fifties with individual backstamps included "Winchester, 73" (14) (later changed to Frontier Days), "Chatelaine" (15), "Imperial" (16), and "Tickled Pink" (17). There were many others.

[1] M. Nelson, *Versatile Vernon Kilns (Book II)*, p. 25.

(1)

VERNON KILNS
MADE IN
U.S.A.
CALIFORNIA

(2)

(3)

(4)

MADE IN U S A
VERNONWARE
dishwasher and ovenproof

(5)

BIRD POTTERY
VERNON KILNS
CALIFORNIA
MADE IN USA
PAT. PEND.

(6)

MAY and VIEVE HAMILTON POTTERY
VERNON KILNS
CALIFORNIA

(7)

JANE F. BENNISON
VERNON KILNS CALIFORNIA
MADE IN U.S.A.

(8)

HAND PAINTED
UNDER GLAZES
BY
Gale Turnbull
VERNON KILNS
CALIFORNIA

(9)

CORAL REEF
Designed by
Aloha
Don Blanding
VERNON KILNS
Made in U.S.A.

(10)

SALAMINA
Designed by
Rockwell Kent
VERNON KILNS
Made in USA

(11)

Designed by
WALT DISNEY
Copyright 1940
VERNON KILNS
Made in U. S. A.

(12)

NUTCRACKER
Designed by
WALT DISNEY
Copyright 1940
Vernon Kilns
Made in U.S.A.

(13)

Winchester
73
Hand Painted Under Glaze
By Vernon Kilns
U.S.A.

(14)

Chatelaine
a Sharon Merrill
Design
Vernonware
California USA
Made

(15)

vernon
ware
Imperial
made in
california

(16)

vernon
ware
california-usa
TICKLED PINK
dishwasher
and
oven proof

(17)

One example of the many full-page advertisements Vernon placed in prominent periodicals in the late thirties. This one appeared in the November 1939 issue of *House Beautiful*.

Early California mixing bowl set in mixed high glaze colors, $175.00 set.

Jane Bennison designed this nesting set of Ring Bowls. #1 blue, 11¾", $150.00; #2 ivory, 10", $100.00; #3 pink, 8", $75.00. Stamped "Bennison" mark, ca. 1935.

The Rippled dinnerware created by May and Vieve Hamilton, stamped "Hamilton" mark, ca. 1935. Plate, 10½", $50.00+; sherbet, $50.00+; cup and saucer, $50.00+; plate, 7½", $40.00+; plate, 9½", $40.00+.

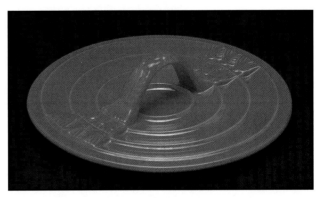

Handled tray, 16", by May and Vieve Hamilton, is an outstanding example of functional art. Possibly part of their Rhythmic dinnerware design, ca. 1937, it is stamped with the Hamilton trademark. $650.00+.

Pierced plate, 16½", in blue, $650.00,+ and goblet, 8½", $150.00, in pink, have stamped May and Vieve Hamilton mark.

Vase with carved handles, 12", by May and Vieve Hamilton is, like most of their finer pieces, very difficult to find today. Stamped Hamilton trademark. $1,000.00+.

From May and Vieve Hamilton's Rippled dinner service, ca. 1936. 4-cup teapot in white, $350.00+; handled platter, 17", in blue, $250.00+. Stamped Hamilton trademark.

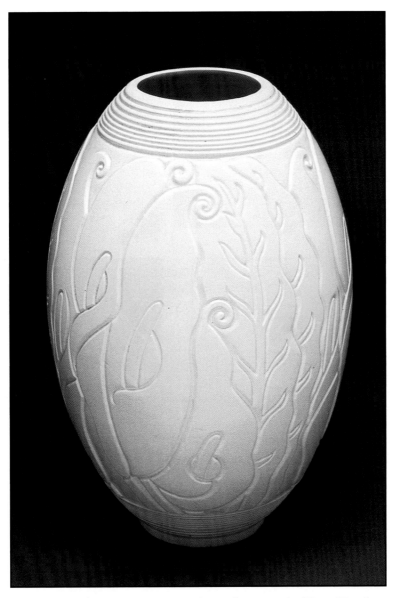

Carved Ovoid vase, 13", is an Art Deco showpiece by Vieve Hamilton issued by Vernon Kilns, ca. 1936. Extremely rare. $1,500.00+.

Wings bowl and candlesticks by May and Vieve Hamilton combine for an exciting centerpiece. Bowl measures 16½" in length. Stamped Hamilton trademark. Bowl, $350.00+; candlesticks, $200.00+ set.

Floral artware designed for Vernon Kilns by the Hamilton sisters. Rose Bowl #4, in yellow, $150.00; Calas #2, in white, $150.00; Cylinders #2 in pink, $150.00. Stamped May and Vieve Hamilton marks.

Phoenix Bird is what Jane Bennison titled her elegant 10" x 18" art deco planter. Stamped Bennison trademark. $600.00+.

Pierced pedestal comport, 12", in turquoise, is a Jane Bennison design produced by Vernon Kilns, and bears her stamped trademark, $250.00+.

Whaling pattern chop plate, 17", designed and decorated by Gale Turnbull, one of many he produced for Vernon Kilns in the mid thirties. Stamped mark. $300.00+.

Fluted pedestal bowl, 6" x 14", by Jane Bennison in two views and versions. Bowl in turquoise, $225.00, and bowl in white with Rockwell Kent's Moby Dick pattern in blue on the inside, $500.00+. Stamped marks.

Sally Rand, 7", by Janice Pettee, was part of a large series of celebrity figurines produced by Vernon Kilns in the thirties and forties. Stamped mark at right. $600.00+.

Harry Bird ware, employing his patented "inlaid glaze" technique of hand decoration, was some of the first decorated dinnerware produced by Vernon Kilns in the thirties. Left to right: Chowder bowl (early design, missing cover) with Tropical Fish pattern (see mark at right), $65.00+; 14" chop plate with Trumpet Flower pattern, $300.00+; chowder bowl (redesigned) with decorated cover, $125.00+; coffee server with stopper in Tropical Fish pattern, $200.00+.

Pitchers by Vernon Kilns. Don Blanding's Ecstasy pattern 2-quart disk pitcher, $175.00; Early California 1-quart pitcher, $45.00; Early California 1½-quart pitcher, $65.00; Calico pattern syrup pitcher, $95.00.

Ultra California dinnerware. One-pint bowl in buttercup, $30.00; luncheon plate, 9½", in aster, $20.00; bread and butter plate, 6½", in gardenia, $8.00; chowder bowl, 6", in carnation, $30.00; cup and saucer in ice green, $30.00.

Egg cup lineup: Modern California, $35.00; Early California, $35.00; B-310 pattern by Harry Bird, $45.00; Casa California pattern by Gale Turnbull, $40.00.

FROM ONE GIFT PACKAGE

COME 45 PIECES OF CALIFORNIA COLOR

SERVICE FOR EIGHT—ONLY $14.95!

Imagine the thrill of opening this exciting gift box and lifting out piece after piece of delicate, pastel dinnerware…Vernon "Modern California" pottery…in azure, pistachio, straw, and orchid. The package itself is adorned with typical California designs…and the pottery it contains is the finest ware made, every piece flawless, durable and craze-proof.

A SPECIAL GIFT PACKAGE AT A SPECIAL PRICE

Just think—for only $14.95 you get eight 9½-inch plates, eight 7½-inch plates, eight chowders, eight cups and saucers, a 12-inch chop plate, a large vegetable dish, covered sugar bowl and cream pitcher. Each of the forty-five pieces is individually packed without messy cut paper or excelsior, making your gift even more fastidiously perfect!

The Vernon Gift Package solves the problem of the perfect wedding, birthday, or Christmas gift for the truly smart woman, and also makes it possible for you to start your own new pottery service at a real saving of money.

If you prefer gay, vivid colors—for the same price you can buy a 45-piece Gift Package set of Vernon "Early California" ware in green, orange, turquoise, brown and other brilliant tones. At the left are just a few of the many exquisite hand-decorated lines made by Vernon, which blend so well with the solid colors of Modern and Early California.

A beautifully illustrated folder in full color showing these and many other distinctive patterns will be sent to you without cost upon request. Address Vernon Kilns, 2300 East 52nd Street, Dept. 10-R., Los Angeles, California.

VERNON

AUTHENTIC CALIFORNIA POTTERY

Phone to Find
WHO SELLS IT
SEE LAST PAGE

Another full-page Vernon ad that appeared in national magazines like *Better Homes & Gardens* in the late thirties.

VERNON'S Gingham

OPEN STOCK	LIST PRICE	OPEN STOCK	LIST PRICE	OPEN STOCK	LIST PRICE
Bowl, 1 Pt.	$1.15	Coffee Server, 10-Cup	$4.30	9½" Platter	$1.95
Butter Tray and Cover	2.95	Coffee Server Stopper	.70	12" Platter	2.65
Butter Tray	1.20	Creamer	1.85	14" Platter	4.75
Butter Cover	1.75	Custard Cup, 3"	.95	Salad Bowl, Ind., 5½"	1.25
Butter, Ind., 2½"	.55	Egg Cup, Double	1.35	Salad Bowl, 10½"	4.00
Casserole, Cov'd. 8"	5.75	3" Flower Pot & Saucer	1.50	Sauce Boat, Reg.	2.90
Casserole, Cov'd., Ind. 4"	1.95	3" Flower Pot only	1.00	Shaker, Pepper, Reg.	1.00
Casserole, Open, Ind. 4"	1.20	4" Flower Pot & Saucer	1.75	Shaker, Salt, Reg.	1.00
Chicken Pie, Cov'd., Ind. 4"	2.25	4" Flower Pot only	1.20	Shaker, Pepper, Large	1.35
Chicken Pie, Open, Ind. 4"	1.50	5" Flower Pot & Saucer	2.00	Shaker, Salt, Large	1.35
12" Chop Plate	2.50	5" Flower Pot only	1.40	Soup, Rim	1.00
14" Chop Plate	4.25	Fruit	.65	Spoon Holder	1.35
Chowder	1.00	Lapel Plate, with Pin	1.00	Sugar, Cov'd.	2.45
Coaster, 4"	.65	Mug, 9 Oz.	1.35	Tea Cup and Saucer	1.65
Coffee Cup & Saucer, Jumbo	2.40	Pepper Mill	8.15	Tea Cup	1.10
Coffee Cup, Jumbo	1.60	1 Pt. Pitcher	2.00	Tea Saucer	.55
Coffee Saucer, Jumbo	.80	1 Qt. Pitcher	3.15	Tea Pot, Cov'd.	5.00
Coffee Cup and Saucer, A.D.	1.55	2 Qt. Pitcher	5.25	2-Tier Plate, Wooden Fixture	9.95
Coffee Cup, A.D.	1.00	6½" Plate	.65	3-Tier Plate, Wooden Fixture	7.95
Coffee Saucer, A.D.	.55	7½" Plate	.80	Tumbler, 14 Oz.	1.05
Coffee Server & Stopper, 10 Cup.	5.00	9½" Plate	1.05	9" Vegetable, Round	1.95
		10½" Plate	1.30	Vegetable Dish, Double	5.25

STARTER SET

16 Pieces, Service for 4:
4 cups, 4 saucers, 4 – 9½" plates,
4 bread and butter plates.

List Price **$13⁴⁰**

SPECIAL
RETAIL **$10⁴⁵**
PRICE

Add to your starter set at any time from the large selection of colorful open stock service pieces designed for multiple uses.

Promotional brochure for the Vernon Kilns Gingham dinnerware line.

Promotional brochure for the Vernon Kilns Barkwood dinnerware line.

VERNON'S *Barkwood*

OPEN STOCK	LIST PRICE	OPEN STOCK	LIST PRICE	OPEN STOCK	LIST PRICE
Butter Tray & Cover	$3.25	Mug, 9 Oz.	$1.40	Shaker, Salt	$1.00
Butter Tray	1.30	½ Pt. Pitcher	2.00	Soup, Coupe	1.00
Butter Cover	1.95	1 Pt. Pitcher	2.25	Sugar, Covered	2.95
Casserole, Cov'd, 8"	5.95	1 Qt. Pitcher	3.25	Syrup Pitcher, Drip-cut Top	3.75
"Casserole Hot"	8.95	2 Qt. Pitcher	5.50	Tea Cup & Saucer	1.70
13" Chop Plate	3.95	6" Plate	.65	Tea Cup	1.15
Chowder	1.00	7½" Plate	.85	Tea Saucer	.55
"Coffee Hot"	7.50	10" Plate	1.20	Tea Pot, Covered	5.50
Coffee Server & Stopper, 10-Cup	5.25	9½" Platter	2.00	2-Tier Plate	8.95
Coffee Server, 10-Cup	4.50	11" Platter	2.50	3-Tier Plate	7.95
Colossal Cup & Saucer	12.95	13½" Platter	3.75	Tumbler, 14 Oz.	1.25
Colossal Cup	8.45	Salad Bowl, Ind., 5½"	1.25	7½" Vegetable, Round	1.75
Creamer	1.95	Sauce Boat	2.95	9" Vegetable, Round	2.00
Fruit	.75	Shaker, Pepper	1.00	Vegetable, Double	5.25

Vernon Kilns dinnerware patterns designed by Don Blanding. Left to right: Jam jar with Lei Lani pattern, $200.00+; 17" chop plate with Coral Reef pattern, $250.00+; disk pitcher with Hawaiian Flowers pattern, $175.00. Stamped marks.

Rockwell Kent's Salamina dinnerware line of 1939 included this 17" chop plate, hand-tinted transfer-printed design, stamped "Kent" mark, $750.00+.

Walt Disney lines of 1940 from the movie *Fantasia*. Nutcracker 6-cup coffee pot, $500.00+, and mug, $250.00+, with 4½" satyr figurines, $250.00+ each. Stamped "Disney" marks.

Photo courtesy Tony Cuñha.

Don Blanding's Lei Lani 14" chop plate, $200.00, and iced tea tumbler, $75.00. Hand-tinted transfer-printed designs, stamped "Blanding" marks.

Disney patterns based on the film *Fantasia* produced by Vernon Kilns. Fantasia tumbler, $200.00+; Nutcracker coffee pot (in back), $500.00+; Fantasia creamer and covered sugar, $200.00 – 300.00+ each; Enchantment teapot (in front), $500.00+. Stamped marks.

Ostriches executing ballet moves from Walt Disney's *Fantasia* were captured in clay by Vernon Kilns. Ostrich (#30), 9", $1,800.00+, and ostrich (#29), 6½", $1,200.00+. Stamped marks.

Walt Disney's colorful Enchantment pattern enlivens this 17" chop plate, $500.00+. Tumbler with Disney's Flower Ballet pattern in foreground, $200.00+. All Disney designed dinnerware from *Fantasia* is extremely difficult to assemble into sets.

Designed by Walt Disney, under exclusive license with Vernon Kilns, this teapot in the Autumn Ballet pattern was inspired by the animated feature *Fantasia*. Stamped mark at right. $500.00+

Figurines based on *Fantasia,* produced under exclusive license granted to Vernon Kilns in 1940 – 41 by Walt Disney, included (left to right) centaur (#31), 10", $1,500.00+; Nubian centaurette (#23), 8½", $1,500.00+; centaurette (#22), 8", $1,500.00+. Stamped marks.

The stork (#42), 8¾", $2,000.00+, and crow (#39), 5¾", $2,000.00+, were featured in Walt Disney's *Dumbo*. Impressed and stamped marks.

Disney's Dewdrop Fairies salt and pepper shakers of 1940. $150.00+ set.

Vernon Kilns teapots from different decades. Left: Imperial pattern of the mid fifties, $150.00. Right: Rockwell Kent's Our America pattern of the early forties, $300.00+. Stamped marks.

This 8½" plate commemorated the opening in 1948 of Vernon Kiln's newly rebuilt factory in Vernon. Artwork by L. Hicks. $85.00.

Hollywood souvenir plate, 10½", by Vernon Kilns, ca. 1940, $50.00.

Contrasting Vernon Kilns casserole designs. Left: Early California, $65.00. Right: Chintz, $65.00. Stamped marks.

The eccentric Chatelaine dinnerware, designed by Sharon Merrill in 1953, included these teapots, in jade (left), $350.00+, and platinum glaze effects, $350.00+.

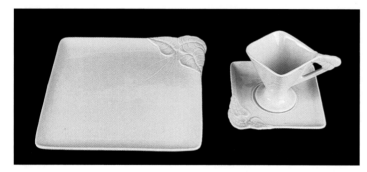

Chatelaine, Sharon Merrill's dinnerware design of 1953. Dinner plate, 10½", $35.00, and teacup and saucer, $35.00, in platinum.

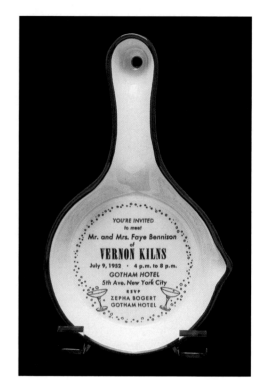

Skillet-shaped spoon rest with printed invitation to meet Vernon Kilns' Faye Bennison and wife in New York City at the Gotham Hotel, $50.00.

The Winchester, 73 dinnerware pattern designed by Paul Davidson included this 14" chop plate, $200.00, and large ceramic/wood shakers, $150.00 pair. Stamped mark, ca. 1950.

Souvenir plate made for San Francisco's famous Fisherman's Wharf, 11", $30.00. See special backstamp below.

Vernon Kilns souvenir plate, 10½", of Yellowstone National Park, with printed legend on back side (above), $30.00.

Early 9½" Vernon Potteries plate with decal decoration suggestive of California's Spanish heritage. See stamped mark below. $25.00.

Mayflower pattern, 10½" dinner plate, with "Mayflower" backstamp, $25.00.

WALLACE CHINA

The Wallace China Company was founded in 1931 by Wallace B. Wood, his son Frank R. Wood, and other former stockholders in the Poxon China Company of Vernon. The business specialized in vitrified heavy-grade hotel and restaurant china and was one of the leading manufacturers of this type of ware in the western states.

The Wallace China Company was housed in a 60,000 square foot factory, located at 5600 Desoto Avenue in Huntington Park. George Poxon, former owner of the Poxon China works, was hired by Wallace soon after it began operating, and a number of his designs were used. Loren Trabue, yet another graduate of the University of Illinois, was ceramic engineer for the business. With a beginning crew of about thirty-five, the company grew in size and prosperity producing both plain and transfer-printed chinaware for institutional purposes. Patterns tended toward time honored English Staffordshire designs at first. Various decal decorations were also produced in the early years and the best of these were continued in suc-

ceeding years. The popular Willow pattern (in blue, green, brown, and red) was manufactured in great quantities in the thirties and forties. During World War II, the company made china for the army and naval training centers located in the western states. Most of this ware was plain, but insignias were added to china destined for the officers' mess.

In 1943, the M. C. Wentz Company of Pasadena, a distributor of gift and house wares, commissioned Wallace China to produce a special line of heavy grade Barbecue Ware to enlarge their exclusive Westward Ho line of household goods with a western theme. Well-known western artist Till Goodan created the patterns Rodeo, Boots & Saddle, Pioneer Trails, and Longhorn. A special three-piece Little Buckaroo Chuck Set was made for children. The Wentz company described their Rodeo pattern this way, "Appealing Western Ranch brand dinnerware with authentic Ranch brand border. Four color pattern, hotel weight vitrified china. Background color is buckskin, design work is saddle brown, enhanced by

Wallace China chop plates, 13", with artware by Till Goodan. Left: Boots & Saddle, $250.00. Right: Rodeo, $250.00. Stamped marks.

two-color handwork. A profitable, attractive, fast-moving pattern." The Westward Ho line was very popular and widely imitated, and resulted in another Goodan design, El Rancho, which became a Wallace stock-in-trade pattern. The Boots & Saddle and Rodeo patterns had the longest production runs at Wallace. In a sales brochure dated May 15, 1961, twenty-four separate items, in addition to the three-piece Little Buckaroo Chuck Set (which retailed at that time for $7.70), were still available from the company.

Numerous hotels and restaurants in California and throughout the western states enlisted the services of the Wallace designers for custom-made dinnerware patterns. Shadowleaf, designed for a Los Angeles restaurant chain, was so well-liked that it eventually was made available as an open stock pattern. Other generalized china patterns included Dahlia, Bird of Paradise, and Hibiscus.

In 1959, the greatly expanded Wallace China business became a West Coast subsidiary of the Shenango China Company of Newcastle, Pennsylvania. The company was finally liquidated in 1964.

A variety of backstamps was used by the Wallace China Company through the years. One of the earliest stamps contained the words "Wallace China" in an oval, with "Los Angeles, Calif." below. Somewhat later a circular stamp that included these same words was added. The trade name "Desert Ware" appeared

on the undersides of numerous items produced in the thirties, forties, and fifties. One of the Westward Ho backstamps (for the Rodeo pattern) is shown along with the Westward Ho paper label. A modernized logo featuring a stylized "W" was adopted by Wallace in the early sixties. It was incorporated into their subsequent backstamps. Till Goodan's western lines have generated such strong collector interest in recent years, with price tags climbing to rather lofty positions, that reproductions of the ware have recently appeared. But those observed have not included the Wallace China backstamp, so confusion between old and new should not result.

Westward Ho Barbecue Ware items, pattern designs by Till Goodan. Left to right: 12" oval vegetable bowl, Rodeo pattern, $250.00; 9" luncheon plate, Boots & Saddle pattern, $75.00; large salt and pepper shakers, Rodeo pattern, $150.00 set. Stamped marks.

Plate, 9", from the Little Buckaroo Chuck Set. See backstamp below. $200.00+.

Rodeo pattern ashtray, 5½", with original packing box. Stamped mark. $100.00+.

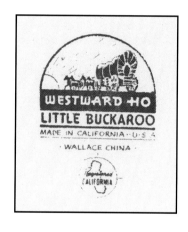

Popular Rodeo pattern by Till Goodan was part of the Westward Ho line produced by Wallace China. 7½ oz. cup and saucer, $75.00; dinner plate, 10¾", $100.00; bread and butter plate, 7¼", $50.00. Stamped marks.

Chuck Wagon restaurant china bowl, 6¾", stamped mark, dated 1955, $35.00.

Westward Ho items made by Wallace China, stamped marks. Top row: Mark Twain ashtray, $75.00; cowboy ashtray, $95.00; Kit Carson ashtray, $75.00. Bottom row: Rodeo pattern large covered sugar bowl, $75.00, and cream pitcher, $50.00.

Eaton's Rancho dinner plate, 10½", by Wallace China, from full line produced for the noted Southern California restaurant. Stamped mark. $45.00.

El Rancho pattern dinner plate, 10½", from the Last Frontier Village, Las Vegas, $100.00+, and Boots & Saddle pattern water pitcher, $400.00. Stamped marks, see backstamp on El Rancho pattern plate below.

49er pattern (on white) dinner plate, 10½", $85.00. See backstamp below.

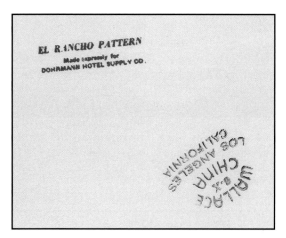

Lunch plate, 9½", made for Apache Land Village, Globe, Arizona, $100.00+.

Pioneer Trails 13" chop plate, artwork by Till Goodan, stamped mark with Apple Valley Ranchos added, $250.00+.

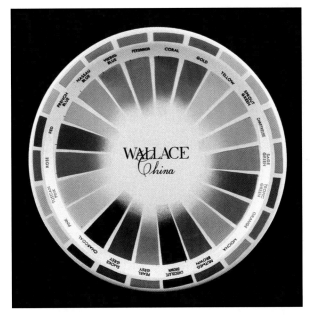

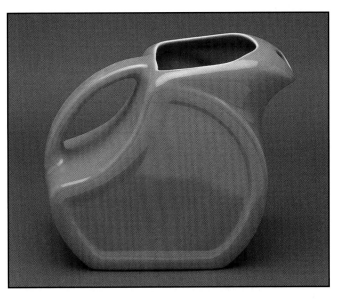

Plate displaying the colors available for pattern decoration, stamped mark, $50.00+.

Wallace China water pitcher in pink. Great for pink lemon-
ade. Stamped mark. $50.00.

Wallace China restaurant ware. Left to right: Gray/white soup bowl, 5¾", $20.00; Paris Inn, Los Angeles plate,
9½", $65.00; California Missions cup, $30.00. Stamped marks, see backstamp on Paris Inn plate (above).

Surfer Girl restaurant china dinner plate, 10½", by Wallace. Airbrush and stencil pattern on white background, stamped mark, $50.00.

Ashtray, 5½", made for the Chi Chi Club of Palms Springs, California, $50.00+.

Desert Ware restaurant line bowls. Traditional Blue Willow pattern in brown on right. Stamped marks. $20.00 – 25.00 each.

Commemorative ashtray picturing Los Angeles' Biltmore Hotel. Stamped mark, dated 1949, $50.00.

Wallace restaurant china with stamped marks. Left to right: Shadowleaf pattern individual creamer, 3½", $25.00; Shadowleaf butter pat, $20.00; Seafood salad plate, 7", $25.00; Shadowleaf shakers, $75.00 set.

Hibiscus pattern dinner plate, 10½", $35.00, and serving bowl, 8½", $35.00.

Water pitchers by Wallace China. Left: Bird of Paradise, $150.00. Right: Shadowleaf pattern, $150.00. Stamped marks.

Wallace China Hibiscus pattern dinner plate, $35.00.

Ashtray with Christmas greetings from the Wallace China company, stamped mark, ca. 1950, $50.00.

Many of the smaller Southern California potteries were family owned and operated. The Climes family business, originally known as Will-George, was a typical example. Started "on a shoestring" in the family garage by two art-minded brothers, with financial backing it blossomed into one of the state's hallmark companies in terms of design and technical proficiency.

George Climes was the motivator behind Will-George. He was born in Ohio, three years after his brother Will, in 1909. After the Climes family moved to Los Angeles in the late twenties, George worked for the Catalina pottery on Catalina Island. There he learned the pottery trade, especially glaze chemistry, as an assistant to ceramic engineer Virgil Haldeman. Will, after a year or two of study at the Chicago Art Institute, returned to Southern California and joined his brother for a short time on the island.

Back in Los Angeles, the Will-George business began officially in 1934 in Will Climes' garage. Will designed, modeled, and decorated the various figurines that were initially produced. George formulated the clay body and glazes and made molds, Will's wife Frances helped out with the finishing, and a third brother, Lloyd, joined them in 1937 as salesman.

The first real success came with a charming artist and model set of figurines produced in a combination

Will Climes of Will-George at work in his studio in the fifties. *Archival photo.*

of bisque and glazed slip decoration. In 1938, the company received a much-needed boost when entertainer Edgar Bergen, who was an avid ceramics collector, discovered the Climes family. So impressed was Bergen that he immediately invested in their business. With his backing and influence, improvements in production were implemented and new markets were opened up.

In 1940, the operation was moved to a much better facility equipped with two kilns at 2966 East Colorado Boulevard in Pasadena. At this time a corporation was formed with Bergen as the major stockholder. New items in the Will-George line were introduced with increasing frequency as imports disappeared during the war.

Will Climes' colorful, exquisitely crafted figurines of birds were produced at this time with a supplemental work force that included five full-time decorators. Many of the figurines required complex eight-piece molds and as many as six separate firings. Due to this extreme attention to detail and its added cost factor, Will-George creations were not inexpensive and were carried by the more exclusive gift shops and department stores.

Howard Ball was hired as a modeler in 1945 and worked a short time before establishing a competitive business. His designs included a large pair of Great Danes and a smaller set of cocker spaniels. Will Climes, in addition to birds, sculpted a number of human figures in a style akin to the Royal Doulton works of England. George also modeled during the busy war years, contributing one of the company's best-selling lines with his elegant flamingos.

After the war and a split with Bergen, the business became known as The Claysmiths and was relocated to 400 South San Gabriel Boulevard in San Gabriel. The San Gabriel plant was very large and equipped with a continuous tunnel kiln in addition to two periodic kilns.

In its final decade, the output of the pottery included a series of Oriental figures and figural flower holders with matching bowls. A line of lamps was also produced. The post-war flood of Italian imports was largely to blame for declining sales during the last few years of the business, which was liquidated in 1956. Will Climes died in 1960 while employed as a designer for Hagen-Renaker. George worked for the Redondo Tile Company of Torrance from 1956 to 1959, and for Gladding-McBean as a lab technician from 1959 until his death in 1966.

A variety of incised and stamped marks was used over the years. The one most often seen is the stamped "Will-George Pasadena." A paper label has also been noted. The "Claysmiths" designation was apparently never used on the ware.

Will-George's novel Flower Vendor, 10", included eight separate flower containers. NPE. *Archival photo.*

Early Polynesian female figurines. Erect figure, 7½", $100.00; seated figure, 5½", $100.00. Incised mark reads "Will-George/Made in California."

Exquisitely detailed Will-George figurines of children on footstools. Boy holding frog, $150.00, and girl holding doll, $150.00. Both 9½" in height. Stamped marks.

This well-dressed girl in pigtails is named Faith. She measures 10" and is stamped "Will-George Pasadena." $150.00.

Child-like artist and model set of figurines, incised marks, ca. 1939, $250.00+ set.

Small bird on branch, 2" x 5", paper label, $60.00.

Young Pan figure with attendant forest creatures measures 7" in height, stamped mark "Will-George Pasadena," $100.00.

Pair of large giraffes by Will-George. Male, 14½", $150.00; female, 13", $150.00. Stamped mark "Will-George Pasadena."

Cardinal on branch, 13", stamped mark, $150.00.

273

Brown cocker spaniel, 7" x 9½", $250.00+, and black cocker spaniel, 7½" x 9½", $250.00+, were produced during World War II by Will-George. *Archival photo.*

Dachshund, 6½" x 9", stamped mark, ca. 1945, $250.00+.

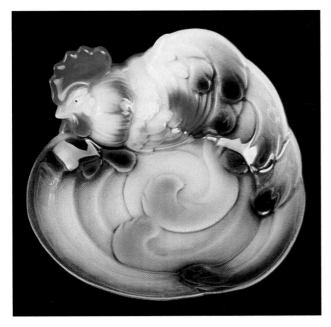

Small rooster tray by Will-George, stamped mark, $75.00.

Rooster-shaped pitcher, 8", $150.00, and wine or cordial glass with rooster-shaped ceramic base, 5", $50.00, by Will-George. Stamped marks.

Three rooster-shaped items by Will-George, stamped marks. Left to right: pitcher/vase, 7", $150.00; tumbler, 4½", $50.00; wine or cordial, 5", $50.00.

"Rooster, white. Brahma cock in toned white, multicolored tail with red comb and wattles. Neutral base, 14" high." This is the way Will-George described this imposing example of their distinguished artware. $200.00+. *Archival photo.*

Large pink cockatoo, 12", by Will-George, $200.00.
Archival photo.

This highly naturalistic red macaw on tree trunk (with two openings for flowers) is 14½" in height. Stamped mark. $250.00+.

Small pink cockatoo by Will-George dates from the late forties. $150.00. *Archival photo.*

Cardinals measure, left to right, 10", 13", 7", and 4". They all have openings for flowers, and stamped marks. 10", $125.00; 13", $150.00; 7", $100.00; 4", $60.00.

Will-George's elegant, naturalistic flamingos, ca. 1945. Male, 11½", female (head in wing), 10", $200.00 each. Stamped marks.

Colossal flamingo, 15½", standing inside matching low flower bowl, $350.00+. Bowl is 15" in length, $75.00. Matching candle holder in foreground is 6¼", $75.00. Stamped Will-George marks (mark on candle holder reads "W-G.")

Pair of graceful flamingos by Will-George, stamped marks. Male (head up), 9½", $150.00; female (head down), 6½", $150.00.

Flamingos, flamingos, and more flamingos! Will-George was in the forefront of the flamingo trend and in terms of product excellence, was never outdone. *Archival photo.*

Chinese girl with pots for flowers, 8¼".
Partial overglaze red decoration, stamped
"Will-George." $95.00.

Will-George Chinese girl attached to pillow vase.
$95.00. *Archival photo.*

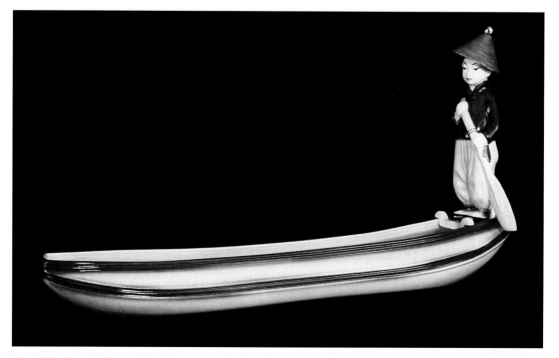

Gondola-shaped flower bowl, 20", with detachable Chinese boy oarsman figure of the late forties, stamped mark, $175.00.

Left: A corner of the productive Will-George studio with a pair of completed figures on display. Right: Close-up of the harlequin figures visible in the Climes' studio view. NPE. *Archival photos.*

Unusual female Harlequin figure, 16", in satin matte black, presumably has missing mate. Incised mark reads "Will-George." $150.00.

This Will-George horse-shaped covered container, 8½" x 7", in speckled matte glaze, likely dates from the fifties. In-mold mark reads "Will-George 80." $75.00.

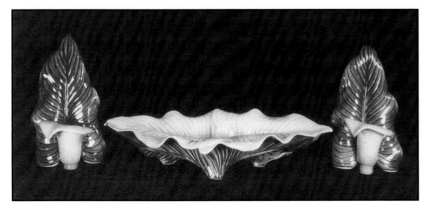

Lily themed flower bowl, $85.00, and matching candle holders, $150.00 pair, by Will-George. *Archival photo.*

BARBARA WILLIS

Barbara Willis pioneered and popularized a style of ceramic production rooted in the work of famed California ceramists Glen Lukens and Laura Andreson. Her mass-produced output provided the average American household with a level of ornamental wares that might otherwise have been beyond their reach.

Born in Bakersfield in 1917, Barbara Willis was fortunate to study ceramics under Laura Andreson at UCLA. By the time she obtained an undergraduate degree in art in 1940, pottery had become Willis' first love. She envisioned operating her own successful ceramics business, and with the help of her father who constructed a small studio behind the garage of their Los Angeles home, Barbara Willis produced a number of prototypes which she showed to respected sales representative Dick Knox. After he agreed to represent her, she began production of her original line in the summer of 1942.

The trade name "Terrene Pottery" was selected for her line of vases and flower bowls that were designed with both the amateur and professional flower arranger in mind. Her ware was unusual and appealing to the buying public because her smooth brightly-colored crackle glazes, like those of her mentors, did not entirely cover the earthy clay body. The highly tooled clay surfaces on Barbara Willis items were accentuated with stains (usually brown), but hers alone were rendered waterproof by a unique

Exceptional early ware by Barbara Willis with yellow crackle on brown, incised signature. Cache pot, 7" x 10", $350.00+; cone vase, 8", $200.00+.

method of wax application. The early Willis glaze colors were turquoise, yellow, chartreuse, and white, and were confined to the insides of bowls and vases, with only a portion of the exterior of a vase showing the glaze. Coral and bright red set off by a gray-toned clay body were two of her later glaze treatments. Other early items included candle holders, chargers, cigarette/match holders, ashtrays, covered boxes, planters, salt and pepper shakers, wall pockets, and a limited assortment of figural ware.

The figural items modeled by Barbara Willis included a small horse figure, a native (Mexican) boy bust, a set of native (Hawaiian) boy/girl wall pockets, and a set of two Oriental figures designed as bookends. These items, with the exception of the horse, met with limited sales acceptance and were made for a short time only.

In 1946, Barbara Willis introduced new lines of ware characterized by a bolder use of the glazed areas on the exteriors of items. The new decorative patterns were called Chinese Character and Scroll; the latter, exhibiting a more spirited use of glaze, was the more successful. By this time, the pottery had been relocated twice, first to a larger facility located at 8366 3rd Street in Los Angeles, and about five years later, to its final site, at 5536 Vineland Avenue in North Hollywood. The 3,000-square foot North Hollywood facility included four or five small periodic kilns and a tunnel kiln. But the Willis work force at any given time numbered fewer than twenty. Therefore, much of the work was accomplished by herself and her husband Walter.

Some Barbara Willis lines of the post-World War II period employed decals centered on the fully glazed exteriors or obverse sides of the ware. The decal decorations were given names like Provincial, a single stylized bird and/or floral spray, and Swedish Modern, featuring a simple repetitious leaf design. Although these decorations added variety to the Willis line of household goods as a whole, they tended to compromise the aesthetic distinction of the pivotal undecorated wares and never achieved the same level of acceptance.

In the early fifties, her trustworthy representative and friend Dick Knox died. After this Barbara Willis aligned herself with the Registered California organization and largely represented herself at the various semi-annual gift shows throughout the country. Her business, like many others, was beginning to feel the pressure from imports, and a few years later she decided the only choice was to end her successful ceramics career. After closing shop in 1958, Barbara Willis sold some of her molds to the Cleminsons, who used them and others in combination with Hedi Schoop's drip glazes to produce a striking new line of modern household accessories.

Barbara Willis items were diligently marked with her signature incised by hand or recessed in-mold. Ink stamped marks and paper labels were also used. In 1996, a second phase of Willis' career began, with

a variety of new pieces being completed at her Malibu beach studio. The new ware — mostly small scaled at present — is incised with her full name and the date so that new items will not be confused with old.

Barbara Willis in the shipping room of her North Hollywood plant, ca. 1945.

Barbara Willis' Terrene Pottery, ca. 1949. *Archival photo.*

A selection of Barbara Willis ware decorated with Provincial decals. *Archival photo.*

Barbara Willis items, ca. 1943, turquoise crackle on brown, incised signature. Left to right: Leaf bowl, 12", $200.00; square vase, 5", $125.00, and cylinder vase, 5", $125.00.

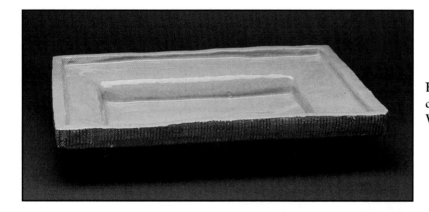

Left: Footed square bowl with Scroll design, 10", in chartreuse crackle/gray, $150.00. Right: Square cigarette box, 6", in yellow crackle/brown, stamped mark (right photo), $135.00.

Early double flange bowl, 14½" x 11½", in chartreuse crackle on brown, incised "Barbara Willis," $300.00+.

Floral artware by Barbara Willis, incised signatures. Left to right: Flared pillow vase, 4" x 6", in white crackle/chartreuse, $125.00; compressed cylinder vase, 7", in yellow crackle/brown, $200.00; sphere bowl, 4½", in turquoise crackle/brown, $150.00.

A choice array of Barbara Willis ware, incised and stamped marks. Low cylinder bowl, 14", in red crackle/gray, $400.00; native boy bust, 9", in chartreuse crackle/brown, $250.00; modern pillow vase with Scroll pattern, in white crackle/brown, $100.00; jug, 7", in turquoise crackle/brown, $200.00.

Square vase, 7", in chartreuse crackle/brown, $150.00; modern pillow vase, 7½", in chartreuse crackle/brown, $150.00; Chinese pillow vase, 7½", in yellow crackle/brown, $165.00; cigarette box, 4" x 4½", in white crackle/brown, $100.00. Incised "Barbara Willis."

Very rare figures by Barbara Willis called Flute (right) and Lute (left) in chartreuse crackle on brown. Both 6" in height and incised "Barbara Willis." $350.00+ each.

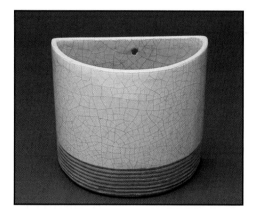

Barbara Willis crescent wall pocket, 5", in pale green crackle on brown, with stamped mark, $135.00.

Barbara Willis' most popular figurals were her 5" horses. Pictured are yellow and white crackle examples, $175.00 – 225.00 each. Also pictured is flared bowl, 4" x 11½", in white crackle/Scroll pattern, $175.00. Bowl is stamped "Barbara Willis 36A;" horses are unmarked.

Two modern pillow vases by Barbara Willis. Vase #42B in coral crackle measures 5½" x 6½", $145.00. Vase #42C in red crackle is 4" x 6¼", $200.00. Incised marks (see mark on vase #42B above).

An 8½" square vase with two very different decorative treatments. Left: Vase in Scroll pattern/yellow crackle on grey, incised "Barbara Willis 720A," $200.00. Right: Vase in red crackle on gray with glaze covering most of the outside of the form, unmarked, $250.00.

Decal decorated ware in Provincial design by Barbara Willis. Pillow vase, 6", $65.00, and low cylinder bowl, 14", $125.00, in white crackle/brown. Stamped and in-mold marks.

Decal decorated kitchenware from the fifties phase of the Barbara Willis business. Back row: (left to right) Large canister with wood cover in Festive, $175.00; paprika shaker with wood cover in Provincial, $65.00; large canister with wood cover in Provincial, $125.00; condiment jar with wood cover (notched for spoon) in Provincial, $65.00. Front row: Cigarette box, 8½", in white crackle on brown with Provincial decal on lid, $95.00.

Large batter bowl in nutmeg glaze with Festive decal decoration, in-mold mark, $250.00.

A sampling of the new wave of ware now being produced by Barbara Willis. Low bowl in background is 12" in diameter. Incised marks include date.

WINFIELD

The Winfield Pottery of Pasadena was founded by Lesley Winfield Sample in 1929. Sample was born in England in 1897 where he received a wide-ranging education, including instruction in ceramics. He immigrated to the United States in the twenties, locating in Southern California. The original site of the Winfield Pottery was the Cloisters of El Padre, a Spanish-style structure financed and built by Sample at 1432 North Foothill (now Altadena Drive) on the northeastern fringe of Pasadena in 1929. The business began as a studio and "School of Clayworking," a service he rendered during evening hours. Despite limited experience in ceramic production, Sample managed to turn out an exceptional line of cast porcelain vases and bowls, many of which were modeled on the same principles as classical Greek vessels. One small muffle kiln capable of firing up to 1,950° F. was utilized in a one-fire process in which body and glaze matured simultaneously.

Lesley Sample's glazes were particularly noteworthy and included both opaque and transparent types, including crystallines, in a wide range of colors. Experiments in glaze application were carried out, with many subtle and unusual effects achieved.

In order to expand productivity, the Winfield Pottery was moved a short distance in 1935 to 1635 North Foothill where it occupied an authentic California adobe. Designer Margaret Mears Gabriel joined Sample at the new location and fashioned some utilitarian items that were favorably received in the shops that already handled the artware. This aspect of production was greatly expanded over the next few years with two complete dinnerware designs and about ten decorative patterns introduced between 1936 and 1941.

Initially, a set of coupe-style dishes was made. This was followed in 1937 by the first square-shaped dinnerware lines made in California. Most of the pieces in the line were square with softly rounded corners and required unorthodox production methods and molds. The numerous hand-painted patterns created by Gabriel to embellish her shapes included Bamboo, introduced in 1937; Tulip, Avocado, and

Workers bringing a new supply of clay into the Winfield factory on Union in Pasadena, ca. 1959. *Archival photo.*

Winfield decorator painting Citrus pattern on round dinner plate, ca. late fifites. *Archival photo.*

Geranium in 1938 and Citrus in 1939. Bamboo was by far the most successful design and remained in production until the business closed. Some of the simple but attractive color combinations marketed in dinnerware were yellow-sage, pink-grape, turquoise-white, chartreuse-olive rim, and linen-pine.

With the passing of founder Lesley Sample in 1939, Margaret and her husband Arthur C. Gabriel became the owners of Winfield. In 1941, they constructed a new 12,000 square foot factory at 150 West Union Street in Pasadena equipped with three large periodic kilns. More dinnerware patterns were initiated at this time, including Yellow Flower, Weed, Acorn, and Fallow. Tyrus Wong, a talented Chinese-American artist, created a number of dinnerware patterns in the late forties and early fifties. In addition, he personally decorated many large plates with graceful Oriental motifs.

Other Winfield artware consisted of glazed vases, candle holders, planters, and low flower bowls. More than four hundred separate articles comprised the Winfield line at this time, three hundred of which were designed for use in food preparation and dining.

In 1946, an unusual arrangement was worked out with American Ceramic Products of Santa Monica, enabling them to assist the Pasadena plant with a huge backlog of dinnerware orders accrued during the war. The trade name "Winfield China" (along with the manufacturing rights) was licensed to the Santa Monica business, with the Winfield Pottery adopting the trademark "Gabriel Porcelain" to distinguish its product. Overwhelming war-time demand had severely disrupted the owners' original marketing philosophy. What they originally intended to produce was hand-crafted casual china of high quality for the discriminating buyer, and as such catered to exclusive outlets in the West such as Gump's, Neiman-Marcus, and Joseph Magnin. Their larger accounts were therefore assigned to American Ceramic Products, which expanded the line even further into the lucrative direct sales market.

The Winfield business was incorporated in 1947 following the retirement of owners Arthur and Margaret Gabriel. Investors in the closed corporation were son-in-law Boucher Snyder, nephew Nathan Mears, and Douglas Gabriel, Margaret's stepson. The latter became

A view of the casting department of the Winfield Pottery on Union Street in Pasadena.

the sole owner when the other partners withdrew in the mid fifties.

Winfield's business slowed considerably after the reappearance of imported china, and a continued sluggish trend led to the closing of the Pasadena plant in 1962. At most, just fifty people had been employed. China clay from England combined with certain domestic materials was used in production. Over the years, a number of custom-designed dinnerware sets were made for well-known personalities including Bing Crosby, Boris Karloff, Pearl Buck, the Duke and Duchess of Windsor, and Mr. and Mrs. Franklin D. Roosevelt.

Winfield obviously took pride in its product and diligently marked it. Unmarked pieces are extremely uncommon. The early studio production of Lesley Sample was impressed "Winfield Pasadena" (1). Very early work was sometimes dated, and the initials

"L.S." have been noted on rare occasions. Other impressed marks used on Winfield tableware and artware in the early years are shown (2) and (3). The block lettered designations were superseded by hand-incised versions (in various script handwriting styles) around 1941 (4). After 1947, the words "Gabriel Pasadena" were incised in script (5). In addition, a shape number was nearly always incised on Winfield ware. The American Ceramic Products Company used "Winfield," "Winfield Ware," and "Winfield China" printed in ink or recessed in-mold.

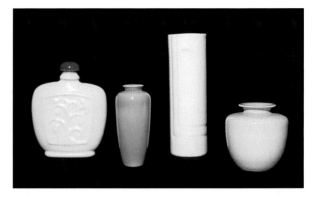

Early artware with impressed "Winfield" marks. Bottle with stopper, 6¾", $75.00; vase 5½", $75.00; cylinder vase, 8½" (from three-piece stepped set), $50.00; vase, 4", $65.00.

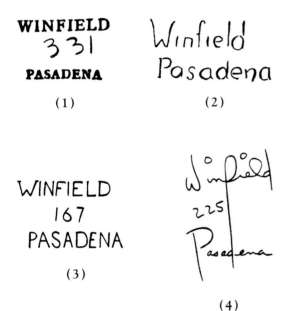

WINFIELD
3 31
PASADENA

(1)

Winfield
Pasadena

(2)

WINFIELD
167
PASADENA

(3)

Winfield
225
Pasadena

(4)

Gabriel
Pasadena
308

(5)

The Primitive Pony pattern, incised "Gabriel" mark. Square design serving bowl, 9", $45.00; cup and saucer, $35.00.

Individual casserole in chartreuse, $30.00, along with 9" square plate with hand-painted fruit pattern, $50.00. Incised "Gabriel" marks.

Early period artware from Winfield of Pasadena. Left to right: Footed bowl #257, 2¼" x 3½", $35.00; vase #1 with iris in low relief, 6½", $150.00; vase with test glaze, 5½", $100.00. Impressed "Winfield" marks.

Footed Winfield vase #33, 6½", with raised cactus motif in green-yellow high glaze, dated July 1931. $175.00+.

Footed bell-shaped vase #283, 6½", $65.00, and rectangular planter #325, 4", $50.00. Impressed "Winfield" marks.

Superb early period Winfield artware with in-mold relief decorations. Left to right: Vase #1 with ethereal Art Deco archer motif, 6½", $200.00+; vase with wispy wisteria motif, 5½", $150.00+; and vase with delicate fern motif, 4", $150.00+. Incised marks. Right and center vases are dated 1931.

This exceptional Winfield vase with poinsettias in low relief, in a subtle blending of cobalt blue and medium green, measures 10". Incised mark reads "Winfield Pasadena/Aug-1931/#32-P/73-78" (last two numbers indicate glazes). $250.00+.

This advertisement for Winfield Pottery appeared in the November, 1932, issue of *California Arts & Architecture.*

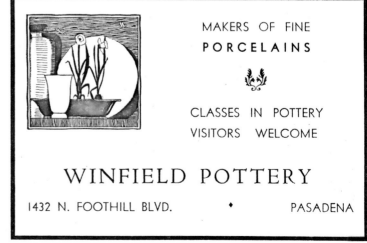

MAKERS OF FINE
PORCELAINS

CLASSES IN POTTERY
VISITORS WELCOME

WINFIELD POTTERY

1432 N. FOOTHILL BLVD.   ◆   PASADENA

Two Winfield vases in commonly found glaze combination of satin matte white exterior-pale green or turquoise interior. Vertically ribbed vase #126, 9", $100.00; rectangular vase #143, 5", $65.00. Impressed "Winfield" marks.

Winfield ware seemingly well suited to the boudoir. Tray #186, 3½", $20.00; bottle with stopper #196, 11", $100.00; covered jar #111, 2" x 4½", $65.00. Impressed "Winfield" marks.

Early hot chocolate set included covered server, $150.00, and small handled mugs, $50.00 each. Impressed "Winfield" marks.

A few of the many Winfield accessories. Left to right: Covered mustard jar, $35.00; covered honey jar (note bear knob), $100.00+; covered jam jar, $35.00; turtle-shaped cigarette box, $65.00. Various period marks.

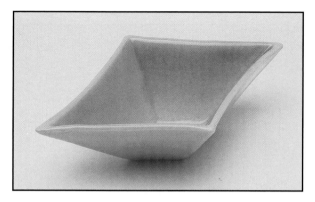

More accessory items. Double boat-shaped relish, $35.00; scoop, 7½", $30.00; single boat-shaped relish, $30.00. Various marks.

Irregular diamond-shaped bowl, 2¼" x 8", in green-yellow high glaze, dated 1931, $100.00+.

Winfield porcelain artware of the thirties. Vase, 4¾", $50.00; vase, 4¼", $45.00; vase, 8½", $150.00; deer, 4¼" x 4¾". $200.00+. Impressed "Winfield" marks.

Winfield casual porcelain was offered in a variety of glaze color combinations. Row 1: Coffee pot in yellow-sage, $50.00; 1-quart pitcher in chartreuse-olive rim, $40.00. Row 2: Coffee/teapot in azure-brown rim, $45.00; scuttle in yellow-sage, $40.00. Various marks.

Square platter, 14", with hand-painted Tulip pattern, $150.00. Incised "Winfield" mark.

Square platter, 14", hand decorated by Tyrus Wong, incised "Winfield" mark, $250.00+.

Square dinner plate, 10½", hand painted by Tyrus Wong, incised "Winfield" mark, $150.00+.

Round design dessert/breakfast plate, 8½", in hand-painted Geranium pattern, $35.00, along with undecorated individual coffeepot, $50.00. Incised "Winfield" marks.

Winfield's square design dessert/breakfast plate, 9", $25.00; salad plate, 7½", $20.00; dessert bowl, 4¾", $20.00, with small cream pitcher, $35.00. Impressed "Winfield" marks.

Plate, 7½", with hand decoration of Siamese cats by Edo Mita, incised marks indicate experimental design, $100.00+.

Large Winfield oval casserole #424, 10", in adobe (pebbly matte finish) and yellow, $65.00; small oval casserole # 397, 6½", in adobe and turquoise, $50.00.

Winfield coffee/teapot #268, in Fallow pattern, $65.00.

Winfield raised cherry/grape motif shakers #366, 3", $45.00 set; bowl #404 with contrasting colored bands, $65.00; rose-shaped shakers #275, $55.00 set. Impressed and incised marks.

ADDITIONAL COMPANIES

Listed here are more than fifty additional Southern California potteries that are worth considering. Some of them are already very collectible. Many others could have been added to this list, but limited time and resources prevented their being investigated. Companies are listed alphabetically, followed by their principal location, personnel, products, and dates, if known.

AMERICAN POTTERY, Los Angeles, Evan K. Shaw, Walt Disney and Leon Schlesinger (Warner Bros.) licensed figurines and novelties, other hand-decorated giftware, 1940–1946.

ADAMS, MATTHEW, Los Angeles, Matthew Adams, former Sascha Brastoff decorator's Alaska line of hand-decorated household goods, giftware, 1960s.

ARCADIA CERAMICS, Arcadia, inventive miniature salt and pepper shakers, other small-scale hand-decorated novelties, 1940s–50s.

ARCHITECTURAL POTTERY, Manhattan Beach, large-scale glazed jardinieres and planters, some custom made, 1955–1983.

BALL ARTWARE, Inglewood, Howard Ball, finely detailed, hand-decorated birds, other giftware, 1946–1956.

BRAHM, JOHANNES, Los Angeles/Reseda, Johannes Brahm, fine figurines, giftware, florist ware, 1940s–50s.

BROCK, B. J./SOUTHERN CALIFORNIA POTTERY, Lawndale, Bertram J. Brock, dinnerware, 1947–1980.

CALLENDER, JANE, Los Angeles/North Hollywood, Jane Callender, hand-detailed dog figurines, 1940s–50s.

CALIFORNIA ORIGINALS, Torrance, William Bailey, household goods, cookie jars, florist ware, 1955–1982. (See Heirlooms of Tomorrow.)

CEMAR, Los Angeles, Paul Cauldwell/C. J. Malone, figurines, giftware, kitchenware, florist ware, 1935–1955.

CLAY SKETCHES, Pasadena, Cy and Edna Peterson, distinctive bird figurines, 1940s–50s.

COORS, H. F., Inglewood, Herman F. Coors (founder), heavy-duty institutional china, 1925–present.

DE FOREST OF CALIFORNIA, Duarte, Jack and Margaret DeForest, cookie jars, novelties, giftware, 1950s–60s.

DELEE ART, Los Angeles, Jimmy Lee Stewart (later: Kohl), distinctive hand-painted figurines, giftware, cookie jars, 1940s–50s.

DESERT SANDS, Barstow (previously Boulder City, Nevada), Ferrell and Dorothea Evans, handmade pottery articulating various colored clays, 1960s–70s.

DORANNE OF CALIFORNIA, Los Angeles, cookie jars (a specialty), kitchenware, buffet ware, planters, giftware, 1950s–80s.

FLINTRIDGE CHINA, Pasadena, Thomas W. Hogan/Milton E. Mason, fine porcelain dinnerware, 1945–1970.

FREEMAN-LEIDY, Laguna Beach, Leland Freeman/Russell Leidy, very ornate, decorative household goods, giftware, figurines, 1940s–50s.

GILNER, Culver City, florist ware, figurines (pixie line), decorative household goods, 1934–1957.

GUPPY, Corona del Mar, Roy and Harriet Guppy, eccentric square-shaped Island Ware dishes and related articles, 1940s–50s.

HEIRLOOMS OF TOMORROW, Manhattan Beach, William Bailey, artistic line of Dresden-type figurines, 1944–1955. (Became California Originals in 1955.)

HOLLYDALE, Los Angeles (Hollydale), dinnerware (Malibu Modern), 1936–1958.

JACKSON, VEE, Pasadena, Vee Jackson, decorative household goods, giftware, novelties, 1946–76.

JARU ART PRODUCTS, Culver City, Jack and Ruth Hirsch (founders), manufacturers and distributors of decorative household goods, floral artware, giftware (some very large scale and/or abstract), 1950s–80s.

JOHNSON, HAROLD, Glendale, Harold Johnson, graceful low flower bowls, vases, 1940–1952.

JOSEF ORIGINALS, Monrovia, Muriel Joseph George/George Good, cute small-scale figurines, novelties (some produced in Japan), 1946–85.

KAYE OF HOLLYWOOD, North Hollywood, Katherine (Kay) Schueftan, hand-decorated figurines and figurine-vases by former Hedi Schoop decorator (see Kim Ward), early 1940s.

KINDELL, DOROTHY, Laguna Beach/Corona del Mar, Dorothy Kindell, figurines, figural household goods, giftware (some quite racy for their time), 1940s–50s.

KNOWLES, TAYLOR and KNOWLES OF CALIFORNIA, Burbank, Homer J. Taylor, cast and handmade artware (decorative household goods, figurines and novelties), 1937–1948.

KNOX, DICK, Laguna Beach, Dick Knox (representative and manufacturer), giftware, decorative household goods, figurines, 1942–1950.

LA CAÑADA, Newhall, hand-molded colored pottery tableware, kitchenware, florist ware resembling early Brayton Laguna line, 1930s–40s.

LANE, Van Nuys, decorative household goods (TV lamps, planters a specialty), 1950s–60s.

LERNER, CLAIRE, Los Angeles, Claire Lerner, decorative household goods, 1940s–50s.

LOS ANGELES POTTERIES, Lynwood, Dale C. Kennedy, hand-decorated dinnerware, kitchenware (cookie jars a specialty), household goods, 1940s–60s.

MADELINE ORIGINALS, Pasadena, Paul and Madeline Johnson, decorative household goods, florist and garden ware, 1948–present.

MADDUX OF CALIFORNIA, Los Angeles, William Maddux (founder), decorative household goods, figurines (birds a specialty), giftware, florist and garden ware, 1938–1976.

MANLEY, JEAN, North Hollywood, Jean Manley, charming hand-detailed doll-like figurines, 1940s.

MAXWELL, ROBERT, Venice, Robert Maxwell, stoneware (figurines, novelties, giftware), 1960s–1970s.

MEYERS/CALIFORNIA RAINBOW POTTERY, Los Angeles (Vernon), California Rainbow line of colored pottery tableware, kitchenware and artware resembling Bauer ware, 1930s–40s.

McCARTY BROTHERS, Sierra Madre, Lee and Michael McCarty, figurine-planters of children of various nationalities, other related giftware, 1940s.

MIRAMAR OF CALIFORNIA, East Los Angeles, line of colored pottery (dinnerware, kitchenware, floral artware), later switched over to molded plastic ware, 1950s–60s.

MODGLIN'S ORIGINALS, Los Angeles, A. Lois Modglin and Stewart B. McCulloch, distinctive line of hand-decorated figurines, ca. 1940–1945.

PACIFIC POTTERY PRODUCTS, Long Beach, large-scale glazed ornamental garden pottery, 1960s–present (no relationship with Pacific Clay Products Company.)

PADRE, Los Angeles, extensive line of colored pottery tableware, kitchenware, artware, and hand-decorated giftware, 1930s–40s.

ROBERTSON, Los Angeles/Hollywood, Fred and George Robertson, crackle-glazed artware, giftware (precursor of early La Mirada line), 1930s–early 50s.

SANTA ANITA, Los Angeles, mixture of plain and decorated dinnerware lines, kitchenware, 1940s–50s.

SHIREY, ESTHER, Encino, Esther Shirey, terracotta figurines, artware in polychrome glazes, 1930s.

SIERRA VISTA CERAMICS, Reinhold and Leonard Lenaberg, decorative giftware, household goods (cookie jars a specialty), 1942–1958.

Simmons, Robert, Costa Mesa, Robert Simmons, various animal figurines, other related giftware, 1940s – 50s.

S-quire Ceramics, Los Angeles, Del Squire Jonas, hand-decorated figurines, generally male/female sets of children and adults (often in period costume) signed "Zaida," other related giftware, 1943 – 50.

Thompson, Joy, Pasadena, Joy Thompson, refined hand-decorated figures (both handmade and cast), usually males/females of various nationalities, other related giftware, 1940s – 50s.

Treasure Craft/Pottery Craft, Lynwood/Compton, Alfred A. Levin/Bruce C. Levin, diverse lines of decorative household goods (novelty cookie jars and salt and pepper sets a specialty), giftware, novelties, floral artware and garden ware, 1945 – present.

Triangle Studios (Vallona Starr Ceramics), Los Angeles/El Monte, Valeria Dopyera, Everett and Leona Frost, hand-decorated novelty salt and pepper shakers, other kitchenware, decorative household goods, floral artware, 1940 – 1953.

Tudor Potteries, Los Angeles, C. J. Biddle/M. L. Vincent, colored pottery (floral artware, garden ware, figurines, etc.), late 1920s – 1930s.

Vohann of California, Laguna Beach/Capistrano Beach, E. A. Von Helmolt/Charles E. Kauffman, (owners), Charles Chaney, (designer), decorative household goods, artware, giftware in monochome glazes, 1950 – present.

Ward, Kim, Although she did not work for Hedi Schoop, as previously thought, she did produce a rather derivative line of figurines, etc. in the 1940s.

Weil of California/California Figurines, Los Angeles, Max Weil, originally California Figurines Company, hand-decorated figurines and figurine-vases; later Weil of California, hand-decorated dinnerware, kitchenware, artware, 1941 – 1955.

West Coast, Burbank, Lee and Bonnie Wollard, floral artware, giftware, figurines, 1940s – 50s.

Werner, Vally, Los Angeles, Vally Werner, Barbara Willis worker who started own competitive pottery making similar ware, 1940s.

White, Eugene, Bell, Eugene White, decorative crackle-glazed terra-cotta household goods, floral artware, 1940s.

Ynez, Inglewood, Inez Ward, charming small scale, hand-detailed figurines of children (male/female sets), 1940s – 50s.

Yona Ceramics, Los Angeles, Yona Lippin, hand-decorated figurines, figurine-vases, related kitchen items, giftware, some of which closely resembled work of former employer Hedi Schoop, 1940s – 50s.

American Pottery: Elmer Fudd, 6¾", $85.00, and Bugs Bunny, 7", $150.00, figurine-flower holders of the mid forties.

AMERICAN POTTERY: Mickey and Minnie Mouse figurines made after an exclusive license was obtained from Walt Disney in 1942. Both 6", with paper labels. $300.00+ each.

AMERICAN POTTERY: Peter Pan, 2¼", from Walt Disney's *Peter Pan*. American Pottery model on the left, $400.00+; the later Evan K. Shaw Co. (Metlox) model on the right, $350.00+. Paper labels.

AMERICAN POTTERY: Bambi figurines from Walt Disney film of same name. Left to right: Large model, 7½", $150.00; mid-size model, 5", $100.00; miniature, 2½", $125.00; large model, 7¾", $150.00. Paper labels. (Note: Different large Bambi models face in opposite directions.)

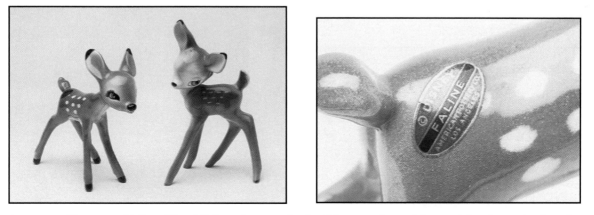

AMERICAN POTTERY: Faline (Bambi's love interest in the Disney animated feature) is often mistaken for Bambi. American Pottery version on left, 7½", $150.00; later Shaw & Co. (Metlox) version on right, 8½", $175.00. Paper labels (see American pottery label at right.)

AMERICAN POTTERY: American Pottery duck rivalry. Warner Bros. Cartoons' Daffy Duck, 5½" at left, $150.00; Walt Disney's Donald Duck, 7", at right, $300.00+. See Shaw & Co. paper label on Daffy figurine at right.

ARCADIA CERAMICS: Miniature novelty salt and pepper shaker sets. Try matching them up. All under 2". $20.00 each. *Photo courtesy Tony Cūna.*

BALL ARTWARE: Pheasant, 7½", stamped mark, late forties, $85.00.

JOHANNES BRAHM: Three boxes with handmade roses on their covers. Two at left are cigarette boxes and came with matching ashtrays inside, $85.00 complete; one at right is a candy box, $65.00. In-mold marks (right).

JANE CALLENDER: Dog figurines were Jane Callender's specialty. Left to right: English setter, $75.00; Pekingese, $55.00; cocker spaniel, $65.00. Cocker is 4½" in height. Stamped and painted marks.

JANE CALLENDER: Poodle, 7", stamped mark includes "46" (model number.), $100.00. Note detailing with numerous strands of finely extruded clay representing fur.

CEMAR: Fish-shaped condiment jar with notched cover, ca. 1954. In-mold mark. Cemar was a spin-off of the Bauer Pottery. $65.00.

CEMAR: Striking Cemar fish figurine, 9¼", in polychrome glaze, with in-mold mark reading "Cemar 564," $150.00.

CEMAR: Deer figurine, 11¾", brown flocking on base, late forties, $85.00.

CEMAR: Phoenix bird, 9½", has felt-like flocking on underside of base, $75.00.

CEMAR: These small scale figurines were intended to complement floral arrangements. Left to right: Peacock, $35.00; cockatoo, $35.00; deer on the rocks, $50.00; horse, $35.00. Deer measures 9¼" and is the only one marked. Clue to identity: many Cemar figurines have had their unglazed bottoms flocked.

CEMAR: These small Catalina Island souvenir ashtrays were made after the Catalina Pottery closed. Sailboat in foreground measures 4" x 4". In-mold "Cemar" mark. $45.00–55.00 each.

DeLee Art: Hand-painted Skunkettes, Mrs. Skunk on left, Mr. Skunk on right. Late forties. $50.00 each.

DeLee Art: This cute Scottie measures 3½" x 4", no mark, $50.00.

DeLee Art: Latino dancers of the early fifties, female, 11½", male 12½". Hand-painted decoration with overglaze gold, in-mold marks. $200.00+ each.

DELEE ART: Two quite different yet easily recognizable deLee models. Left: Young aviator, 6", with in-mold mark reading "deLee USA © 42," $50.00. Right: Woman in period attire named Patsy, 9½", with in-mold mark reading "deLee Art Hollywood © 1950," $65.00.

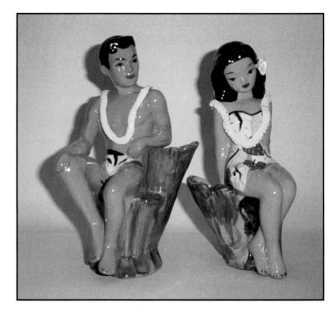

DELEE ART: Seated Hawaiian couple (male named Maui; female named Leilani), 9", by deLee Art date from about 1950. In-mold marks. $750.00+ set.

DELEE ART: This playful Siamese cat, 8½", is unmarked. $75.00.

DELEE ART: These giraffes are 6½" in height and unmarked, $75.00 each.

DESERT SANDS: A select assortment of Desert Sands vases that were handmade in California. Large vase in center is 9"; smallest vase (second from left) is 3". See photos of stamped marks above right. Price range: $45.00 – 200.00.

DESERT SANDS: Two handmade bowls with marbleized blending of various colored clays. Bowl in front, 3" x 4½", $45.00; bowl in back, 3" x 7½", $65.00. Stamped marks.

DORANNE OF CALIFORNIA: Tortoise and hare cookie jar, endemic woodtone finish, ca. 1970, $50.00.

FLINTRIDGE CHINA: Fine china dinner plate, $30.00, and teapot, $125.00, with overglaze silver trim and stamped marks.

GILNER: Childlike "native" pixies were made in the late forties to early fifties as separate figurines and also came attached to planters. Note small metal earrings. Seated boy at right, 3½", $35.00, and girl, 4½", $35.00, are unmarked. Planters have in-mold marks (below). $45.00 each.

GUPPY: Shaker, $25.00, flared tumbler with hand-coiled base, $35.00, and bamboo-shaped tumbler, $30.00. Late forties.

HAROLD JOHNSON: Two examples of elegant low flower bowls, ca. 1948. Top: 13¾" x 12", $50.00. Bottom: 14" x 10¼", $50.00. Incised "Harold Johnson" in script.

GUPPY: Exotic Island Ware of the forties. Service plate, $25.00; stacked saucers, $10.00 each, and cup, $25.00. Painted marks.

JOSEF ORIGINALS: Two examples that were made in California. Left: April, from the Birthday Month series, 3¼", with in-mold mark, $35.00 Right: Pixie and friend, 3½", with paper label, $45.00.

KAYE OF HOLLYWOOD: Soap dish figure, 8", $75.00.

DOROTHY KINDELL: Kindell was known for her female nudes that were rather racy for their time. These goblets with acrobatic nudes attached are very rare, $250.00 each.

DOROTHY KINDELL: This unique 11" ashtray was called "The Beachcombers" when it was introduced in 1951. In-mold mark. $175.00.

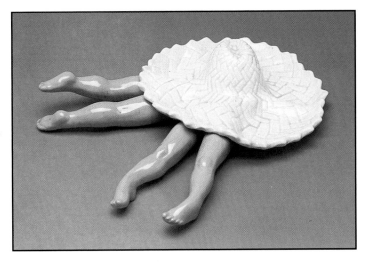

KNOWLES, TAYLOR & KNOWLES OF CALIFORNIA: Decorative pitcher/vase, 6", in blended glaze, incised, "Eileen 1-21-43" (made by Eileen Taylor), $60.00.

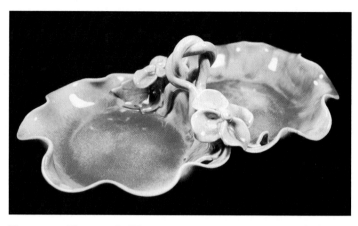

KNOWLES, TAYLOR & KNOWLES OF CALIFORNIA: Divided dish, 10", with scalloped edges, applied flowers and leaves, and handle made from twisted strands of clay. In-mold mark. $60.00.

KNOWLES, TAYLOR & KNOWLES OF CALIFORNIA vase, 10½", in-mold mark reads "K T K/Calif/503," $100.00.

DICK KNOX: Art Creations' Nubian compote, 11", from Dick Knox Productions, painted mark on underside below, $150.00.

DICK KNOX: This rare Dick Knox line of semi-vitreous china was designed by Beatrice Wood. Left to right: two-quart water pitcher, $750.00+; coffee pot, 8½", $1,000.00+; individual coffee pot, 5", $750.00+; dinner plate, 10", $300.00+; bread and butter plate, 7", $275.00+; cup, $300.00+; buffet (large size) shaker, $200.00+. Limited production, ca. 1948, unmarked.

DICK KNOX: Two Dick Knox Productions vases in an Oriental mode, ca. 1948. "Dick Knox" mark hand painted overglaze in gold. Left: pillow vase, 9½" x 5½", $75.00. Right: bottle vase, 8", $75.00.

LA CAÑADA: Handmade dinner plate, $35.00, and small pitcher, $65.00. Incised marks, ca. 1935.

MADDUX: Flamingo line of the early fifties included this double flamingo vase, 5", $85.00, and single flamingo planter, 6", $85.00. In-mold marks.

MADDUX: This idyllic Wynken, Blynken & Nod TV lamp by Maddux of California measures 10" x 10", $250.00.

MADDUX: Cockatoo on floral trimmed branch, 11", ca. 1947. In-mold "Wm. Maddux." $150.00.

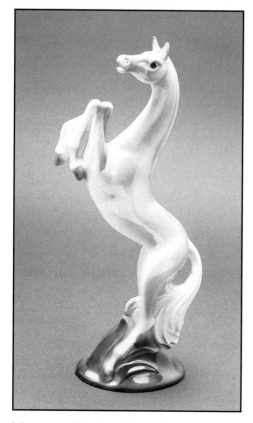

MADDUX: Rearing horse figurine, 13", with in-mold mark reading "Maddux of Calif/© 60/925/Made in USA." $60.00.

JEAN MANLEY: Handmade figurines of seated boy holding duck, 4", $125.00, and girl holding bowl of fruit, 5¾", $125.00. Late forties.

JEAN MANLEY: An exceptional piece of children on horseback, 7½" x 6", unmarked, $250.00+.

ROBERT MAXWELL: Stoneware vase, ca. 1960, paper label, $100.00.

JEAN MANLEY: Doll-like figurine of woman in winter garb, 8½", no mark, $100.00.

ROBERT MAXWELL: These cantankerous looking, unglazed stoneware figurines were made in 1969. Man, 3½", $75.00; woman, 2¾", $75.00.

ROBERT MAXWELL: These unglazed stoneware critters range from 1½" to 5" in height and date from the seventies. Some are marked in-mold "© Robert Maxwell" or "© R. M." but smallest ones are not marked. $45.00 – 150.00 each.

McCARTY BROTHERS: Charming set of Mexican children planters from the mid forties. In-mold marks. $55.00 set.

MEYERS/CALIFORNIA RAINBOW POTTERY: #12 mixing bowl, $50.00, and covered coffee server with wood handle, $75.00, in velvety cobalt blue glaze. In-mold marks.

MEYERS/CALIFORNIA RAINBOW POTTERY: The California Rainbow line of Meyers included these colorful items. Clockwise from top: Large service plate in yellow, $50.00; salad serving bowl in black, $150.00; cup and saucer in green, $35.00; butter dish in dusty rose, $100.00; custard cup in black, $45.00; water tumbler in white, $45.00. In-mold mark "California Rainbow" or no mark.

PADRE: Honey jar in maroon high glaze, in-mold mark, $85.00.

PADRE: Calla lily wall pocket, 7", satin-matte cobalt blue glaze, ca. 1939, in-mold mark, $85.00.

PADRE: This attractive wall pocket measures 9½" and has an in-mold block-lettered mark reading "Padre 241." $75.00.

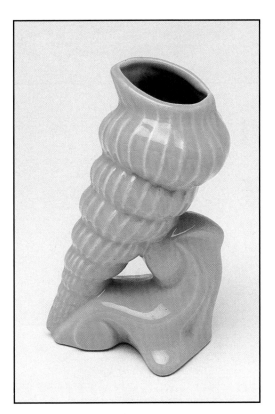

PADRE: Surfing shell vase, 7", in turquoise, in-mold mark includes number "8," $65.00.

PADRE: The hand-decorated Regal line of Padre included this impressive Toby jug, 11", in the likeness of an American Revolutionary. In-mold and handpainted marks. Handpainted mark (below) includes decorator's first name. $150.00.

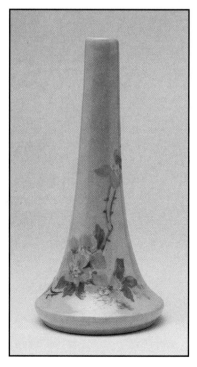

PADRE: Regal rooster with overglaze red-painted cock's comb, decorated and signed by "Muriel" on its underside, $75.00.

PADRE: Regal line bud vase, 7", with skillfully handpainted floral spray, painted mark on bottom reads "Painted by Z," $50.00.

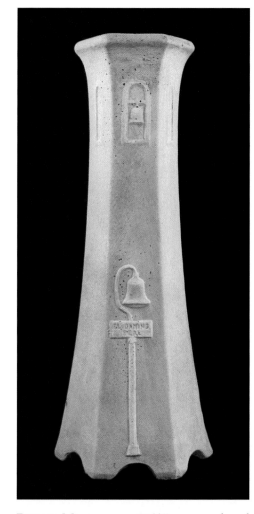

ROBERTSON: Robertson Hollywood vases in exquisite crackle glazes. Left to right: Vase (note skewed perspective), 7", in deep turquoise, $200.00; vase, 5½", in yellow, $85.00; vase, 2½", in deep turquoise, displayed on black-glazed stand, 1" x 2¼", $150.00. Full mark incised on larger vases (below), small vase incised "R.", no Robertson mark on stand.

POXON: Mission vase, 10¼", was produced in a light-colored bisque finish with glaze inside only, ca. 1920. Impressed "Poxon Los Angeles." Marker reads "El Camino Real." (Bauer and Padre produced later versions of this design.) $250.00+.

ROBERTSON: Elegant covered box, in pinkish crackle glaze, with applied rose on cover is 5¾" in length and incised "Robertson Hollywood." $125.00.

ROBERTSON: Little lamb, 4" long, in unusual mottled matte glaze, incised "Robertson Hollywood," $150.00.

ROBERTSON: Hand-decorated 10½" plate of silhouetted antelope. Artwork by George Robertson, signed "Robertson Hollywood 149." $250.00+.

ROBERTSON: Table lamp, ca. 1945. Ceramic base measures 11½". White crackle high glaze with hand-painted design. Signed "Robertson Hollywood." $500.00+.

SANTA ANITA: Dinner plate, 10½", $20.00, and cup and saucer, $20.00, from the Vreniware line in Stylized Spirals pattern. Fifties period stamped marks.

SANTA ANITA: Bird of Paradise dinner plate, 10½", from Flowers of Hawaii series of the fifties. Stamped mark. $45.00.

S-QUIRE CERAMICS: Dutch boy and girl set includes pint-size potted tulips. Boy holding cap, 7"; girl holding potted tulip, 6½". Stamped marks include legend "Figurine by Zaida." $100.00 set.

JOY THOMPSON: Madonna figure in arched niche with radiating rays of light in low relief, 12" in height. Incised "Joy T." $150.00. Reverse side has raised "tree of life" motif (right).

JOY THOMPSON: Handpainted and embellished female harvester figure is 11½". Incised "Joy Thompson Pasadena." $250.00.

319

VOHANN OF CALIFORNIA: Tissue box cover, 7" x 7", has paper label on inside, $35.00.

KIM WARD: Peasant girl candleholder, 8½", with painted mark, $100.00.

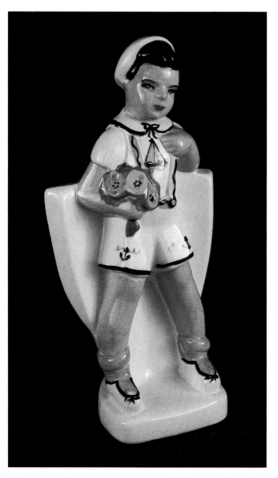

WEIL OF CALIFORNIA: Hand-decorated sailor boy vase, 10¾", ca. 1943. Stamped mark. $75.00.

WEIL OF CALIFORNIA: These two early term Max Weil-produced California Figurines also function as flower holders. Blonde female holding parasol, 10", $65.00, and brunette in bonnet, 10½", $65.00. No marks.

WEIL OF CALIFORNIA: Charming Dutch children flower holders. Boy (#3040), 7¼", $45.00; girl (#3041), $45.00. Stamped marks.

WEIL OF CALIFORNIA: Dinnerware of the late forties by Weil. Malay Bambu round design chop plate, 13", $60.00, with Malay Blossom square design dinner plate, 9¾", $25.00; lug soup, $40.00; cup, $10.00; fruit bowl, $50.00.

WEIL OF CALIFORNIA: Pensive lady holding horn of plenty is a wall pocket, measuring 9". Stamped Weil logo. $75.00.

VALLY WERNER: Hand-decorated vase, 7½", ca. 1949, incised "Vally," $50.00.

VALLY WERNER: Vase with under-tray, 8" x 7¾", $50.00, and small round jar (cover missing), $35.00, from the studio of Vally Werner, ca. 1942. Incised. "Vally."

WEST COAST: Pleasing peacock vase, 11", has in-mold mark, $65.00.

VALLY WERNER: Small oval vase and liner in white crackle glaze over dark brown clay body, in-mold marks, $40.00.

WEST COAST: Stylized pheasant, 7¾", $25.00; rose bowl, 4¼", with in-mold mark, $25.00.

WEST COAST: Ball-shaped vase, 7½", with spirited hand-painted decoration on one side only. In-mold mark reads "West Coast/California/Designed by Ken Wheeler/602." $75.00.

EUGENE WHITE: Utilitarian artware, incised "Eugene White." Tray, 11", dated 1942, $100.00; handled dish, 2¾" x 11", $75.00; small bowl with hammered copper lid, $200.00.

YONA: Striking set of Siamese dancers with abundant overglaze gold embellishment. Female, 13½", $100.00; male, 12½", $100.00. Painted marks read "© Yona." Fifties period.

YNEZ: Jennifer figurine, 5½", hand decoration with added hair curls and lace trim, ca. 1946. Incised mark. $40.00.

GLOSSARY

Over the years that I have been a dealer, it has become apparent that many pottery collectors, especially beginners, are unfamiliar with the terminology of the ceramic industry. The following glossary is included for them.

Airbrush Decoration: Decorative process whereby an atomizer employing compressed air is used to spray paint in a fine mist.

Bisque: Ware that has been fired but not glazed.

Body: Structure of a ceramic object.

Cast: See slip cast.

Ceramics: All-inclusive term for the art of making objects of fired clay.

China: Ware made from a vitrified body. See porcelain.

Clay: Earthy mineral substance composed largely of a hydrous silicate of alumina, which becomes hard and rock-like when fired.

Crackle Glaze: Decorative glaze having intentional crazing (a fine network of cracks) which is sometimes augmented with stain.

Decal Decoration: Process of decorating china or other types of ware with printed decals. Also known as decalcomania.

Earthenware: Relatively low-fired pottery, usually buff, red or brown in color.

Engobe: A layer of slip applied to objects to alter body color.

Faience Tile: Polychromed decorative tile. Originally the tin-glazed ornamental earthenware of Faenza, Italy.

Finishing: Process of removing mold marks and rough edges from cast ware prior to firing.

Glaze: Glass-like coating on a clay surface.

Green: Ware that is dry but unfired.

Hand Thrown: Objects formed by hand on a potter's wheel.

Jiggered: Objects formed between a revolving mold that shapes the inside and a template that shapes the outside. Semi-automated pottery.

Jobber: Individual or organization that obtains ware directly from producers (sometimes under exclusive contract) and sells it to retailers.

Kaolin: Relatively scarce, non-plastic type of clay which is indispensable in the making of porcelain.

Kiln: Oven designed specifically for the high temperatures required for baking and glazing clay objects.

Metallic Oxide: Elemental mineral combined with oxygen which is used to impart color to glazes or clay bodies.

Modeling: Process of sculpting an original object from which molds are made for production purposes.

Mold: A hollow plaster of Paris form into which plastic clay is pressed or liquid clay is poured.

Periodic Kiln: Kiln in which ware is heated in a gradual cycle and allowed to cool before removal.

Porcelain: Objects made from a white, vitrified and translucent body. Popularly called china.

Pottery: Objects, especially vessels, that are made from fired clay. General term that includes earthenware, stoneware and porcelain.

Press Molded: Objects that are duplicated by hand-pressing thin slabs of clay into plaster molds.

Ram Press: Fully automated machine for mass-producing clay objects.

Short Set: Basic dinnerware service lacking most or all of the accessories.

Slip: A fluid suspension of clay and water used for casting and decorating.

Slip Cast: Objects that are duplicated by pouring liquid clay into plaster production molds.

Slip Decoration: Underglaze decorative process employing colored slip as a painting agent.

Stoneware: Semi-vitrified pottery made from clay that is dense and usually light in color. Non-translucent.

Talc: Fine-grained mineral that is used instead of clay to produce a body especially suited to commercial production.

Tunnel Kiln: A continuously operating, tunnel-like kiln in which ware is moved through varying heat zones on slow-moving flat cars or slabs.

Vitrified: Ware that has been fired at a very high temperature to the point of glassification.

CREDITS

These generous people loaned choice examples to be photographed, photographed selected pieces themselves, or otherwise supplied photographic examples for the second edition of the book:

Diana Andrews, James Barrett, John and Joanne Barrett, Sharlene Beckwith, Debbie Clint, Chris Crain, Doris Dohn, Jimm Edgar, James Elliot and Patrick Barry (The Pottery Shop, Seattle, WA), Christine Falkenburg, Juan Fernandez and Carl Gibbs, Jr. (California Connection, Houston, TX), Jan Fontes (Antique Gallery, Fullerton, CA), Jerome and Helen Franklin, Clare Graham and Bob Breen, Gary Keith, Gary and Caroline Kent, Ron and Juvelyn Nickel, Christy Prouty, Patti Smith, Paula Soest, Ken Stalcup and Dennis Warden (L. A. Finders Keepers, Los Angeles, CA), Doug Stanton, George and Elaine Stecker, Bill Stern, Marilyn Webb, Marty and LiLi Webster, Scott and Pamela Wells (Wells Antiques, Los Angeles, CA), Mark Wiskow and Susan Strommer, Barbara Willis, Janice Wise, and Donna Yarrell.

These collectors and dealers loaned key examples of California pottery to be photographed for the first book edition: Melinda Avery (Metlox Potteries, Manhattan Beach), Sharlene Beckwith, Fred and Ruth Eilenfield, Delleen Enge (Franciscan Matching, Ojai), Jeanne Fredericks, Van Fryman and Paul Lenaburg, Norman Haas, Wilbur and Virginia Held, Gary Keith, Gary and Caroline Kent, Cynthia Kern, Bill Kochanski, Betty Lopez (Holly Street Bazaar, Pasadena), Jack Moore (Jack Moore Gallery, Pasadena), Stan Palowski, Jerry Robin and Melanie Peterson, Keith Robinson (Manhattan Beach Historical Society), P. A. Roswell, Bob Schmid, Carl and Maire Schrenk, Jack Shafer, Judy Stangler, Alvah Stanley (Slightly Crazed, Los Angeles), Bill Stern, Baron Stoelting, Marilyn Webb, Helen Wenko, Buddy Wilson (Buddy's, Los Angeles).

Most of the photography for the first edition was undertaken by the author. In addition the following photographers contributed: Tony Cuñha, Roger Gass, Bruce Handelsman, Richard N. Levine, C. L. McClanahan, and Julius Shulman. Most of the photography for the second edition was accomplished by Victoria Damrel. In addition, the following photographers contributed: Chris Crain, Shel Izen, Juvelyn Nickel, and LiLi Webster. The remaining photos are of archival nature, drawn from private and public sources, and the photographers are unknown.

BIBLIOGRAPHY

Abelson, Cheryl A.; *Hagen-Renaker Collector's Catalog.* (privately printed, 1980.)

Anderson, Timothy J.; Eudora M. Moore; Robert W. Winter, eds., *California Design 1910.* (Santa Barbara/Salt Lake City: Peregrine Smith, 1980.)

Bray, Hazel V.; *The Potter's Art In California: 1885-1955.* (The Oakland Museum, 1980.)

Chipman, Jack, *Collector's Encyclopedia of Bauer Pottery.* (Paducah, KY: Collector Books, 1997.)

Chipman, Jack; Judy Stangler, *The Complete Collectors Guide To Bauer Pottery.* (Culver City, CA: California Spectrum, 1982.)

Conti, Steve; A. DeWayne Bethany; Bill Seay, *Collector's Encyclopedia of Sascha Brastoff.* (Paducah, KY: Collector Books, 1995.)

Derwich, Jenny B.; Mary Latos, *Dictionary Guide To United States Pottery & Porcelain.* (Franklin, MI: Jenstan, 1984.)

Duke, Harvey, *The Official Price Guide to Pottery and Porcelain.* (New York: House of Collectibles, 1995.)

Enge, Delleen, *Franciscan Ware.* (Paducah, KY: Collector Books, 1981.)

_____, *Franciscan: Embossed/Hand Painted.* (privately printed, 1992.)

_____, *Franciscan: Plain & Fancy.* (privately printed, 1996.)

Evans, Paul, *Art Pottery Of The United States.* (New York: Charles Scribner's Sons, 1974.)

Foland, Doug, *The Florence Collectibles: An Era of Elegance.* (Atglen, PA: Schiffer Publishing, 1995.)

Frick, Devin, *California Kilns.* (Anaheim Museum, 1994.)

Frick, Devin; Jean Frick; Richard Martinez, *Collectible Kay Finch.* (Paducah, KY: Collector Books, 1997.)

Fridley, A.W., *Catalina Pottery: The Early Years 1927-1937.* (Long Beach, CA: Privately printed, 1977.)

Gibbs Jr., Carl, *Collector's Encyclopedia of Metlox Potteries.* (Paducah, KY: Collector Books, 1995.)

Harris, Dee; Jim & Kay Whitaker, *Josef Originals.* (Atglen, PA: Schiffer Publishing, 1994.)

Held, Wilbur, *Collectable Caliente Pottery.* (Claremont, CA: privately printed, 1987.)

_____, *Collectable Caliente Pottery* (Updated Edition). (privately printed, 1997.)

Henzke, Lucile, *Art Pottery Of America.* (Exton, PA: Schiffer Publishing, 1982.)

Lehner, Lois, *Complete Book Of American Kitchen and Dinnerwares.* (Des Moines: Wallace-Homestead, 1980.)

_____, *Lehner's Encyclopedia Of U.S. Marks On Pottery, Porcelain & Clay.* (Paducah, KY: Collector Books, 1983.)

Nelson, Maxine Feek, *Collectible Vernon Kilns.* (Paducah, KY: Collector Books, 1994.)

_____, *Versatile Vernon Kilns (Book II).* (Paducah, KY: Collector Books, 1983.)

Nickel, Mike; Cindy Horvath, *Kay Finch Ceramics: Her Enchanted World.* (Atglen, PA: Schiffer Publishing, 1996.)

Piña, Leslie, *Designed & Signed.* (Atglen, PA: Schiffer Publishing, 1996.)

Posgay, Mike; Ian Warner, *The World of Head Vase Planters.* (Marietta, OH: Antique Publications, 1992.)

Rhodes, Daniel, *Clay And Glazes For The Potter.* (Philadelphia: Chilton, 1957.)

Roerig, Fred; Joyce Herndon Roerig, *Collector's Encyclopedia of Cookie Jars (Book II).* (Paducah, KY: Collector Books, 1994.)

Roller, Gayle; Kathleen Rose; Joan Berkwitz, *The Hagen-Renaker Handbook.* (Vista, CA: privately printed, 1989.)

Stiles, Helen E., *Pottery In The United States.* (New York: E.P. Dutton, 1941.)

Webb, Frances Finch, *The New Kay Finch Identification Guide.* (privately printed, 1996.)

INTERVIEWS

Sascha Brastoff, John Herbert Brutsche, Carlotta (Mrs. George) Climes, Frances (Mrs. Will) Climes, Kay Finch, Betty Davenport Ford, Douglas and Claudia Gabriel, Anna (Mrs. Virgil K.) Haldeman, Bunny (Mrs. Thomas F.) Hamilton, Ida Harris, Victor Houser, Tracy Irwin, Marie (Mrs. Harold) Johnson, Phil Keeler, Brad Keeler Jr., William Manker, Ray Murray, Howard Pierce, John and Maxine Renaker, Hedi Schoop, Stan Skee, Richard Steckman, Roger (Bud) Upton, Jack White, Barbara Willis, Don and Bruce Winton.

INDEX

ABOUT THE AUTHOR

Over 20 years ago, Jack Chipman began collecting California ceramics. In time, he amassed a huge collection of the ceramics of his native state. This led to extensive research on the subject.

By the 1980s, Chipman was an expert on California pottery, particularly Bauer pottery. In 1980, he published the *Bauer Pottery Price Guide*, which was co-authored with Judy Stangler. This book was so popular that Jack was urged to publish a second book, and the *Complete Collector's Guide to Bauer Pottery* was published in 1982, again co-authored with Judy Stangler.

Jack Chipman's research on California ceramics continued and soon he was a known and respected authority on every aspect of California clayware. This knowledge culminated in the publication of a third book, the *Collector's Encyclopedia of California Pottery*, published in 1992 by Collector Books.

For several years after the publication of his third book, Chipman was able to devote himself to his "other life." Few people in the world of collectible ceramics realize that Jack is also a talented fine artist whose work is in the collections of several museums. Vestiges of his years of involvement with ceramics come through in the textures and coloration of his paintings. His assemblages are a series of witty and sardonic one-liners aimed at topical issues of American culture.

As Chipman focused on his art, another book was being written on Bauer pottery. Mitch Tuchman put together an elegant volume on Bauer pottery for Chronicle Books and asked Jack to be a contributing writer. Chipman wrote the section on Bauer's late-period artware. With the public's growing interest in Bauer pottery, Chipman felt the urgent demand, not only for an historical perspective on the colorful clayware, but also for an up-to-date comprehensive price guide; hence his latest book on Bauer, the *Collector's Encyclopedia of Bauer Pottery* was published in 1997 by Collector Books.

This updated and expanded second edition of the *Collector's Encyclopedia of California Pottery* by Jack Chipman is the result of a burgeoning interest in all facets of California ceramics among collectors and dealers throughout the country.

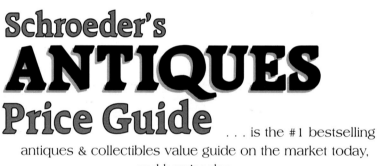